THEATRE
IN THE
AMERICAS

A Series from
Southern Illinois University Press
ROBERT A. SCHANKE
Series Editor

"That Furious Lesbian"

"That Furious Lesbian"

The Story of Mercedes de Acosta

Robert A. Schanke

Southern Illinois University Press
Carbondale

Library of Congress Cataloging-in-Publication Data
Schanke, Robert A., 1940–
     "That furious lesbian" : the story of Mercedes de Acosta / Robert A. Schanke
     p. cm. — (Theater in the Americas)
     Includes bibliographical references and index.
     1. Acosta, Mercedes de, 1893–1968. 2. Women and literature—United States—
History—20th century. 3. Authors, American—20th century—Biography. 4. Lesbians—
United States—Biography. I. Title. II. Series.
     PS3501.C7 Z87 2003
     818'.5209—dc21
     ISBN 0-8093-2511-X (cloth : alk. paper)   2002011762
     ISBN 0-8093-2579-9 (pbk. : alk. paper)

To Madi
"such a dear little, good little, sweet little girl"
described of my beloved mother
as I recently paged through her high school yearbook
I wish now to pass this on to my precious granddaughter,
Madilynn Ruth Lyford

Contents

Illustrations

Preface

first stumbled upon the name of Mercedes de Acosta in the early 1970s, while conducting research for my Ph.D. dissertation on the actress Eva Le Gallienne. While reading Le Gallienne's two autobiographies, *At 33* and *With a Quiet Heart,* I was struck by her mention of close, emotional friendships with so many women but few men. Even though I was not yet fully aware of my own sexual orientation, I became curious about Le Gallienne's. Whenever I asked people I was interviewing about Le Gallienne's personal life, they chose to remain silent. The actress was still living, and they preferred not to divulge any personal information.

One woman Le Gallienne mentions briefly in *At 33* is Mercedes, who wrote two plays that the actress starred in—*Sandro Botticelli* and *Jehanne d'Arc.* Even though she had been involved in a deeply intense, romantic affair with Mercedes, Le Gallienne avoids all reference to their relationship. The most personal she ever allows herself is when she writes that *Sandro Botticelli* contained "many beautiful and poetic passages . . . [and] was very lovely."[1]

I remember thinking when I finished reading her two books that it seemed odd she discussed the two productions, especially the exhausting problems of mounting *Jehanne d'Arc* in Paris, but said so little about the woman who had written two of her starring vehicles. I confess that a major oversight on my part was having neglected to read Mercedes's autobiography, *Here Lies the Heart,* published in 1960, for I would have been better alerted to their relationship, even though Mercedes discussed it discreetly.

Almost twenty years later and after I had become much more comfortable accepting my own orientation, I interviewed Le Gallienne's younger lover, Anne Kaufman Schneider, for a book-length biography I was writing about the actress. When I asked her whether she knew anything about Le Gallienne's earlier, five-year relationship with Mercedes de Acosta, she snapped, "Well, you know Mercedes was a professional lesbian." Author Diana

McLellan, who had never met Mercedes, describes her as a woman who "planned her seduction like a military strategist."[2] Although a definition of "professional lesbian" still eludes me, it seems that McLellan's description comes closest to what Kaufman Schneider meant. She considered Mercedes an evil seductress, a femme fatale who was always on the prowl for a new victim. Since Kaufman Schneider never met Mercedes, her opinion was obviously based on what her lover and others had told her and on what she had read.

My interview with Kaufman Schneider intrigued me. I knew I would have to discuss Le Gallienne's romance with Mercedes in this new book I was writing, but there was so little information to go on besides Mercedes's account in her own autobiography. I proceeded cautiously, but in my book, *Shattered Applause: The Lives of Eva Le Gallienne* (1992), I candidly addressed their relationship.

About two years after the book's publication, I learned that Mercedes had sold her vast collection of correspondence to the Rosenbach Museum and Library in Philadelphia in 1960. At first, I was relieved that Mercedes directed her correspondence from Le Gallienne to be sealed in a vault until after the actress died. Even if I had learned about the collection earlier, I would not have had access to it while I was preparing the biography. Le Gallienne was still alive, and by the time she died in 1991, my book was already in production. About the most I was able to add at the time of her death were a few pages about her final days. I knew that I had to examine the letters for myself as soon as possible. Truth be told, I was fearful that the correspondence might prove some of my statements about her relationship with Mercedes were inaccurate. Fortunately, I was relieved to discover that, for the most part, this was not the case.

The week I spent at the Rosenbach in the summer of 1994 set me on a deeper course. At that time, I began a collaboration with historian Kim Marra that had actually been precipitated by my biography of Le Gallienne. I had learned, much to my dismay, that Le Gallienne's lesbianism had influenced her selection of scripts, management practices, and style of acting and ultimately affected her work's critical reception. Her love of other women became a nemesis that defined her great need for privacy. "What prominence LeG might have realized," I concluded, "if circumstances had not forced her to waste so much precious energy on her shame and seclusion."[3]

Marra and I set out to examine other theater artists and how their same-sex sexual desires, like Le Gallienne's, had shaped their personal and professional lives. It was our profound conclusion that such "knowledge of the role of same-sex sexual desire in historical figures' theatrical careers is central to understanding their contributions and essential both to writing a fuller and more accurate account of history and to changing current attitudes."[4] We wanted to examine how social and cultural sentiments shaped both their self-worth and public reception. Our efforts resulted in two volumes, *Passing Performances: Queer Readings of Leading Players in American Theater History* (1998) and *Staging Desire: Queer Readings of American Theater History* (2002). In these two volumes, we examined the lives and careers of twenty-eight artists.

Although my primary goal in visiting the Rosenbach Museum was to relieve my mind about Mercedes's relationship with Le Gallienne, I found myself becoming more and more fascinated with this exceptional woman. She was born into a wealthy family that hobnobbed with the Astors and Vanderbilts, yet when she died, she was living in a tiny, two-room apartment and was nearly destitute. She was an intelligent woman who, by the age of thirty-five, had published three books of poetry and two novels and had had four plays produced—two Off-Broadway, one in Paris, and one in both New York and London. I discovered she was a confidante to many stars, and her friends included such internationally known figures as Greta Garbo, Marlene Dietrich, Eva Le Gallienne, Cecil Beaton, Alice B. Toklas, Igor Stravinsky, Tamara Karsavina, Isadora Duncan, Janet Flanner, Natacha Rambova, and John Barrymore.

Quite coincidentally, during one of my lunch breaks from the museum, I saw a new book displayed in the window of a nearby bookstore, Hugo Vickers's *Loving Garbo: The Story of Greta Garbo, Cecil Beaton, and Mercedes de Acosta*. For the next few days, I spent every lunch period lying out in the sun of Rittenhouse Square while reading Vickers's account of a complicated web of relationships. By the time I left Philadelphia, I was energized and certainly in agreement with Alice B. Toklas: "You can't dispose of Mercedes lightly."[5] An essay about this forgotten and neglected woman became part of the publishing project that I was conducting with Marra.

In many ways, Mercedes's intriguing story seemed more interesting than that of Le Gallienne's. Mercedes had the advantage of money and name recognition to open doors, and yet she ended her life so pitifully. During the final stages of preparing the essay for publication, I fully realized that I needed to write this more complete biography and to greatly expand upon the ideas I had already set forth in my essay.

I began to question the disparaging, yet common references to Mercedes and wondered why her friendships and relationships had been used to condemn her rather than simply describe her. Why was she being dismissed so lightly? Was there something about Mercedes's personality and behavior

that encouraged such harsh words? Was her known desire for women so
repugnant that it prejudiced all responses to her and her work? I was determined to discover whether there was more to this woman's story than
had been revealed.

Closely aligned with her dim reputation is the accusation that Mercedes's
autobiography is full of lies, half-truths, and distortions. This charge is not
an unusual indictment of autobiographies, a literary genre that is commonly
labeled narcissism and self-adoration. After all, don't we all want to be liked
and remembered with admiration? One critic, however, argues, "In
autobiography the reader recognizes the inevitability of unreliability but
suppresses the recognition in a tenacious effort to expect 'truth' of some kind.
The nature of that truth is best understood as the struggle of a historical rather
than a fictional person to come to terms with her own past."[6] In other words,
it is difficult, if not impossible, to establish in any autobiography the firm
and infallible authority of truth.

This dilemma is not necessarily due to an author's intent to deceive.
According to one scholar,

> Events we witness do not always, or even usually, remain unchanged
> in memory; we fill in missing details by inference, or alter them in
> accordance with questions we are asked or suggestions made to us, and
> have no way of retrieving the original—and are not even aware that
> anything had happened to it. . . . [A]ll of us continually revise our
> memories of our lives to harmonize with the events that have happened
> or are happening to us; we are unable to distinguish between what
> really happened and what we now think happened, since original
> memory no longer exists.[7]

Two of Mercedes's former lovers, Greta Garbo and Eva Le Gallienne,
denounced her memory of the past and would not speak to her after her
book appeared. Le Gallienne never forgave Mercedes. When Anne Kaufman
Schneider found a gold wedding band in Eva's attic some ten years after
Mercedes had died and asked what it was, Eva snatched it away, threw it down
a well outside her house, and grumbled, "It was from Mercedes."[8] Garbo
snubbed her on the sidewalks of New York and refused to see her even when
she was on her deathbed.

The responses of Garbo and Le Gallienne, to be completely fair, must be
put into perspective. Both were closeted and private women. Until the day
they died, neither of them admitted to ever having had same-sex sexual
desires. Even though Mercedes wrote with discreet and sometimes coded
language, her lovers obviously felt betrayed and "outed." Just as stars today

vehemently resist their same-sex sexual desires being made public and often deny the truth, so did her lovers. Indeed, by claiming that Mercedes had lied, Garbo and Le Gallienne were clearly culpable in trying to dismiss their past and distort history.

Mercedes admitted there may have been errors in her book. "I may have made mistakes in some dates or minor incidents," she confessed, "but if so, I do not too much regret it since I feel that I have held to the spirit of my statement if not to the letter."[9]

In my research, I discovered two kinds of errors. The first is Mercedes's description of incidents with no corroborating evidence and whose veracity seems suspicious. For example, she describes dramatically how her father arrived in New York from Cuba. He supposedly escaped from a firing squad by leaping over the walls of Havana's Morro Castle into the sea and swimming to safety. Yet anyone who has visited Morro Castle, as my partner and I have, knows that this probably never happened the way she described it. The castle is surrounded by huge, sharp, jutting rocks, and the sea is teeming with sharks. Mercedes had visited Cuba when she was a teenager, so even if this story is what her father had told her, she must have sensed it was inaccurate. Unfortunately, the records in the National Archives in Cuba provide no clues as to how her father escaped or even that he was ever arrested in the first place. So why did she create or continue this family legend? Was it her desire to be more dramatic? Was she trying to create a better image of her father, who actually may have been a traitor rather than a quasi martyr? Was she trying to portray a more noble family for future generations?

The second kind of error includes blatant inaccuracies. For instance, Mercedes writes that in 1935, Garbo sent her a telegram inviting her to join her in Stockholm. Correspondence in the de Acosta Collection tells a decidedly different story. Mercedes had been advised by friends to cable Garbo and request an invitation. A letter from Garbo to Mercedes states her position clearly: If Mercedes really insisted on coming there for just a dinner, Garbo would agree to join her. The decision was Mercedes's to make.[10] Mercedes was not invited; she invited herself. Why the inaccuracy? Did she forget the actual details, or was it intentional? Did she look through the correspondence she had saved and decide to distort? Did she think her version would rest better with family, friends, and historians?

Of course, her motivations will always remain clouded. Psychologists have concluded that autobiographers such as Mercedes "tend to seek information that confirms their theories about themselves and to revise their autobiographical memory so as that it accords with their current self-concept."[11]

When her autobiography appeared in 1960, many readers were offended. They did not want to read about all of Mercedes's female friends and former lovers. Sales were slim. Even at the age of sixty-seven, "that furious lesbian," as Cecil Beaton once described her, had done it again; she had refused to conceal her love for other women.[12] Through the years, however, the book has found an audience, especially in the homosexual community. In 1998, Ayer Company Publishers selected to reprint it as one of the fifty books in their series Homosexuality: Lesbians and Gay Men in Society, History and Literature.[13] Jonathan Katz, editor of the series, chose it because it was one of the few period autobiographies in which the author "sounded fairly 'out'."[14] The inclusion of Mercedes's book with those of Natalie Barney, Romaine Brooks, and Renée Vivien gave *Here Lies the Heart* even more credibility and visibility. It is now recognized as an important historical and social document. The book is a testament to a culturally influential lesbian life at a moment in history when most lesbians stayed in the closet.

Where does that leave the biographer? For more than forty years, even though they may have doubted some of Mercedes's accounts, writers have emblazoned them repeatedly in their own books. Through my own extensive archival research and personal observation, I have labored to point out the errors and distortions wherever I suspected them. I must agree with Georges Gusdorf, who writes in his classic essay "Conditions and Limits of Auto-biography" that "the biographer remains uncertain of his hero's intentions; he must be content to decipher signs, and his work is in certain ways always related to the detective story."[15]

I acknowledge that my conclusions, like the decisions and opinions of historians before me, are subjective. I confess that I decipher signs. For example, I had been struggling to determine the social position of the de Acosta family in New York society. I had little hard evidence. At one point, when I finally managed after weeks of investigation to determine the burial plot for Mercedes at Trinity Cemetery in New York City, I felt I had to witness the site myself. I wanted to view the plot but also wanted to establish birth and death dates of family members according to cemetery records. There had been a torrential rainstorm the night before I arrived, so that when the cemetery attendant drove me up the hilly, winding road in his pickup truck to the de Acosta plot, we discovered a large, majestic maple tree had crashed down, missing the stone marker by inches. Small branches and leaves were strewn everywhere. A chill ran through me, as though I had been suddenly transported into a Gothic novel. When I scanned the area from the hillside and discovered through the tall trees that the de Acosta vault was near the mausoleum of the Astors, it confirmed for me the status of Mercedes's family as well as her own personal desire for status and recognition.

For weeks at a time, spread over several years, it seemed as though I camped at the lovely Rosenbach Museum. For seven hours each day, I waded through the voluminous amount of correspondence from friends and lovers Mercedes had preserved, in addition to earlier drafts of her autobiography, an unpublished novel, endless clippings, essays she had written, and film scripts. I dissected set designs and photographs, even thirty years of passports. Often I felt as if I were an intruder, a "peeping Tom" reading love letters and poetry intended only for Mercedes. I remember especially the time I asked a staff member to help me decipher an extremely intimate and sensual poem that Isadora Duncan had written to Mercedes. It had been composed with a pencil in long hand, so I wanted to make sure I was reading it correctly.

Although Mercedes preserved thousands, yes, thousands of letters and telegrams written to her, very few of the letters she sent out to people were similarly preserved. This discrepancy meant, of course, that I often felt I was privy to only one side of a conversation and needed to very carefully reconstruct the other side. I hope that in my sincere desire to write a lively biography I misrepresented neither Mercedes nor anyone else.

I admit that my imagination was piqued when I examined some of her precious memorabilia. There is a little yellow anklet of Marlene Dietrich's with a lipstick smudge on its heel. Was it a gift to Mercedes? Was it unintentionally left behind when Marlene returned to her own home? What was the occasion? Where were they at the time? Why only one anklet? Where is the other one? Who kissed the heel? If it was a gift, what was said between them when it was presented? If it was left behind by accident, did Mercedes ever inform Marlene? Was there a message when one of them kissed the anklet? Why did she keep it for thirty years? How often did she hold it and bring the lipstick smudge to her own lips? What memories did it evoke? And a thousand more questions. What opulence for a biographer! What a treasure!

Many of Mercedes's photographs of her lovers and friends are in frames covered with black velvet. Where were they placed in her home? In a sitting room? In her bedroom? Why the choice of the sensual black velvet? Did the feel of the velvet stir up memories? Did she ever pick up a photo and kiss it or talk to it? Or run her hand up the soft velvet as she gazed at a photo? Why did she keep photos of women, such as Garbo and Le Gallienne, who had shunned her? What were her thoughts and feelings as she looked at these photographs? Again, what wealth for the biographer!

Although most of my research was productive, of course I encountered my share of brick walls. I wanted to confirm the report that Mercedes's mother had come to New York from Spain originally to regain a fortune that her uncle had stolen. Mercedes claimed that the New York Supreme Court awarded her mother four million dollars. I could find nothing to substantiate this account. The state archives in Albany, New York, have no record of a lawsuit. Officials in New York City told me that it could have happened but that a fire had destroyed many of their records years ago.

Also, I wanted to learn the truth about Mercedes's socialite sister, Rita Lydig, who was rumored to have been addicted to drugs. On several occasions, she had been hospitalized at the Mayo Clinic in Rochester, Minnesota, so I thought records there might provide some answers. The clinic would not release the files. Much to my surprise, I discovered that even though Rita had been dead for more than seventy years and there were no living relatives, the state of Minnesota will not release medical records without approval of a family member.

I spent several days at the Municipal Archives in Lower Manhattan. The first day was taken up poring over census records, trying to determine when and where the de Acosta family lived and the value of the property. Another day I was able to hold and read the actual decree and proceedings for the divorce of Rita from her first husband. In New York such papers are not public information but are always sealed for one hundred years after the divorce. When the dusty, folded pack of dried papers tied with a red ribbon was handed to me, it was sobering to realize that I would be the first person to read these proceedings since the divorce in 1900. And do they ever read like a soap opera, complete with charges of adultery, hotel witnesses, attempts to cover up and bribe, and fiery testimonials. Even more delight for this historian.

One of my discoveries, my most blessed, occurred in August 2000 while I was attending the national convention of the Association for Theatre in Higher Education in Washington, D.C. At one session, a panelist who represented the Manuscript Division of the Library of Congress happened to mention that they had several cardboard boxes of old, copyrighted plays that they were in the process of sorting for either destruction or recording on microfilm. He noted that in one of the boxes were some plays by a woman named Mercedes de Acosta. As far as he knew, nobody was aware that these scripts existed. I was not there, but as the gods have it, my dear friend Kim Marra was, knew I was working on this biography, and shot down the hall to find me minutes after the session ended. Minutes later, I connected with the Library of Congress and arranged a meeting with Alice Birney, Literary

Manuscript Historian. With her assistance, I was able to photocopy every one of the plays before I left the city.

Originally, I had written a detailed synopsis of these unpublished plays for this biography, since they were not available to the public. However, since Southern Illinois University Press decided to publish a collection of them titled *Women in Turmoil: Six Plays by Mercedes de Acosta,* I only summarize them here.

I hope this biography and the companion volume of plays will correct many myths and will help position Mercedes de Acosta in her proper place in history. She was not hugely famous. Her contributions to the theater were not substantial. Yet her story reveals a woman who stood up courageously for her beliefs and values. She seldom stumbled, even when her friends and peers turned against her. She lived her desire and paid the price. Perhaps the description of her as "that furious lesbian" should become an admirable attribute rather than a scornful slur.

Acknowledgments

To the following people, I say, "Many, many thanks!"

Jack C. Barnhart for inspiring, supporting, and editing this manuscript

Kim Marra for her continuing encouragement and advice

Mary Jo Sodd, the chair of the Theatre Department at Central College, for her understanding and advocacy

Val Hedquist, a former associate professor of art at Central College, for tracking down the location of a portrait of Mercedes painted by her husband

Alice Birney, Literary Manuscript Historian of the Library of Congress, for assisting in the discovery and photocopying of scripts

Hugo Vickers for hosting me twice at his country home in England, where he shared information about Mercedes and Cecil Beaton

Elizabeth Fuller, librarian at the Rosenbach Museum, and her staff for assisting in my research and for their loving supervision of the de Acosta Collection

Nicholas Scheetz and Scott Taylor of the Lauringer Library of Georgetown University for assisting in my research

George Ann Huck, a professor of Spanish at Central College, for serving as my interpreter and translator in Cuba

Jim Simmons of Southern Illinois University Press for his encouragement of this book and suggesting publication of a collection of Mercedes's plays

Elizabeth Brymer of Southern Illinois University Press for serving as a wise, patient, and gracious editor

Wayne Larsen, a former student of mine at Midland Lutheran College, for his meticulous and careful copyediting for Southern Illinois University Press

Lisa Merrill for accompanying me on a rather challenging afternoon in
  Washington, D.C., following our research at the Library of Congress

Abram Poole Jr. for hosting me at his home in Old Lyme, Connecticut,
  and sharing his memories of his creative father

Patricia Andre for providing information about her grandmother, who
  just may have been Mercedes's nanny

Nathaniel Weyl for sharing his memories of his Aunt Mercedes

Jan Mostowski for sharing his memories of a luncheon with Mercedes
  as she promoted her new autobiography

Lisette Coly, the executive director of the Parapsychology Foundation,
  for providing information about Mercedes's work with *Tomorrow*
  magazine

Ruth Schanke, my former wife, for her encouragement as I first began
  my interest in Mercedes in the early 1970s

Julie Lyford, my daughter, for her continued curiosity and interest in my
  research and many publications

Richard Glendening, a professor of economics, and Suzanne Wallace, an
  associate professor of economics, both at Central College, for translating
  historical dollars into contemporary terms

Robin Martin, the director of the Central College Library, and her staff
  for all their assistance in gathering materials

Terri Vander Molen, the director of campus services at Central College
  and her staff, especially Diane Schuring and Tammy Way, for all their
  clerical assistance

Rich Joens, a licensed independent social worker and dear friend, for
  helping me understand Mercedes

Central College for subsidizing my research

Joseph Kissane for supplying me with information and for conducting
  some research for me at Columbia University

The authors who contributed to *Passing Performances* and *Staging Desire*
  and who provided me with case studies about other artists who had
  same-sex sexual desires

Alberto Milanes Suarez for accompanying me on a memorable trip to
  Matanzas, Cuba

During my research at the Rosenbach Museum and Library in Philadelphia,
I read and studied all the letters written by both Greta Garbo and Eva Le
Gallienne to Mercedes. It is unfortunate that Garbo's niece, Gray Horan, has
not permitted the letters to be quoted directly. Le Gallienne's literary
executor, Eloise Armen, and Le Gallienne's former agent, Mitch Douglas,

also denied permission. Their objections, perhaps rooted in homophobia, may reflect fear that the reputations of their cherished icons will be tarnished and the value of their art negated.

All others, however, graciously granted permission to quote directly:

Jeff Lotman of TM & ©2001 Marlene, Inc. Licensed by Global Icons, LLC for Marlene Dietrich letters. All rights reserved.

Maria Riva, Marlene Inc., USA, and Marlene Dietrich Collection GmbH, Germany, for Marlene Dietrich letters

Edward Burns for permission to quote Alice B. Toklas letters from his *Staying On Alone: Letters of Alice B. Toklas*

Ray Pierre Corsini of the Anita Loos Trust for Anita Loos letters

Ellen T. M. Craig and Marie Taylor for Edward Gordon Craig letters

Justine A. Tenney for the Estate of Norman Bel Geddes, Edith Lutyens Bel Geddes, Executor, for Norman Bel Geddes letters

David Higham Associates for Tamara Karsavina letters

Amy Bishop and the Springer Opera House for an Alla Nazimova letter

Hugo Vickers for letters and diary entries of Sir Cecil Beaton © The Literary Executors of the late Sir Cecil Beaton, 2002

Ram Gopal for permission to quote from my interviews with him

Elizabeth E. Fuller, Rosenbach Museum & Library, Philadelphia, Pa, for permission to quote from the de Acosta Collection

Every effort has been made to obtain the necessary permissions with reference to copyright material, both illustrative and quoted; should there be any omissions in this respect I apologize and shall be pleased to make the appropriate acknowledgments in any future edition.

"That Furious Lesbian"

᠆ 1 ᠆

"Mother Complex"

On February 3, 1930, Mercedes's friend, the photographer and designer Cecil Beaton, wrote in his diary that he was embarrassed to be seen with Mercedes when he accompanied her to the theater that night. They had attended the Broadway premiere of Donald Ogden Stewart's *Rebound,* which starred Hope Williams, one of Mercedes's former lovers. As they found their seats in the crowded Plymouth Theatre, he sensed people looking at him and questioning why he associated with "that furious lesbian."[1] In more contemporary publications, she has been damned as "starstruck," a "lover to the stars," and more outrageously, "the greatest starfucker ever."[2] One of the documents at Philadelphia's Rosenbach Museum and Library that is intended to describe the vast de Acosta Collection even characterizes her as a "social butterfly." The fact that her roster of former lovers included the most eminent artists of the era has been used to portray Mercedes as something of a perverse psychopath.

So fascinated was Truman Capote by the amorous lifestyle of Mercedes de Acosta that he even devised a card game called International Daisy Chain. The challenge was to link people sexually, using as few beds as possible. "Mercedes is the best card to hold," he quipped. "You could get to anyone from Cardinal Spellman to the Duchess of Windsor."[3]

Mercedes was notorious for walking the streets of New York in mannish pants, pointed shoes trimmed with buckles, tricorn hat, and cape. Her chalk-white face, deep-set eyes, thin red lips, and jet black hair slicked back with brilliantine prompted Tallulah Bankhead to call her Countess Dracula.

1

She often boasted of her sexual prowess: "I can get any woman from any man."[4] Among her conquests were such international beauties as Greta Garbo, Marlene Dietrich, and Isadora Duncan, as well as Alla Nazimova, Eva Le Gallienne, Tamara Karsavina, Pola Negri, and Ona Munson. Additional, unsubstantiated chatter included Eleonora Duse, Katharine Cornell, Alice B. Toklas, and Eleanor Roosevelt. There was perhaps justification for Toklas's observation, "Say what you will about Mercedes, she's had the most important women of the twentieth century."[5]

The years 1916–1920, when Mercedes was experiencing her first adult relationships with other women—namely, Alla Nazimova, Isadora Duncan, and Hope Williams—she would not have been derided as "that furious lesbian." Indeed, owing in part to the popularity of Freudian psychology, the period signaled the beginning of "self-conscious sexual experimentation between women" who loved women. Women bobbed their hair, shortened their skirts, resisted Prohibition laws, and explored sex openly. As Lillian Faderman has suggested, "sex with other women was the great adventure . . . [and] many women did not hesitate to partake of it."[6]

Mercedes was no exception. During those years, she not only experienced love with other women but also wrote novels, volumes of poetry, and plays that revealed her same-sex sexual desires. Even though she usually avoided direct representation of same-sex eroticism in her writing, she freely "smuggled in" subaltern desires through other kinds of transgression. This indirect representation is what David Van Leer calls "queening," that is, "the ways in which gay men and to some extent women shape dominant cultural forms by silently importing into heterosexual plots rhetorics and motifs more common to their own homosexual community."[7] Mercedes writes about loneliness, social ostracism and prejudice, thwarted loves, and women with strong spiritual yearnings.

It is shortsighted to conclude that her importance might be dismissed with a simple shrug since most of her plays were never produced. Her good friend of thirty years, Indian dancer Ram Gopal, confided that "when she met men who ran the theaters, they did not want to work with a strong woman who loved women. Men found her too overpowering."[8] Mercedes absolutely refused to camouflage her desire for other women. As historian Felicia Londré has pointed out, even with the improved status of women in the theater, it remained important for a woman dramatist to demonstrate that her "essential femininity—her attractive appearance, her social position as a wife, her ability to run a household, her maternal devotion, and so forth—had not been impaired by her writing career."[9]

Indeed, the career of Rachel Crothers shows how a lesbian could succeed on Broadway by concealing her same-sex sexual desires. Although Crothers never married, she carefully "scripted a public identity of herself . . . that not only explained away the lack of a husband and children, but to some degree even celebrated her lack of conformity to a traditionally feminine, domestic role." The press always portrayed her "as married to her work and too busy for a social or personal life." As historian J. K. Curry points out, Crothers clearly felt "compelled to limit the subject matter of her plays in order to maintain public approval and commercial appeal."[10]

When suggestions were offered to Mercedes on how to make her scripts more commercial, however, "she would say, 'To hell with them.'" Mercedes "did not give a damn for the men in power," Ram insisted. "She was just herself and would not hide and conceal herself. She would not pander to anyone's taste. Because she insisted on being the dominant person in any production, interest always fell apart."[11] Not much had really improved since a few years earlier when playwright Marion Fairfax argued, "The best and first thing for an aspiring playwright to do is to be born a man."[12]

Even though the New York state legislature in 1927 passed a bill prohibiting any play from "depicting or dealing with, the subject of sex degeneracy, or sex perversion,"[13] Mercedes persisted in trying to mount a production of her play *The Dark Light* (1926) wherein there is an incestuous love between a brother and sister, and she wrote *Illusion* (1928), which is the story of a prostitute in a waterfront bar.

With the onset of the Great Depression at the end of the decade, lesbians came to be regarded as social outcasts. They were considered sick and sinful. Those like Mercedes who aspired to careers came under greater attack. They were accused of eroding the American family and taking jobs away from men. "Lesbians," writes Faderman, "were . . . considered monstrosities in the 1930s."[14] Little wonder, then, that Mercedes had become known as "that furious lesbian."

Many lesbians chose to marry, hoping for economic security and social acceptance as well as a safe cover for continuing their same-sex sexual practices. But Mercedes refused to buckle under and conform. She had married in 1920, but the union was certainly unconventional. She maintained her maiden name, reportedly invited a woman to join her and her husband on their honeymoon, and never concealed her love for women. In fact, her husband's son by a second marriage insists that she and her husband never consummated their marriage during their entire fifteen years together.[15] She often traveled and lived with other women and refused to conceal her romantic relationships with Eva Le Gallienne, Greta Garbo, Marlene Dietrich, and Ona Munson.

After World War II, when men returned from the battlefront, women were encouraged to renounce their wartime jobs and resume their place in the home. Lesbians, especially those who needed to work, were considered ill. One author, Frank Caprio, concluded that lesbians have "only a surface or pseudo happiness. Basically, they are lonely and unhappy and afraid to admit it."[16] He argued that lesbians were prone to suicide. Contempt for lesbianism generated books and journal articles that detailed accounts of conversion of homosexuals into heterosexuals and of cures for lesbianism. This image of the typical lesbian as a "sicko" convinced most of them of their need for secrecy. They were forced into the closet.

Soon after Senator Joseph McCarthy began his witch-hunts for Communists, he turned his wrath on homosexuals, claiming they were threats to national security. By April 1950, ninety-one homosexual women and men were fired from the State Department. Gays and lesbians in all walks of life were hunted down and encouraged to undergo treatment to cure them of their disease. One woman recalls, "If anyone ever asked if you were a lesbian you knew that you needed to deny it to your dying breath."[17] Mercedes, however, did not deny it. To Mercedes's credit, she never concealed her sexual orientation even though her openness brought her heartache and misery.

A highly illuminated, three-inch-thick, leather-bound family genealogy, with gold-embossed edging and numerous colorful coats of arms, traces the proud and noble history of the de Acosta family as far back as 1797.[18] Mercedes's mother, Micaela Hernandez de Alba y de Alba, was descended from the Castilian families of the dukes of Alba. The story of Mercedes's grandmother reads like a soap opera. Rita was a beautiful heiress living in Madrid. Known as "la Linda," she established a free, public medical clinic for the poor and was often seen dispensing money to beggars on the streets. She knew that her entire inheritance would revert to her evil uncle, Rodriguez, if she bore no children. At twenty-four, she married Rafael de Alba, who was the distinguished Commander and Chevalier of the Royal Order of Calatrava. Ruthless and determined to gain her fortune, her uncle poisoned Rita's husband, causing his impotency and a mental breakdown. As legal head of the family, the uncle had him committed to an insane asylum and even refused Rita's repeated requests for visitation. When he learned that his niece was already pregnant with Mercedes's mother, he fled to Paris with the fortune.

Three months after her baby was born, which was probably around 1853, Rita, along with a maid and a wet nurse, set off to find her uncle and to demand he sign a document that would release her husband from the asylum. Just as the ship was to leave the harbor at Cadiz, Rita received a letter saying that her husband had died of a heart attack. Already ill and exhausted, Rita collapsed and died before the ship reached France. A loyal friend of the family, Don Delgado, raised the little girl Micaela. When she was fourteen years old, the villainous uncle died, and they learned the fortune had been invested in banks in America. Accompanied by Don Delgado, Micaela sailed the following year to New York, where they hoped to regain the family fortune. In a typically happy ending to a seemingly unreal, melodramatic story, the Supreme Court ruled that Micaela was the rightful owner and awarded her nearly four million dollars.

While she was in New York in the late 1860s, Micaela met Cuban-born Ricardo de Acosta, who served as her translator. He had an equally sensational background. His father had migrated from Spain to Cuba, where he had established at La Jagua, near Matanzas, a coffee plantation that he named "Dolores" in honor of his first wife, whom he had met in Havana. It was supposedly one of the most beautiful plantations in all of Cuba, landscaped with flowers and tropical fruit trees. When guests came to visit for holidays, Ricardo's father threw vines across the tree-lined boulevard leading to the house and hung fruits and flowers from them for the guests to gather. The plantation was surrounded by a hedge of lemon trees. The couple had six children, four sons and two daughters.

Soon after Dolores died, her husband remarried. Mercedes's father was an offspring from this second marriage. When Ricardo was still an infant, the family returned to Madrid, but as he was growing up, he often heard accounts of how the Spanish authorities abused, intimidated, and terrorized not only the native Cubans but also African slaves. Through the centuries, Cuba had evolved from a sparsely populated island to a thriving land of large sugar, coffee, and tobacco plantations that relied on a slave population that by 1841 actually outnumbered the whites. They were huddled into crowded barrack buildings. Working conditions for the slaves on the large, impersonal estates were deplorable. Death from overwork was common. Especially during the harvest period, they often had less than four hours of sleep each day. They were sent into the fields in gangs and might work sixteen to eighteen hours before even given a break. Accidents were frequent. Slaves were often beaten and whipped to keep them from falling asleep. It was common for slaves to be left in stocks for days at a time.

A dozen years before Ricardo was born, in 1825, a slave rebellion near his family's plantation was overthrown, but forty-three slaves were killed and some twenty-four plantations were destroyed. In 1843, more uprisings near their home involved nearly one thousand slaves; hundreds were hunted down by trained bloodhounds, tortured, and killed. Indeed, it may have been this rebellion that convinced his parents of the need to return to Spain. One account reported that "slaughter-houses" were established in Matanzas "where the accused were subjected to the lash to extort confessions. . . . A thousand lashes were in many cases inflicted on a single negro; a great number died under this continued torture, and still more from spasms, and gangrene of the wounds."[19] In addition, seventy-eight were condemned to death, 1,292 sent to prison, and more than four hundred exiled.[20] Even slave owners who were suspected of opposing the government were seized, imprisoned, and beaten.

Mercedes writes that her father "made up his mind before he was eight years old that he would fight for the liberation of Cuba as soon as he was old enough, even though the Spaniards, his own people, would consider him a traitor."[21] His actual involvement is less than clear. Mercedes wrote that when her father and his parents returned to their coffee plantation when he was fifteen years old, Ricardo went almost immediately to Havana to see his Spanish fellow students who were involved in the struggle against the Spanish government.[22]

It is likely that Ricardo was more interested in the movement to have Cuba annexed by the United States than in liberation. As early as 1783, President John Adams had written that Cuba was clearly a natural extension of United States borders and that annexation was inevitable, and Thomas Jefferson was "a constant spokesman for incorporation of Cuba into the Union."[23] It was looked on as part of America's Manifest Destiny, a justification for imperialist expansionism. American annexationists, especially those in Southern states, hoped that by strengthening the slave system in Cuba they could counter the growing abolitionist movement. A few years later, when Stephen A. Douglas was a candidate for president in 1852, he argued for annexation, not because he was proslavery but because he believed annexation would strengthen slavery in the South and, thus, put the slavery question to rest.

The movement in Cuba for annexation may have begun as early as 1810, but it escalated in 1837 when a compelling, widely distributed essay declared that if Cuba were forced "to throw herself into foreign arms" she could not "fall with more honour or glory than in those of the great North American Confederation."[24] As the frequency of and destruction from slave uprisings escalated, wealthy plantation owners lived in constant fear that slave revolts would destroy their way of life. They saw annexation, therefore, as the best means of preserving slavery and their prosperity. It seems logical to assume that Mercedes, writing in 1960, preferred to describe her father as a young man fighting for liberty from Spain rather than for the preservation of slavery.

Whenever Ricardo went to Havana, he attended revolutionary meetings and helped to distribute political pamphlets. Unfortunately, during one of those trips around 1852, one of the members informed the authorities, and Ricardo, along with eighteen others, was arrested and condemned to the firing squad. When his mother visited him in prison in Havana, she told him that she cut off her beautiful hair and vowed to "La Señora de la Merced" that she would live the rest of her life with a shaven head if her son's life would be spared. She had already sent her hair to the priest at the church in Matanzas and instructed that it be used for the statue of the Virgin. When a Spanish guard saw Ricardo's mother's shaven head and overheard her story, he instructed Mercedes's father in how he might escape.

According to Mercedes's account, as the convicts were lined up to be executed on the battlements of Morro Castle overlooking the sea, Ricardo leaped over the wall just as the captain shouted "Fire!" He barely escaped smashing against the jutting rocks and swam until he was rescued by an American schooner headed for Boston.

Although the 1871 tragedy of eight martyred medical students and their Cuban classmates is well documented and commemorated by Cubans each year in November, there is no evidence of Mercedes's account of her father's arrest and escape. During the Spanish-American War at the end of the century, the Spanish authorities destroyed thousands of official documents; others they confiscated when they fled the country. Proof of Mercedes's story certainly may have been among those papers. However, the likelihood of her father's escape by jumping into the sea is problematic. The castle had been designed so that it was surrounded on three sides by monstrous, sharp, jutting rocks that would deter enemy ships from approaching and attacking. Sharks swarm the waters below. From no point along the battlement is there a spot where someone could jump into the sea and swim to safety. Official tourist guides at the castle argue that firing squads were never used. In fact, they claim that as late as the 1950s during the infamous Batista regime, enemies of the state were thrown alive over the battlement to be killed by the spiked rocks and the hungry sharks.[25]

One distant relative who wishes to remain anonymous supplied another story. He indicated that many family members believed Ricardo was arrested but that his supposed escape was total fiction. They concluded that after he was arrested, he negotiated his release by supplying evidence against the other prisoners. Since he would then have been considered an outcast by both the liberation and annexation forces, the Spanish government enabled his escape to the United States.[26]

Regardless of how and when he arrived, Ricardo settled in New York, where he became a highly paid executive for a steamship line running between New York and the West Indies. He was introduced to Mercedes's mother in the late 1860s when he was asked by a lawyer friend to serve as an interpreter in Micaela's lawsuit.[27] As she prepared to return to Spain with Don Delgado after the lawsuit was settled, she decided, instead, to accept Ricardo's marriage proposal. She was only sixteen years old. "This union in America of a de Alba and a de Acosta," Mercedes wrote, "was to be the bridge between the Old World and the New over which their children were to cross back and forth in ceaseless search of a home."[28]

When they were not vacationing in Europe or in Southampton, they lived in a house at 48 West Forty-seventh Street, between Fifth and Sixth Avenues. According to the 1870 New York census, the house was valued at forty thousand dollars.[29] In terms of 2001 dollars, that would amount to just over one-half million dollars.[30] Residing in the heart of the fashionable area on the West Side restricted to private houses, they had as nearby neighbors Joseph Choate, who was America's ambassador to Great Britain, and Theodore Roosevelt. Only a few blocks away, the Vanderbilt mansion stood at the northwest corner of Fifty-second Street. It was common to see Alfred Vanderbilt riding in his brightly painted coach with the "two small footmen standing at the back dressed in gay green livery, wearing high silk hats and blowing lovely notes on long, golden horns."[31]

Mercedes's parents undoubtedly took part in the genteel social activities of the neighborhood and probably attended one of the most famous parties ever given in the United States. On March 26, 1883, Alva and William K. Vanderbilt opened their new house with a fancy-dress ball. Although such events had been popular in New York since the 1820s, during the 1865–1866 season, there had been six hundred such balls. The average cost of a striking costume, without jewelry, was estimated at one thousand dollars (twenty-one thousand in 2001 dollars).

But none of those earlier parties even rivaled the Vanderbilt extravaganza. As the twelve hundred guests began to arrive at about seven o'clock in the evening, hundreds of sightseers lined the streets to see the likes of Mary Stuart, Gilbert and Sullivan's Fairy Queen, Don Carlos, Charles IX of France, Venetian princesses, and Neapolitan fishermen enter the mansion. Cornelius Vanderbilt was Louis XVI, while his wife Alice was "The Electric Light" in a costume that lighted up at intervals from batteries in her pockets. Inside, the halls and drawing rooms were lined with roses, while the upstairs gymnasium had been transformed for the banquet into a tropical garden with palms, orchids, and bougainvillea.

The chief attraction was the "hobbyhorse quadrille," a sort of stately square dance in which the dancers wore costumes that made them look as if they were sitting astride horses. The life-size horses took two months to construct and were covered with leather, flowing manes, tails, and false legs attached on the outside of embroidered horse blankets. The *New York World* calculated that the ball had cost the Vanderbilts $55,730 for costumes, four thousand dollars for carriage hire, four thousand dollars for hairdressers, and $65,270 for champagne, catering, and music![32] In 2001, this party would have cost more than two million dollars![33]

It is conceivable that the de Acostas attended the 1880 debut of Corinne Roosevelt at which six hundred guests danced to the music of a full orchestra in a library decorated with pink carnations and dined with baskets of roses on all tables. And they undoubtedly joined the Vanderbilts, Roosevelts, Harrimans, and others of elite society for the lavish "housewarming" that Mayor and Mrs. Abram Hewitt hosted on the afternoon of February 16, 1888. Thirty-two musicians of the Ladies Amateur Orchestra entertained the guests as they surveyed the elaborate architectural achievements of Stanford White.

Although the de Acostas may not have basked in quite the same vast wealth as some of their neighbors, they were certainly accepted in the setting. Mercedes, who was born in 1893, was the last child in a family of three boys and five girls.[34] The first child, her brother Joaquin, died before Mercedes was born. Her four sisters were Rita, Aida, Maria, and Angéla, who was always known as "Baba." Her surviving brothers were Ricardo (Dick) and Enriqué (Hennie). Three women servants managed the household— Catherine (Katie) Coffey, Annie Cahill, and Maggie Kelly. Katie really served as companion to Mercedes's mother, teaching her English, helping her dress, and accompanying her to Mass. She also took care of Mercedes as she had all of the other children. Annie Cahill, who had run away from her home in Ireland, would chaperone Mercedes to parties. She "believed in romance and she understood all my problems of the heart," Mercedes disclosed. "She would discuss them with me and weigh them from every angle, always advising me wisely, but at the same time with daring. She would say, 'Be as wise as a serpent and as gentle as a dove.'"[35] Maggie was the nanny and laundress. Completing the staff was Bridget Sweeney, their Irish cook; José Arias, the butler; Adelaide Barling, who acted as duenna to Mercedes's mother; and a man simply called Pancho, who was an office assistant to Mercedes's father and spent many hours with the family.[36]

Another important component in the household was Ezequiel Rojas, the former president of Venezuela. Having fallen in love with Mercedes's mother years earlier, he became Mercedes's godfather. During the many years he served as an ambassador in Washington, he spent all of his available time in the de Acosta home. Mercedes's mother "was the love of his life and, because of her, he never married or even looked at another woman."[37]

In her autobiography, Mercedes mentions that she "felt a disharmony" between her parents but that it was not until years later, "by piecing together certain facts and evaluating feelings and intuitions of my childhood, that I [was] able to weigh and partially determine their relationship."[38] Perhaps Mercedes was cautiously concealing the truth when she describes her godfather as a "great gentleman . . . a charming, interesting man, very small, with the most delicate hands and feet. . . . I never knew anyone more considerate of the feelings of others."[39] Yet he continued his long, extended visits in their home, which must have created rather unusual dynamics and tensions. One can only speculate as to what Mercedes thought about the arrangement and what she discussed with the servants. What did she think about the devotion and loyalty Mercedes's father had toward Pancho, whom Mercedes described as seeming "close to an idiot?"[40] Were her parents maintaining no more than just the facade of a marriage?

Regardless of her current life in the New World and her management of a rather unconventional household, Mercedes's mother was unadaptable and retained her Old World, Spanish, and Catholic views—daily Mass, speaking in her native tongue whenever she could, and holding on to the view that women should marry well, lead quiet and pampered lives, and draw no attention to themselves. She certainly subscribed to the position voiced by Rev. Charles Parkhurst that it was a disease for women to ape "everything mannish." To retain their "supremacy," women should make "more and more of their womanliness."[41] She was rarely seen without a fan and would punctuate her ideas with its clicks and flutters. Except for music, she regarded most art as 'trash' and objected to her daughter's interest in reading and writing.

Mercedes believed that her father had little influence over her and even described him as "a weak man unable to assert his own tastes as against my mother's."[42] Yet the picture she paints of him in her autobiography, whether accurate or not, is quite different. It was clearly not a weak, spineless man who, she claimed, participated in life-threatening student revolts in Cuba and barely escaped with his life. His battles against the oppressive Spanish regime, his determination to survive, and his creation of a way of life in the New World for his family that introduced them to wealth and love of lit-

erature and the arts cannot be regarded as legacies from a weak and ineffective father. His fighting for his freedom and standing up for his beliefs
were values he handed on to Mercedes.

If it is true that Mercedes's father "did not interest me as a person,"[43]
the same could not be said of her mother. When she was about fifteen, she
revealed her great adoration by dedicating a collection of poems to her
mother:

I

Pure as a lily, as white as snow,
Spreading sunshine, where e're
    she may go,
Spotless beautiful, and sweet,
Giving her wisdom to whom she
    may meet.

II

Lovely as the morning sun;
Bewitching as the evening sky,
Always striving, working to conquer,
    At least to try.

III

How much more can I tell of this
    wonderful being
How much more can I tell of the
    love and the feeling
That is in my soul and in my
    heart
Conquering and holding me in every
    part.

IV

Thank God! He has made me to
    know her so well.
Thank God! He has made me this
    story to tell
And may we all tell our love
    for one another
As I, my love here have told for
    my mother.[44]

As Mercedes admitted in her autobiography, "I unquestionably had a mother complex . . . an extravagant feeling for my mother."[45]

When Mercedes was about four years old, Maggie began taking her to daily Mass at St. Patrick's Cathedral, where she always made faces and stuck out her tongue at one particular parishioner in a pew behind her. Charmed by the precocious little girl, he went to the mother superior of the orphanage next to the church and asked whether he could adopt Mercedes. Since she always sat next to the orphans, he had thought she was part of that collection of children. When he persisted even after the mother superior identified Mercedes, she arranged a meeting between him and Mercedes's mother. In the end, it was agreed that this man, who was none other than the famous theater producer, Augustin Daly, could fetch Mercedes every Sunday afternoon so she could spend the day with him. Daly did not take Mercedes to his home, however. Instead, unbeknownst to Mercedes's mother, he would transport her to the home of actress Ada Rehan where the three of them would create little toy stages and reenact plays.

An American playwright and theatrical manager, Daly had been a drama critic for New York City newspapers from 1859 to 1869, when he began producing revivals of old English comedies at the Fifth Avenue Theater. He wrote a number of melodramas, including *Under the Gaslight* (1867), *A Flash of Lightning* (1868), and *The Red Scarf* (1869). In 1879 he renamed the Broadway Theater after himself and, with such stars as John Drew, Ada Rehan, and Otis Skinner, presented adaptations of French and German dramas at Daly's Theater. After 1893 he produced Shakespearean comedies in London and New York.

Shortly after Rehan joined Daly's company in 1879, she became his leading lady until his death in 1899. It was well known that Rehan and Daly were lovers. Her more than two hundred roles included many from Shakespeare as well as from several European comedies adapted by Daly for the American stage. Rehan's greatest role, first played in New York City in January 1887, was Katherine in *The Taming of the Shrew*. In 1894 she starred in a phenomenally successful London production of *Twelfth Night*. She appeared in San Francisco in 1896 as part of an American tour but frequently returned to London during her last years on the stage. Mercedes undoubtedly saw her starring in *Sweet Nell of Old Drury* in 1901 and as Katherine in a revival of *The Taming of the Shrew* in 1904.

When Mercedes's mother learned where her daughter was spending Sunday afternoons, the visits ceased. Mercedes was allowed, however, to go backstage with Daly during matinees at his theater. Sometimes she would sit on his lap and watch a rehearsal; other times, Daly would carry her around on his shoulders and tell people that Mercedes was going to become a great actress. Her visits to the theater left a strong stamp on the impressionable young girl: "I remember distinctly being perched on Mr. Daly's shoulder in the wings and listening to the overture. I remember the excitement of the curtain going up and the hush that fell over everyone in the wings. Mr. Daly would put his finger to his lips to make sure I would be quiet. I remember the footlights and the 'spots' and the smell of grease paint and the continual coming and going of actors and actresses in strange costumes."[46]

The American theater was thriving. More than four hundred companies were touring the country. New York City had forty-one legitimate theaters, more than any other city in the world. The star system flourished with productions on Broadway featuring Richard Mansfield, Mrs. Leslie Carter, Mrs. Fiske, Lionel Barrymore, and Maxine Elliott. Foreign stars such as Sarah Bernhardt, Eleonora Duse, J. Forbes-Robertson, Lily Langtry, Rejane, Alla Nazimova, and Mrs. Patrick Campbell were attracting full houses. Mrs. Fiske, Mary Shaw, and Nance O'Neil were presenting Ibsen. Julian Eltinge, clearly the most famous of all female impersonators of his day, made his stage debut.

By 1903, the Theatrical Syndicate, which had been formed nine years earlier, had become a powerful monopoly, owning seventy theaters, controlling nearly half of the professional theaters in the country, demanding that managers book only their shows, insisting on booking fees, and stifling competition. The aim, of course, was profit. Major stars such as Mrs. Fiske who resisted the Syndicate were forced into second-rate theaters. Brooks Atkinson has called it "the unseen monster that hovered over Broadway."[47] In 1905 the Shubert brothers began their rival company and soon became almost as ruthless as the Syndicate. For the next fifteen years, the two organizations battled for control of the American stage. They promoted the star system, type casting, and the "long run." They paid "puffs" to promote their shows, they hired press agents to advertise them, and they wined and dined the critics.

Infatuated by all the hype, Mercedes, along with childhood chum Alice de Zaldo, would walk along Fifth Avenue and hope to catch glimpses of her favorite actors. They would swoon if they saw John or Ethel Barrymore. Although Mercedes might have passed up lighter offerings such as comedian Eddie Foy in *Up and Down Broadway* and the seductive Anna Held in Ziegfeld's *Miss Innocence,* she undoubtedly would not have missed seeing Ethel Barrymore, who starred in both *Captain Jinks and the Horse Marines* and *Alice Sit by the Fire.* "Alice and I had a mania for going to the theatre. On the sly we went to matinees when our families thought we were out exercising in the air."[48]

Particularly memorable was their catching a performance of Maude Adams, who lived nearby. She had appeared in New York in *The Midnight Bell* (1888), then spent three years with the Charles Frohman acting company. She had starred in Sir James Barrie's *The Little Minister* (1896) just three years after Mercedes's birth and as the Duke of Reichstadt in *L'Aiglon* five years later. In 1905, she created the role of Barrie's Peter Pan, probably her most popular performance. Opening night was phenomenal. "Maude Adams is Peter," raved the *New York Times*.[49] It played thirty-one weeks on Broadway for 237 performances, the longest continuous engagement Maude Adams had ever enjoyed. "Every child was hysterical about her as the little boy who never grew up and I was no exception," Mercedes confessed. "To me she *was* Peter Pan and when I saw her in the part I was thrown into a state of ecstasy."[50]

Is it coincidence that at least four leading ladies who have played Peter Pan were lesbian or rumored to be—Maude Adams, Eva Le Gallienne, Jean Arthur, and Mary Martin? How historian Stacy Wolf explains the character's fascination for Mary Martin might speak for all these actresses: "Peter Pan's setting in a world of make-believe gave Martin a freedom to play gender, bound only by the lengthy and complex (although always played by a woman) history of the role. There was no heterosexual romance to play."[51] Perhaps Mercedes, though only twelve years old at the time, was attracted to the role for the very same reason.

~2~

"I Will Be Lonely All My Life"

What with her beauty, her singular allure, her personal extravagances, and the long success of tragedies that befell her, ...she was not, in her essence, a true embodiment of her time: that she belonged, rather, to the days (and to the novels) of Balzac, to the pages of Turgenev, the stories of Maupassant. There was even, in her battle with destiny, a haunting suggestion of the tortured and heart-broken Emma Bovary. . . . Rita Lydig was certainly a dominant influence in the life of her day.[1]

Until she died in 1929, Rita was also a dominant influence on her sensitive and impressionable younger sister, Mercedes.

Born in 1875, 1879, or 1880,[2] by 1894 she was making headlines on the society pages. "Rita could have married any number of men," Mercedes maintained. "There were always so many who were in love with her, and many who were her friends and who—as the expression then was—were 'attentive' to her. She had American admirers and many foreigners, both titled and untitled who, at this time, hung in masses around eligible and, especially, rich American women."[3]

Nearly every evening of the prestigious, annual horse show at Madison Square Garden, where all of high society wanted to be seen, Rita was observed in the box of millionaire William E. D. Stokes. Among such social trendsetters as Mrs. Astor, Mrs. Levi P. Morgan, and Mrs. "Willie" Vanderbilt, she was singled out as "the most beautiful young woman in New York" and praised for her "dark, soulful beauty which is found only among the fair

15

women of Spain or Italy."[4] Her flashing eyes, voluptuous lips, impudent chin, shiny black hair brushed up into a loose pompadour, and her alabaster-like skin dusted with lavender powder attracted attention wherever she went.

On January 4, 1895, Rita provoked headlines again: "Wedding of Miss Acosta." The *New York Times* reported that "no wedding this season in New York has attracted more interest among society people generally than the marriage of" Rita de Acosta to William E. D. Stokes. Because the groom was not Catholic, the wedding took place at the home of the bride, with Archbishop Corrigan of Saint Patrick's Cathedral officiating. Even though she was an infant less than two years old, Mercedes claimed she could remember Rita descending the stairway in their house. "Few brides of the past year have showed such excellent taste," commented one reporter. Her wedding gown was

> cut simply, and was of the richest ivory white satin, with trimmings of rare point lace. Lilies of the valley in pretty sprays were caught on the skirt. A superb necklace of pearls, the gift of Mr. Stokes, encircled the bride's throat. The bridal veil was of tulle, fastened to the coiffure by a coronet of natural orange blossoms. The bride carried a large bunch of orchids, held together by a band of chiffon to match. American Beauty roses in great profusion, orchids, and orange blossoms brought from Florida, thousands of violets, carnations, countless other flowers of the season transformed every room on the first floor into a fairy-like floral bower. . . . The large yard at the rear of the bride's home was placed under a canopy, and it was there that the reception was held.[5]

One thousand guests attended. No wonder it was described by the *New York Times* as one of the highlights of the social world. And no wonder Mercedes could remember the occasion, for she darted out of the sidelines and promptly sat down on the train. "Needless to say I was snatched up and carried away kicking violently."[6]

Many people believed that Rita was pressured into the marriage by her father, who recognized the financial advantages.[7] Her mother, a staunch Catholic, opposed her daughter's marrying outside the faith, and many people questioned Rita's decision to marry this man who was twenty years her senior. Regardless, he was a graduate of Yale University, a multimillionaire who was the president of the Chesapeake Western Railway, which ran across the Shenandoah Valley; he also owned a large racing stable and stud farm outside Lexington, Kentucky, and shared her love of breeding prize horses. Also in his favor, he owned a handsome cottage in fashionable Newport.

Rita, who was probably only twenty at the time, surely felt that her husband would be her passport to a life of elegance and style.

Mercedes writes in a typescript draft of *Here Lies the Heart* that when her sister lived in Kentucky during her pregnancy with her son, she saw all of Stokes's shady friends—bookies, horse dealers, jockeys, and so forth. "Rita was made aware that Stokes was carrying on a number of affairs behind her back with servant girls and the daughters of neighboring farmers."[8]

Stokes's personality and activities attracted unsavory people. After a house party in the spring of 1895, for instance, Stokes was awakened about midnight by loud cries of "Help! Murder!" Rita and he ran to the window but saw no one. Looking over the stair rail, they saw a man with a knife and heard him shout, "Let me get at that Stokes till I kill him!" Stokes went downstairs, ordered the man from the house, and eventually struck him with a broken bottle and had him arrested. Although Stokes was accused in open court of alcoholic intoxication, the intruder, who was their maid's brother, was found guilty of assault in the third degree.[9] Rumors spread that the intruder was seeking revenge for Stokes's having seduced his sister.

For all his vast wealth, Stokes had a reputation for being incredibly stingy. Three months after their marriage, it was reported that Stokes was dodging process servers for back taxes and that he was being charged with contempt of court. The back taxes amounted to only $464.46. And when twenty-two large boxes of his European purchases of furniture, china, porcelain, and statuary arrived from Rome after their honeymoon, he refused to pay the freight charges of $634.40, claiming the fee was excessive.[10]

Through the connections of her wealthy husband, however, Rita was able to pursue her love of horses. Set on having the fastest trotter in the world, she purchased the fleet mare, Benzetta, for sixteen thousand dollars, expecting that he would develop into a champion, and she was presented by the Grand Duke Dimitri of Russia with two full-blooded Russian trotters with pure Orloff pedigrees that she planned to use on her Kentucky farm for breeding purposes. She was thrilled when her husband was appointed the Imperial Russian Government's correspondent for horses and horse breeding in America, with rank, uniform, official entree, and permission to wear the uniform in America on official occasions. This appointment was the outcome of a visit she and her husband had when they attended by "special imperial invitation" the coronation of the czar in Moscow.

It must have been a devastating blow, then, when, in November 1896, a major fire burned one of her barns along with nine heads of the choicest stock on her farm, including the two she had received from the Grand Duke of Russia and Josie B., who had just set the world's pacing record of 2:09H at the Trotting Horse Breeder's Association. The fire broke out in a loft, and the total loss was valued at sixty thousand dollars. There were rumors of arson. Rita's comment when she learned of the fire: "I would rather have had the house burned, with all there is in it, than to have lost the barn."[11] It seems an odd comment from a woman married less than two years, but maybe she was already feeling that the future with her husband looked bleak and less than promising.

One wonders what her parsimonious husband thought when Rita decided to host a lavish "Negro Ball." She built a new, huge ten-thousand-dollar barn (240 feet by 60 feet), decorated it elaborately, and hired a "colored" band. Half the floor space was covered with canvas on which the guests danced. The other half was shut off with sliding doors and used as a dining room with a 110-foot-long table decorated with fruits and cakes. There was a menu of roast shoat and sweet potatoes, fried fish and coffee, fruits, pickles, ice cream, and cake with claret punch, whiskey, and sangaree for beverages. Rita sent out two hundred invitations, and all were accepted. "Negroes" from surrounding towns and cities begged for invitations. As the *New York Times* reported, "She is the first white woman who ever gave the colored people such an elaborate entertainment here. They refer to her as the 'Horse Lady.'"[12]

Perhaps by that time, a little more than two years after her marriage, she had decided to defy her husband's stinginess. She had learned that this marriage was not an easy entry into the fashionable life but rather one with untold challenges. After all, he was not fond of society, went out very little, was independent in the matter of dress, and was indifferent to fads and fashion. Some years later, Rita wrote about a millionaire "who used to attend the opera religiously with his wife. [She was] a great beauty who was one of the sights of the Horseshoe with her jewels and her bare shoulders— and, as soon as the music began, he retreated to the sofa in the little room behind the box, and sat with his hands over his ears. 'Why in the world do you come here?' I asked him. He made a face. 'You have to go somewhere,' he said. 'What difference does it make? There are noises everywhere.'"[13] The anecdote was quite probably about her own husband. Although some women may have found him "a very refreshing individual,"[14] Rita considered him an embarrassing bore.

Mercedes recalls that when Rita returned to New York after the birth of her son, William Jr., on January 5, 1896, "she made every effort to conceal the fact that she was unhappy with" her husband.[15] By 1899, it looked as if the marriage was over. By May of that year, Rita had ceased living with her husband and had taken up residency first at the Buckingham Hotel and

then at the Plaza. The *New York Times* was probably accurate in its assess-
ment: "Socially during their recent married life Mr. and Mrs. Stokes hardly
made the headway they desired. . . . [He] had had much litigation with his
family, and several suits have been cause celebres."[16] Although Rita's mother
claimed in a front-page article that there was "not a word of truth in the
story," by March of the next year, Rita had sued for divorce.

   In her petition for divorce, which was registered with the Supreme Court
of New York County on March 13, 1900, Rita claimed that in the previous five months her husband had "committed adultery with one or more
women" in New York, Boston, and Philadelphia.[17] In the court transcript
filed on April 17, 1900, their valet, George Dagneau, testified that the previous November he had accompanied Rita's husband and "a beautiful lady,"
"a very tall lady, [with] blue eyes, black hair and a very white skin" to the
Hotel Lafayette in Philadelphia and witnessed him register under the name
of "Mr. and Mrs. W. E. Coates and servant." He told the court that he saw
Stokes and the lady "retire for the night in the bedroom of this suite" and
saw them come out of the bedroom the next morning. "Everything showed
that they had retired, and the bed," he remembered, "was in a condition as
if it had been slept in." Henry E. Woolsey, a room clerk at the hotel, confirmed this account. The valet also swore that "a tall, dark, young lady" visited Stokes at their home six or seven times. One time in particular, he
remembered, they went upstairs to the bedroom after dinner and stayed two
to three hours with the door shut. When the valet later went into the room,
"the room was in disorder"; the bed "very much in disorder; all upset." Mary
Taaffe, who was employed by Stokes as a waitress and laundress in their home,
testified that Stokes received "lady callers" at his house. She recounted that
on one occasion she found a lady's hairpin between the bed pillows and a
handkerchief under the dinner table.

   Though Rita had known for years that her husband had been unfaithful to her, she had tried to remain in the marriage, even if it meant living
separately. There were obvious financial benefits. After all was said and done,
she enjoyed a maid of her own, a nurse for their son, servants, a valet, butler, cook, and four grooms. How could she give up the glamour of living
at the Plaza Hotel? Whether or not she had ever considered divorce before, on February 22, 1900, she was forced to act. In a letter she wrote to
her husband, she asked, "I suppose you recognized me on 5th Ave. today?"

   I can not be mistaken about the character of the woman with whom
   you were driving! Her appearance plainly shows what she is—I should
   <u>think</u> that you would have too much respect for yourself to parade

about Fifth Ave with <u>such</u> a woman in broad daylight—but I want
you to understand once for all—I will not tolerate this kind of thing!
This last insult is more than I can bear! and I am determined to divorce
you <u>at once</u>—if you think that I am the kind of woman who would
particularly submit to public insults of <u>this kind</u>—you are mistaken!—

That same day, Stokes replied, "My beautiful Rita":

What a proud girl you are! Your suspicions are correct.—Blame me,
don't trouble the woman. . . . Never have I lied tricked or deceived
you. . . . But why should you find fault with me who till now has been
true to you since the moment we met. I have loved you with all my
heart & soul. I simply lived on your smiles. I never even called on a
woman or rode in a carriage with one except you were with me. I
have been your slave, fairly worshiped you and the ground you stood
on. Never an unkind word or an unkind act did I say or do. I was so
proud of you. I know the sweet side of your confiding child-like
nature. . . . Day and night I worked and planned for you. . . . We were
so happy together, until as it were this cloud came between us.

Regardless of his defense, on May 7, 1900, Justice Bischoff signed the
decree, which was certainly among the largest divorce settlements on record.
Rita was awarded custody of their son and the right to remarry and to resume her maiden name. She was granted alimony of twelve thousand dollars annually "during her natural life, or until she shall again marry." Stokes
was prohibited from marrying during her lifetime, was awarded visitation
rights, and could apply for custody of their son if she ever remarried.[18] It
was speculated that Stokes gave Rita an additional two million dollars in
return for giving up the custody of their son. But years later, she put a different spin on the proceedings, arguing that she had not "sold" her son back
to his father: "I had been too proud to contradict the lie in the past. I gave
the boy back to his father so that he might inherit his father's estate, which
he has."[19] But it was no secret that she had a strong distaste for Stokes and
wanted no reminders of their marriage, including her own son.[20]

With her fortune in hand, Rita bought luxurious antiques, art objects,
and the latest Parisian fashions. She purchased a house on the Avenue d'Iéna
in Paris, drove her own four-in-hand in New York and Paris, exhibited prize
horses at shows in Madison Square Garden, and continued her interest in
racing trotters. As Annette Tapert and Diana Edkins have described her in
The Power of Style, "Marriage, divorce, maternal neglect, passionate consum-
erism—all these made Rita a much-discussed personage in New York so-

cial circles."[21] Her cavalier behavior bothered Mercedes, who was only seven years old: "During this time Rita's situation was one more thing to make me feel uneasy and nervous."[22]

Mercedes certainly had other things to make her feel out of step. She was convinced she was a boy. "More often than not," she wrote, "I was dressed as a boy, generally in a sailor suit. I remember well a photograph of me in this suit which has since been destroyed. In my hand, for some unknown reason, I held a small walking stick. I seemed to be making a great effort to be manly."[23] Her mother called her "Rafael" and encouraged her to play boys' games. But one day, a boy challenged her:

"Have you got this?" he demanded.

I was horrified. I had heard about grown people and children being deformed. . . .

"You're deformed!" I shouted.

"If you are a boy and you haven't got this, you are the one who is deformed," he shouted back.

By this time the other boys had joined us, each boy speedily showing me the same strange phenomenon the first boy had exhibited. . . . They demanded that I produce the same "phenomenon."

"Prove that you're not a girl," they screamed.

She stumbled away and rushed to her nurse.

I flung myself upon her shouting wildly and crying. . . . While I still shouted and screamed she contrived to rush me home and tried to appease me until my mother arrived. When she did, and it was finally admitted that I was a girl I fell into a delirium. For three days I raged in bed and ran a high temperature. An American doctor was summoned to take care of me. He tried to talk reason into me. He tried to make me think it was better to be a girl, but my mental suffering was such that nothing he said remotely impressed me. . . . I pleaded with the doctor to operate upon me or give me some medicine to make this mysterious part grow upon me. . . . Later when I was better, and able to go out, I did not want to go to the beach and face the boys. I would not play with girls either. . . . After this I became very religious. Instead of playing, I used to steal to church and pray that I would become a boy. Each morning when I woke up the first thing I did was to see if the miracle had happened.[24]

Like the girl discussed by Sigmund Freud a few years later in "The Psychogenesis of a Case of Homosexuality in a Woman," Mercedes's comparison of a boy's genital organs with her own "left a strong impression on her and had far-reaching effects. . . . [S]he had developed a pronounced envy for the penis."[25] She played at being a newsboy, running from the basement to the top floor of their house with newspapers under her arm and shouting out headlines. Like most little boys her age, Mercedes planned to become a sailor or fireman or even a great general. "I had a sort of 'folie de grandeur' in all the games I played. I imagined myself performing some heroic deed such as saving drowning children, scaling the highest mountain in the world or leading a victorious and invincible army toward world conquest."[26]

Her parents were naturally concerned that their daughter was not showing enough signs of proper femininity. Studies published at the time, in fact, warned them that when young girls spent too much time with boys and playing boys' games, they could, indeed, grow up to be masculine women. To prevent such a disorder, it was actually recommended that girls "should be strictly confined" to the company of their own gender.[27]

A few years earlier, front-page headlines in the *New York Times* reported "A Most Shocking Crime/A Memphis Society Girl/Cuts A Former Friend's Throat." The subtitle read: "Alice Mitchell, Daughter of A Wealthy Retired Merchant, Jumps From A Carriage, Seizes Freda Ward, And Kills Her." A few days later, the motive was announced: "I killed Freda because I loved her, and she refused to marry me."[28] Several novels and short stories soon appeared, focusing on masculine women who killed their female lovers.

Mercedes's parents were greatly concerned over this image of the masculine woman. Fearful of what might lie ahead for their youngest child, they decided to follow the current research and to promote the company of her own sex. They sent Mercedes to a New York convent school run by the Sisters of Charity "to make a girl" of her. Of course, they never suspected that this might actually focus their daughter's sexual desires.

While at the school, Mercedes soon befriended two lesbian nuns, Sisters Isabel and Clara, delivered notes between them, and even stood guard in the corridors while they stole some privacy. Mercedes witnessed in grief and horror when the mother superior announced that they must be separated: "For a second they stood mutely." Then came "a cry like the cry of death."[29] Mercedes ran down the hallway screaming hysterically, "I am not a boy and I am not a girl, or maybe I am both—I don't know. . . . I will never fit in anywhere and I will be lonely all my life."[30] The astonished nuns repeated this conversation to the mother superior, and Mercedes was gravely punished for her outbursts.

In an unpublished draft of her autobiography, she recalls her bewilderment at the convent: "I cannot understand these so-called 'normal' people who believe that a man should love only a woman, and a woman love only a man. If this were so, then it disregards completely the spirit, the personality, and the mind, and stresses the importance of the physical body."[31] In still another draft of her autobiography, she continues this theme. "How am I to convey to the reader the diverse people I feel within me," she pleads? "Who of us are only one sex? I, myself, am sometimes androgynous."[32]

After the trauma at the convent, her affliction with what she called "moaning sickness" began. She would hide in a corner of a room, put her face to the wall, and moan. The attacks would start about five o'clock in the morning when she would awaken with a sense of fear and fatigue. Sometimes she would lie listless for hours and become obsessed with thoughts of ending her own life.

The next year, she was sent to a boarding school at a convent outside Morristown, New Jersey, where her sister Baba had been living. But she disliked so much being away from her mother that she went on a hunger strike and refused to talk. After three days of not eating or speaking and very little sleep, she was discharged, and her mother enrolled her in a school in New York run by the Order of the Sacred Heart. This school proved academically inadequate for the young girl who was already reading Kant, Spinoza, Goethe, and Schopenhauer. Perhaps a major reason why Mercedes was rebelling against these schools was her devotion to her sister Rita, who had convinced Mercedes "that whereas European convents provided good education and friendships for future life, convents in America did neither."[33]

Having spent much of her youth in France, the newly divorced Rita returned often to Paris, a city she loved for its sophistication and style. It was during one of those trips that she met the handsome, wealthy, and socially prominent Philip M. Lydig. Like her first husband, Lydig was twenty years her senior. An 1889 graduate of Harvard University, he had volunteered in the Spanish-American War and was commissioned as a captain. Because Lydig had learned German military methods while studying at Berlin University, he was "valuable to the Allies" during World War I and was eventually cited by the French government for his services. After the war, he first served in Honolulu as chief and purchasing commissary but eventually wound up in Paris. When they married in 1902, Mercedes's mother wept bitter tears as Rita swept up the aisle of Grace Church, wearing a close-fitting black princess dress covered over with ancient black lace and a great black hat, worn rakishly over her right eye. To make matters worse, she was marrying another Protestant.

Although this marriage, like her first, was not a happy one, it afforded Rita easy reentry into the exclusive high society to which she aspired. She quickly replaced her passion for horses with a concerted effort to build an image of herself as an exotic social figure, as she split her time between Paris and New York, always traveling with a hairdresser, masseuse, chauffeur, secretary, maid, valet, and forty trunks. One time, she returned to New York from Paris flaunting a chapeau twelve inches from crown to brim but only an inch and a half in height. Always preferring to wear black or white, she gloried in deviating from the mandates of the current mode. "With her black dress curling about her little feet, a black hat slanting over her romantic eyes, and a sable scarf wound four times about her throat, she was like no other woman in New York," remarked one reporter, "—like no other woman in America."[34]

Soon after the wedding, she commissioned famous architect Stanford White to design a house for her in the most fashionable district in New York, at 38 East Fifty-second Street, which proved to be one of White's last designs before he was tragically murdered. Beautifully proportioned in Italian Renaissance style, the three-story house displayed her wealth of art treasures "in that each and every piece merits individual attention, the distinguished impression of the whole having been achieved by an assemblage of the choicest original pieces. . . . [E]ach object is appropriate to the position it occupies."[35] In a retrospective written a decade after her death, Frank Crowninshield claimed that "during the years of her hey-day . . . [it was] the most beautiful small house in New York."[36]

While on summer vacations with her parents in Houlgate, Normandy, Mercedes would spend all the time she could visiting her older sister in Paris. She watched with fascination as Boldini, sometimes wearing a bowler hat, completed fourteen portraits of Rita. Several times she accompanied her sister on her visits to the home of Sarah Bernhardt and listened to the actress recite long passages from *Phèdre* and *L'Aiglon*. She remembered especially watching her sister pose for Auguste Rodin at his studio at Meudon, outside Paris. The sculptor was "a man of extraordinary vitality, constantly absorbed with the human body—especially woman's. A typical scene in his studio was a lavish nudist spectacle."[37] Nude women walked freely about the studio. Others reclined while he drew sketches. He had a reputation for working very closely with his female models, hovering over them and even kissing them tenderly as he worked. When Isadora Duncan met him in 1900, just a few years before Mercedes and Rita visited the studio, she confided that he ran his hands over his statues and caressed them fondly. "Finally he took a small quantity of clay and pressed it between his palms. He breathed hard as he did so. The heat streamed from him like a radiant furnace. In a few moments he had formed a woman's breast, that palpitated beneath his fingers." Then, he turned to Duncan. "He gazed at me with lowered lids, his eyes blazing, and then, with the same expression that he had before his works, he came toward me. He ran his hands over my neck, breast, stroked my arms and ran his hands over my hips, my bare legs and feet. He began to knead my whole body as if it were clay, while from him emanated heat that scorched and melted me."[38] To experience Rodin was undoubtedly unique and unforgettable for the curious young Mercedes as well. As she recorded years later, "Awe was my reaction to Rodin—awe for the man for his superhuman work."[39]

While the family was vacationing in Houlgate the summer of 1907, Mercedes's father announced he needed to return to New York. Because he had complained of not feeling well, Mercedes's mother, brother Dick, and sister Aida accompanied him. He had been melancholy in recent years, often lamenting the guilt he felt for escaping from Cuba with his life while his friends had not been so fortunate.[40]

Soon after their return, Ricardo retreated to the Adirondack Mountains, ostensibly to rest. A few years earlier, J. P. Morgan had acquired a camp in the mountains and developed it into a "rustic fantasy in which the super-rich could play at roughing it" in a paradise of fishing, boating, hunting, and hiking. Guests would "arrive in their private railroad cars laden with all the necessities of life in the wilderness, such as the finest bed linens, silver trays, cutlery, serving pieces, china, Champagne flutes, snifters; port, sherry, and brandy decanters; not to mention the appropriate vintage liquids with which to fill them. The servants often outnumbered the employers and their guests by 3 to 1."[41] On August 24, 1907, just a few days after he had arrived at the camp, Mercedes's father threw himself from a cliff and was killed instantly. The *New York Times* obituary described him as "a wealthy Cuban," who "in half a century accumulated a fortune in importing sugar from Cuba."[42] He was seventy years old. It was Mercedes's first experience with suicide. There were many more to come.

Although the specific reason for her father's suicide will never be known, the status of the family fortune might have been a factor. The U.S. economy had taken a major downturn in 1906. On March 12, 1907, the Dow Jones Industrial Average stood at 86.53. Two days later the market crashed, losing 8.3 percent of its value, and the next six months saw steady erosion of the market, a run on the banks, and a recession. Jobs were cut, and many solvent businesses went bankrupt. Because there was not enough currency, some banks actually adopted illegal substitutes for cash. Mercedes's father, a man never known for frugality, may have panicked as he saw his savings disappear.

Soon after the funeral, Mercedes returned to Europe. Persuaded by Rita's arguments about better educational opportunities in France, their mother agreed to send Mercedes and her sister Baba to a school at the Château de Dieudonné, near Beauvais, France, which had been built during the reign of Louis XIV. When she was not studying history, mathematics, and the French classics or practicing on the piano, Mercedes enjoyed escaping into the forest that surrounded the school. "This forest played an important part in my life at the school," she confessed. "It was here . . . that I became aware of the first signs of spring. . . ."[43]

It was also at this school where she became more aware of her sexual interests. The youngest daughter of the head teacher was Catalina, called Catiche by her classmates. Mercedes wrote that "she had dark limpid eyes and in profile looked strangely like Dante. Many of the pupils had crushes on her and were continually writing her silly love letters." Although Mercedes recorded in an early draft of her autobiography that "I did not like her and she did not like me,"[44] letters that were tucked away in her schoolgirl's prayer book reveal otherwise. Folded inside the book was a letter from Catiche that read:

> Darling darling old sweet. This is just a line to my [sic] good night & to tell you how very much I love you. Oh! darling I do so much want to see you again & you don't know how much I miss not being able to kiss you. Anyhow I will kiss you in my dreams & in my heart. I can only keep on telling you the same thing in all my letters & that is that I love you, love you oh! so very much. I kissed this letter lots of times before I folded it up & send the kisses wrapped in it so you must take them before you go to sleep tonight. . . . Good-night darling "Seedy," all my very best love from the very bottom of my heart. . . . God-bless you darling. I do love you so much.[45]

A card safely tucked away in the prayer book reads, "Para mi muy querida Mercedes de su amiga. [For my very dear Mercedes, from her friend.] Catiche. 18 June 08." On still another page is written "Catiche, I think of you always and I'll never forget you! Mercedes."

Before the year was out, Mercedes had penned a poem to Catiche that she titled "To an Old but Not Forgotten friend":

I

Friend of years ago,
Of me I would have you know,
That I have not forgotten you,
    or days of yore,

That I have not forgotten you,
    or day that will come no more.

II

In our old haunts I walk again
    with you.
And the old love in my soul,
    enkindles new,
The old places once more I have
    in mind.
And your face inprinted on
    my heart, I find.

III

Those days have passed,
    Then let them rest,
And if I were asked
I would answer, for you and I
    it is best.

IV

For why wake the dead
    As they sleep in their lonelyness,?
Then why wake the dead of either
    soul or head?
For us it is better forgetfulness.

dated 1908[46]

The more she thought about her feelings for Catiche, the more Mercedes felt guilty for her sexual desires and a need for punishment. Seeking Christ's forgiveness, she would put pieces of glass in her shoes and walk about till her feet bled. "I fasted and mortified myself and in the winter I rose out of bed and knelt with my arms outstretched in the form of a cross before an open window until I was literally frozen."[47] To overcome her guilt, she turned to writing letters and poems to Jesus, Mary, St. Francis, Jehanne d'Arc, and Mary Magdalena.

These letters and poems were a mixture of religious and sexual fervor. In some letters I repeatedly wrote of my longing 'to hold in my arms the naked and suffering body of Jesus' and I wrote letters to Mary Magdalena saying that I longed 'passionately to kiss her beloved and tear-stained face.' . . . I poured out my heart with all its fears and hopes. Their contents were in every case a pathetic and revealing testimony to my religious and emotional dilemma—an expression of my tortured spirit.[48]

Because Mercedes's mother had no income and her father had mismanaged the family fortune, the de Acostas were forced to reduce their number of servants and move to less expensive quarters, first to Sixty-sixth Street and Madison Avenue and then to Madison and Seventy-ninth. Soon, however, Rita, who was sympathetic with her mother's financial reversals but interested in projecting a certain image of social elitism, moved them to a small but more fashionable apartment at 830 Park Avenue and completely furnished it. Then Rita suggested that their mother and Mercedes should travel to Cuba and sell some of the property near Matanzas they had inherited on their father's death.

Until recent years, there had been little opportunity to sell the property. Ever since their father had escaped, Cubans had been enmeshed in struggles for independence: the Little War in 1879, the War of 1895. More revolutionaries had been thrown into the Morro Castle dungeons. Hundreds of thousands of Cubans had been driven from their homes and crowded into towns. An estimated three hundred thousand were denied adequate food and shelter. One traveler to Cuba wrote about his impressions of Matanzas: "The country outside the military posts was practically depopulated. Every house had been burned, banana trees cut down, cane fields swept with fire, and everything in the shape of food destroyed. . . . I did not see a house, man, woman or child, a horse, mule, or cow, nor even a dog. I did not see a sign of life, except an occasional vulture or buzzard sailing through the air. The country was wrapped in the stillness of death and the silence of desolation."[49] Even if Ricardo had contemplated selling his property years earlier, he must have debated the timing of the sale. However, after the explosion, on February 15, 1898, of the American warship *Maine* as it was anchored peacefully in the Havana harbor, conditions changed. War was declared between Spain and the United States. By the end of the year, after tens of thousands of fatalities, the war was over, and Spain, in the Treaty of Paris, agreed to end its sovereignty over Cuba. The basis for American control of the Cuban economy had begun. When President Theodore Roosevelt, in his annual message to Congress on December 2, 1902, urged the need for a treaty with Cuba "because it is enormously in our interest to control the Cuban market and by every means to foster our supremacy in the tropical lands and waters south of us,"[50] it paved the way for the Platt Amendment of 1903, which stipulated the legal right of the United States to intervene if political developments in Cuba threatened American business interests.

So the timing was right for Mercedes and her mother to travel to Cuba. During the trip, Mercedes wrote "My First Impression of Cuba" and dedicated the poem to her father.

I

The sun of Cuba,
Was slowly rising ore a distant hill,
It shone its rays on the sleeping
    flowers,
They stired, then all was still.

II

The blue and pink and spotted houses,
Shone and glisned in the suns bright
    light,
As from sleep they seemed to awaken,
From the dark and gloomy night.

III

The ants began their daily tasks,
The sun rose higher in the sky,
The flowers nodded and awakened,
The birds began to fly.

IV

All the earth seemed filled with
    gladness
The palms they shook their lofty laves [sic]
The little pigs scampered about
    in utter badness
And the cocoa-nuts trembled in the
    breeze.

V

The oxen to the field did go,
Their task soon to know,
The horses seemed filled with glee
And around the field they would like
    to flee.

VI

The work-hands to their tasks did go,
And the wind softly began to
    blow,
The negroes began to sing as they
    went about,
And the breeze took it up and continu-
    ed their lofty shout.

VII

And o're the distant sky,
White clouds appeared, and then
    went by,
The birds soared high in the air,
And the cattle, in the shade they
    went, a protection from the glare.

VIII

The water rippled calmly,
And the air smelt sweet and
    balmy,
Thus did I first see this land,
Inchanted, coming from Gods
    hand.

IX

Thus did I first see this land of
    fruit and trees,
Lying lazyly at its ease,
Thus did I first see this land of
    palms,
In all its beauty and its charms.[51]

The fourteen-year-old Mercedes did not seem to notice the crushing poverty and destruction surrounding her. In the end, the family sold several coffee plantations as well as a large house on the Malecon in Havana for fourteen thousand dollars. "A few years later," Mercedes noted, "this house was resold for a million dollars and the plantations for fabulous sums."[52] "My mother always hated Cuba," Mercedes wrote. "I suppose this was the natural reaction of a Spaniard. I, on the contrary loved it—especially the interior—but as we left its shores she said she hoped never to see it again. She never did."[53]

Another family suicide challenged her youthful innocence. Her brother, Hennie, who was eight years older, had always been delicate, slender, and sensitive-looking. "He had beautiful and poetic hands that were incapable of handling life. Hennie, like myself," Mercedes wrote, "wanted to be a poet. We were both desperately unhappy and unadjusted people, centered in our own despair and unable to help one another. We were like deaf mutes making frenzied signs, but using different symbols and scarcely knowing that we did not really understand each other. If I had known then as much as I do now about life in general and psychology in particular, the whole tragedy for Hennie and myself might never have happened. . . . I should say that both Hennie and I lived in an inner state of melancholia."[54] While Mercedes and Hennie were vacationing with their mother in Hot Springs, Virginia, in September 1911, their "mutual depression reached its peak. . . . (They) talked of death, God, and immortality." Two weeks after they returned to New York, Mercedes was awakened early by the overpowering smell of gas. The *New York Times,* however, reported that he had died of "heart disease" and that a servant had found him dead in his bed.[55] Earlier, reportedly because of his health, he had been forced to give up his position with a Wall Street brokerage. The cause of his melancholia and his decision to end his life remain a mystery, but his sister's guarded description suggests that maybe he, like herself, was left alone to struggle with his gender issues.

~3~

"Beauty She Achieved"

In Paris, Rita continued to move in the artistic and literary circles of the day, frequently attending the salons of several lesbian hostesses: Friday afternoons at the Natalie Barney–Romaine Brooks salon, Saturday evenings with Gertrude Stein–Alice B. Toklas, and Sunday luncheons at the Versailles villa of Elisabeth Marbury–Elsie de Wolfe.[1] These "at-homes," as they were often called, were known not for their culinary delights but rather for the array of artistic and literary personages and the lively, witty, intellectual discussions.

It is likely that Rita, perhaps accompanied by Mercedes, attended a Barney–de Wolfe fete in June 1913 "long remembered for its beauty and originality."

> There were covers set for forty at small tables upon the lawn. Rows of tiny lights marked the flower beds. Garlands of electric bulbs dripped from the trees. Festoons of roses hung from the roof covering the terrace. The fountains played, illuminated by the variety of colored lights. . . . At the foot of the rose garden was the best orchestra to be engaged in Paris. Fortunately the night was perfect. The stars were shining, the silver moon peeping through the branches, and the air soft and caressing.[2]

The de Acosta sisters mingled with official representatives from Great Britain, Greece, Belgium, Italy, Spain, Germany, Austria, Turkey, and Russia, as well as the American ambassador, Myron T. Herrick.

The art collection Rita had acquired was phenomenal. In addition to magnificent, medieval tapestries, exquisite Chippendale furniture, Chinese carpets, rare bronze statuettes, and marble sculptures, she had purchased notable paintings such as Sano di Pietro's *Virgin and Child* and Mazo's *Infanta Margarita*. "There are few in this country, or comparatively anywhere," cited the *New York Times*, "who collect with an idea of the whole scheme into which the separate items of beauty are to be fitted. In a word, there are few collectors who are artists at their task. Mrs. Lydig . . . is one of those few."[3]

One of her most prized objets d'art was Botticelli's *Venus*. Similar to his more famous *Birth of Venus*, the goddess stands on a bluish gray marble base, nude except for a diaphanous white drapery that she holds to cover the lower part of her body. In the main fold of the drapery are roses. Curls of golden hair fall on her shoulders. Standing almost six feet high and two feet wide, this seductive rendering of the voluptuous Venus was prominently displayed in Rita's home and certainly made an impact on Mercedes whenever she visited her older sister. In 1919, she wrote and produced *Sandro Botticelli,* which starred her lover, Eva Le Gallienne; the play was the tragic tale of a model posing for this very painting.

Rita decorated herself just as lavishly and artistically as she did her home.[4] She was particularly fond of rare antique lace with which she enhanced most of her clothing, handbags, and seventy-five Spanish fans. "Her seventeen lace petticoats were reserved for mornings in her bedroom; her favorite was an eleventh-century piece that had cost her nine thousand dollars."[5] She owned 150 pairs of shoes, some never worn, each custom-made by Yanturny, constructed of silk, satin, velvet, and laces, and stored in Russian leather cases—twelve pairs to a case. One of the features of the Metropolitan Museum's 1948 "Turn of the Century" exhibit was a pair of Rita's two-inch-wide, white, pencil-pointed satin shoes trimmed with heavy appliquéd Venetian lace. When Mercedes visited her sister, she was always in awe. "Rita designed most of her own clothes and they were made for her by Callot Soeurs," she marveled. "Whatever style she created or wore was copied by the fashion world, and spies were sent out by the different houses to discover her new creations. She once said to me, 'I should play a joke on these foolish sheep women by wearing some monstrous costume. They would all rush to copy it and then imagine they looked well in it!'"[6] She was so intent on good taste and style that when she learned that her husband was having an affair with a woman who dressed poorly, she ordered, "I can't have you going around with a creature who looks like that" and sent the woman off to Callot Soeurs for new fashions. When Diana Vreeland was preparing her 1975

"American Women of Style" exhibit at the Metropolitan Museum of Art, the first woman she thought of was Rita.

The story goes that when Puccini visited New York in 1910 for the premiere of his opera *The Girl of the Golden West,* he "abandoned his seat and ensconced himself at the back of Rita's loge, where he remained transfixed on her provocative back."[7] She captivated all of New York society when she appeared in her box at the opera in an evening dress with her back bare to the waist. Though some may have considered the gown indecent and scandalous, the décolleté design was soon copied all over the Western world. There was certainly truth in the remark of one critic: "Beauty was her goal, and beauty she achieved."[8]

Rita also entertained. Paderewski, Caruso, Mary Garden, Emma Eames, and Toscanini performed for her guests. Creating her own salons in both Paris and New York for poets and painters, she brought together such artists as Spanish painter Ignacio Zuloaga, John Singer Sargent, Sarah Bernhardt, Eleonora Duse, and Isadora Duncan. Writing several years later, photographer Arnold Genthe remembered Rita's hosting a dinner party for Zuloaga and one of his closest friends, Juan Belmonte, a celebrated Spanish matador. Zuloaga was seated on her right, and Belmonte on her left. Next to Belmonte was Mrs. Charles Lanier, known as a patron of music. When Mrs. Lanier asked Genthe who it was sitting next to her, he replied,

> "He is the most famous bullfighter in Spain. He is just back from a triumphal tour of South America."
> "A bullfighter?" she gasped. "That's even worse than a prizefighter. The idea of his being here!" Turning to Mrs. Lydig, she said, "I'm not feeling very well, Rita; I think I must be going."[9]

Rita did not seem fazed by the sudden exit.

She became such a generous patron of the arts that she arranged the first American exhibition and tour of Zuloaga's paintings and even paid for redecoration of the Duveen Galleries so they would be an appropriate setting. Mesmerized by her beauty and charm, artists begged for her to pose. Zuloaga painted her. Helleu sketched her several times. In fact, the Costume Institute of the Metropolitan Museum of Art used one of these sketches for the cover of its 1963 annual progress report sent to all members.

In spite of her enviable position in "the smart set," Rita's life was sadly unfulfilled. She desired wealth, glamour, and social acceptance but at the same time craved independence and wished she could devote herself to more constructive, social causes. It seemed that her primary emotional outlets were with women, especially with four lesbians—Anne Morgan, Anne Vanderbilt,

Elisabeth Marbury, and Elsie de Wolfe. Anne Morgan was the daughter of J. Pierpont Morgan, who had inherited his father's business in 1890 and was instrumental in financing many enterprises—railroads, steel, mining, and utilities—that established the United States as a modern industrial power. In the years around the turn of the century, he was, arguably, one of the mightiest personal forces in American business life.

Anne Harriman Sands Rutherford became the second wife of William K. Vanderbilt in 1903. The grandson of the shipping and railroad tycoon, he had built his own reputation as a leading yachtsman and breeder of champion racehorses. His divorce from Alva had come only after a front-page scandal that had William K. linked with a mistress in Europe whom he was paying two hundred thousand dollars a year. His aversion to scandal was so strong that he paid twenty-five thousand dollars to be put on a list of "immunes," gentlemen about whom the periodical *Town Topics* would never print anything that was not flattering.[10] Rita was also a recipient of his wealth. Although no evidence cites a reason for the payments nor when they began, an article in the *New York Times* refers to a court document that says "her income of $5,000 a month had stopped with the death of William K. Vanderbilt." The supposed contract had specified the payments would be "for life," but when William K. died in 1920, the Vanderbilt estate successfully argued that it meant for his lifetime only.[11]

Elisabeth Marbury, though not nearly as well-off as the Morgans and Vanderbilts, grew up in an affluent and cultured home. Her father was a successful attorney, as well as a speculator in real estate and the stock market. With her partner and companion, Elsie de Wolfe, who was an accomplished interior decorator, she became a recognized hostess in New York and Paris. After an 1885 amateur theatrical benefit that she organized, "Bessie", or "Granny," as Rita called her, became one of the first women theatrical agents and producers and was the English-speaking representative for playwrights George Bernard Shaw, Victorien Sardou, Georges Feydeau, Oscar Wilde, and Edmond Rostand. Bessie, who was Oscar Wilde's friend as well as agent, undoubtedly kept Rita informed about the plight of her client—the lawsuit, trial, imprisonment.

Inevitably, these women came to know each other, and as one author suggests, "it's likely some of their friendships involved a greater intimacy. The language of their letters and diaries certainly implies much—'Heavenly afternoon with E.M.!'—but nothing more explicit was committed to paper. One kept up appearances."[12]

When Rita's friend Anne Morgan had been asked as a little girl what she wanted to be when she grew up, she replied, "Something more than a rich fool."[13] Rita agreed. She was envious as Anne and these other friends involved themselves in social reform movements and became women of "agency," women of power who could get things done. They became early advocates of workplace safety, campaigned for drug-addiction rehabilitation, supported the employment of women for police work, and financed special housing for the impoverished who suffered from tuberculosis.

Motivated by these women, Rita had joined the Colony Club, the first social club for women in New York, which had been founded by Marbury and Morgan in 1907 and whose founding members included Maude Adams, Amy Lowell, Emily Post, and Jane Addams. The six-story clubhouse designed by Stanford White and decorated by Elsie de Wolfe featured a restaurant, a lounge, a gymnasium, and a swimming pool sunk in white marble and reflected on three sides by Venetian mirrors. Wall sconces of green and white grapes suggested a subtle pagan eroticism.[14]

In 1909 Rita joined other club members in support of the Women's Trade Union League during the shirtwaist strike of 1909. On November 24, two days before Thanksgiving, twenty thousand workers, most of them women and girls, walked off their jobs. Three weeks later, the Colony Club invited some of the striking women to a meeting, and Rita, along with Elsie de Wolfe, passed around hats for contributions and collected thirteen hundred dollars.[15]

A theater production earlier in the year had undoubtedly precipitated the strike. When *Votes for Women* opened on March 15, 1909, it appeared more like a political rally than a theater premiere. Suffragettes representing the Interurban Council of Women Suffrage Clubs, the Union Club, and the Equality League of Self-Supporting Women crowded the theater. Members of the American Suffragettes were conspicuous with yellow buttons pinned to their lapels. Banners flew from the balcony. Women from the Harlem Equal Rights League marched during intermission with placards reading "Women vote in 4 Western states. Why not in New York?"

The plot revolves around Vida Levering, a suffragette who accidentally meets her former lover and his fiancée. Many of the character's lines provided ammunition for the women's movement:

> Some girls think it a hardship to have to earn their living. The horror is not to be allowed to.
>
> We must get the conditions of life made fairer. We women must organize. We must learn to work together. We have all worked so long and so exclusively for men, we hardly know how to work for one another. But we must learn.[16]

Since the playwright, Elizabeth Robins, was a close friend of Bessie's, it is likely that both Rita and Mercedes attended a performance. On May 4, 1912, Rita, along with ten thousand other women carrying "Votes for Women" banners, marched up Fifth Avenue from Washington Square to Fifty-seventh Street and then over to Carnegie Hall for a mass rally.

Even though Rita had become more politically active and had even bought a house on the corner of Fiftieth Street in Beekman Place that she donated as a home for delinquent girls, she was restless to do more. In a somewhat veiled autobiography that she published in 1927, Rita confessed to "the tragic futility of fashionable life."

> I saw a whole generation of boys and girls grow up around me, and wreck themselves in some moral disaster or other, before they reached middle age. What was the matter with us? Why were we so especially hag-ridden by unhappiness and disappointed in our hopes? Was there any difference between us and any other Americans, except a difference in income? Was it just too much money that was killing us all? . . . Marriage without love is a suicide compact. It is death—spiritual and moral and often physical death—for both husband and wife. Marriage without love is most common among our fashionable rich, and it seems to me to be the fruitful source of most of their tragedies. In any marriage that is made without love, there are bound to be re-sistances and revolts and hatreds that become murderous in their tendency even when they do not actually achieve murder in fact.[17]

When she writes about one of her unhappy acquaintances who developed a taste in art to alleviate her disappointments, Rita's words describe her own past: "Art is basically what the psychologists call an 'escape.' It is the dream of those sensitive spirits who take refuge in an imaginary world from the frustrations which are put upon them in their daily existence; and, to enjoy art truly, one must have some of the artist's sensitivity and feel the same need to escape from reality which he has felt."[18] "I think she was only at peace in the presence of beauty," Mercedes recalled. "Then her dual na-ture ceased to battle."[19] Mercedes saw her sister often in Paris and New York, and though there was an eighteen-year age difference, they had a special bond.

> Looking back on my early life I realize now that although we spent hours and hours together, we never talked of practical or everyday things, nor rarely of the actual occurrences in our lives. It was always of fictitious things and people. We often referred to these people and

were as interested in them as though we really knew them. I used to prepare long stories and plots to tell her [Rita], which I remember, were always very tragic and terrible. I was never interested whether anyone else thought I was clever, but I longed to have her think I was clever and I would read and study for hours so as to impress her with my knowledge. Even when a small, and probably very annoying child, I never remember her correcting or scolding me about anything, although in a curious subtle way she was always very high handed with me about what I should or should not do; no one in the world could make me do anything if she advised me to the contrary. . . . It seemed that I always leaned on her, and asked her advice, and took my strength from her.[20]

It was particularly difficult for Mercedes to witness Rita's decline, both financial and physical. On February 23, 1913, the *New York Times* reported, "Mrs. Lydig to Sell Her Art Treasures." The American Art Association announced "the sale as the most important public one of Gothic and sixteenth century art that has ever taken place in this country." Rita was being forced to auction off her art treasures to the highest bidders due to ill health and dwindling finances. The Metropolitan Museum of Art published an extensive catalog. When everything was finally sold on April 2, she collected $362,555: $41,000 for an early-sixteenth-century Flemish tapestry, $11,300 for the Botticelli that was the inspiration for Mercedes's 1919 play, $10,700 for a fifteenth-century walnut chest. Because Rita was in the hospital at the time, Mercedes oversaw the sale. Also present was noted interior decorator and friend Elsie de Wolfe.[21]

No less then ten days before the auction, Rita, whose health had been failing, was driven to the Mayo Clinic in Rochester, Minnesota. She was apparently suffering from an old injury sustained when she was trampled by a horse. It was reported that she planned to "remain for an indefinite period."[22] On the day before the auction, Rita "underwent a very severe operation." A member of the hospital staff reported that "her youth and remarkable vitality favor steady progress toward recovery."[23] In spite of her poor health and financial condition, Rita was still able to leave for France the summer of 1914. It was a dangerous trip. American women were testifying at the time that German soldiers treated them with "barbarous methods" as they tried to flee over the borders into France. So it must have relieved Mercedes to read in the *New York Times* that when Rita arrived from Vichy "she was very ill and came in a motor car, for which she paid $1200, and was attended by two maids and a doctor . . . [and] was always treated nicely."[24]

It was at this time, when Mercedes was in her early twenties, that Bessie Marbury, who had become the "doyenne of Sapphic Broadway,"[25] assumed the role of matchmaker and launched Mercedes into relationships with several available women. One was with the exotic and sensual Russian actress Alla Nazimova.[26] Beginning March 22, 1905, Nazimova had reveled in a year of headlines with performances in New York, Chicago, and Boston as she toured and lived with fellow Russian actor Paul Orlenev. Though the media lauded them as an intriguing married duo, the unmarried couple was advised to offer no correction. After all, this might hopefully serve as a convenient cover for their sinful alliance. Serving as their press agent, translator, and manager was the anarchist, feminist, and advocate of free love and free speech, Emma Goldman. One performance of Ibsen's *Ghosts* was offered as a special benefit to raise money for her new political magazine, *Mother Earth*.[27]

In November 1906, after learning English with remarkable speed, Nazimova opened in the title role of Ibsen's *Hedda Gabler*. Two months later, she added *A Doll's House* and in September 1907, *The Master Builder*. Dozens of articles appeared in major publications, poets penned tributes, and artists painted her portrait.[28] Her fame reached such heights that in 1910 the Shubert brothers remodeled their 39th Street Theatre and renamed it "Nazimova's 39th Street Theatre."

The Shuberts were aware of Nazimova's bisexuality and of her rumored liaisons with Laurette Taylor and Constance Collier.[29] Her stage manager, A. H. Canby, analyzes her androgyny: "She is certainly amenable to reason if you discuss matters with her at the proper time. At such a time she acts with the fairness of a man, but if she is peevish over other matters she is just like any other fool woman and will make a fool woman's mistakes."[30] To create a "neurotic fascination" for the new Shubert star, Canby insisted she shave her boyish moustache so she would not be identified as a "Mannish Lesbian." As they toured, Canby was concerned that it was not the men who rushed to meet her: "The women . . . were enthusiastic about her. . . . She is keeping herself very exclusive and this intensifies the desire of the curious to meet her. [At the hotel, the] ladies' entrance was always crowded with women waiting for her to return from the theatre. It is much better that she should be exclusive and meet no one if possible. They regard her as a mystery. And there are other damned good reasons besides this one."[31] Canby warned her that she must be discreet with her sexual pursuits. Trying to dismantle the rumors, the Shuberts created an image of a dangerous, seductive siren. The roles they gave her to perform were more than just the strong-willed women of Ibsen; they were "invariably those of soul-racked and nerve-shaken women," women of "temperamental extremes."[32]

Because she had embraced the subversive image so completely and had
become notorious in the Broadway establishment as androgynous, producers
were slow to realize her full potential. After a year of failing to sign a contract with any Broadway producer, in early 1915 she decided to become
her own manager and began touring in the vaudeville circuit. Although this
was an embarrassing setback for a serious actress, she at least had the opportunity of playing something other than a vamp.

The one-act play she chose to present was Marion Craig Wentworth's
timely antiwar drama, *War Brides.* According to *Theatre Magazine,* her enact-
ment of a young mother whose husband and brothers have been killed in a
senseless war "was never more natural, earnest and fiery."[33] It was so successful that she played it on the Orpheum vaudeville circuit for over a year.

"After seeing Nazimova in *War Brides,*" Mercedes gushed, "I rushed
back to Bessie's house and announced what she, and everyone else, already
knew—that Nazimova was a great actress."

> Then I told Bessie that I must meet her, and Bessie, who often received
> her in her house and who had never before refused a wish of mine,
> shook her head.
>
> "But why, Granny Pa?" I asked.
>
> "Several reasons," she answered. "Mostly because I'm frightened
> of the two Annes."
>
> By the two Annes she meant Anne Morgan and Anne (Mrs. William
> K.) Vanderbilt.
>
> "But what have they got to do with it?" I asked.
>
> "Plenty. They think they own Nazimova and they would be angry
> with me for introducing her to a young person."[34]

Although Mercedes was attracted primarily by Nazimova's exoticism, she
was undoubtedly stirred by *War Brides,* which suffragists had called "the
Magna Carta of Woman."[35]

A few weeks later, she witnessed Nazimova's performance at a special
Madison Square Garden benefit: "As the band struck up the Imperial Anthem she waved the Russian flag as a great spotlight played over her. Then
the music changed to a wild Cossack strain and, . . . she ran . . . around the
arena, leaping into the air every few steps." When they met in Nazimova's
dressing room a few minutes later, de Acosta felt that Nazimova "seemed
tiny and more like a naughty little boy. We took to each other instantly."

The weeks that followed were exciting ones for starstruck Mercedes.
Since Nazimova was searching for a new play to present, when they were
together she read aloud Hauptmann's *The Sunken Bell,* as well as all the

Ibsen roles she had championed and several plays by Chekhov. "And sometimes as she read," Mercedes recalled, "she acted out the parts."[36] They
talked about Pushkin and Gorky and the similarities between Russian and
Spanish mysticism.

Mercedes was devastated when Nazimova had to leave New York to take
War Brides on a national tour. Although the separation brought an end to
the intensity of their romance, the two remained intimate friends until
Nazimova's death in 1945. When Nazimova returned to New York in January 1927 after a lengthy vaudeville tour with *Woman of the Earth,* Mercedes
greeted her with a huge "Welcome Home" sign. And while she was performing the play in London, Mercedes surprised her one evening by arriving at her hotel with champagne and caviar. A few days later, the two of
them dined together with Mrs. Patrick Campbell and Somerset Maugham.

When they had first met, Nazimova began the relationship with deception. "My family were Spanish Jews who immigrated to Russia," she began. "My actual name is Lavendera, but when I began to study for the theatre with Nemirovich Danchenko I took the name of Nazimova from the
Russian word *zima*—meaning winter."[37] None of it was true! Perhaps it
was this deception that led Mercedes to conclude, "I have known many great
artists but I have only rarely found in their characters the blending of great
art and great spiritual development. Certainly I did not find this blending
in Nazimova's character."[38]

Another liaison was with dancer Isadora Duncan. At the onset of World
War I, Duncan returned to New York from Paris, where she had been living and performing for several years. On November 21, 1916, she received
a standing ovation at the Metropolitan Opera House for her final dance
number, a portrayal of France's national anthem. According to her biographer, Ann Daly, "Duncan's body was enfolded in a blood-colored robe that
bared her shoulders and, according to some reviewers, bared a breast at her
moment of triumph."[39] In the audience for this by-invitation-only performance were such dignitaries as Otto H. Kahn, Anna Pavlova, and Mrs. Dana
Gibson. Duncan repeated her Metropolitan program for the public on
March 6, 1917, enjoying one of the largest audiences of the New York season. As the performance ended, she "peeled away her crimson robe, revealing the silken folds of the Stars and Stripes underneath."[40] The audience
went wild as the orchestra played the "Star-Spangled Banner."

Mercedes met Duncan the summer of 1917 while the dancer was liv-
ing at the seashore on Long Island. In an early draft of her autobiography,
Mercedes remembered that "Many days and nights we spent together. . . .
Often she would dance for me at night, three or four hours at a time."[41]

One occasion was particularly unforgettable, even though she chose to exclude this account in her completed manuscript.

> I don't know how long she danced, but she ended with a great gesture of Resurrection, with her arms extended high and her head thrown back. She seemed possessed by the dance and utterly carried away. When she finished she dropped her arms to her sides and stood silently. I dropped my eyes and did not look at Isadora.... In that pause I think we both lived many lives. Then Isadora seemed to return from a far land and again she became conscious of me. I moved toward her and in a mutual gesture we flung our arms around one another, and stood there clinging to each other in silence and tears.[42]

The two women continued their romantic relationship for many years. When a friend asked Mercedes later how she and Duncan had expressed their desire for one another, Mercedes confessed, "Oh, Isadora liked to kiss my breasts and lick the moisture between my legs."[43]

~4~

"Strange Turmoil"

Although Mercedes had been interested in the theater since childhood, now motivated in part by her romantic fascination with Nazimova and her friendship with Bessie, who had become one of most important literary agents on Broadway, Mercedes began to dabble at playwriting. Perhaps like her sister Rita, Mercedes was also searching for an "escape . . . a refuge in an imaginary world."[1] She must have felt encouraged by the recent developments in the American theater. In 1915 three little theater groups had been founded—the Washington Square Players, the Neighborhood Playhouse, and the Provincetown Theatre. As our country's answer to the art theaters of Europe, they concentrated on new, American plays. The artists were nonprofessionals who usually performed their new works for matinees only. "They wanted whatever the established theater would have none of," explained critic Joseph Wood Krutch, "and in the beginning that included a great deal—the esoteric, the radical, the intellectual, and the merely shocking."[2] Working with these groups were writers Eugene O'Neill, Susan Glaspell, and Maxwell Anderson, as well as designers Robert Edmond Jones and Lee Simonson. Mercedes was determined to be one of them.

Her first attempt was *Loneliness,* a one-act play she had copyrighted on June 10, 1916.[3] Set in a farmhouse in a little country village in France, near the border of Belgium, the story takes place during World War I. As the curtain rises, a young, attractive French peasant woman is knitting by the light of a candle. After an old man greets her from outside the window, he enters the cottage and they share their misfortunes. He and his wife have lost their last boy in the war, and he relates what his wife had cried: "Each one seemed like a flower, their fragrance of which was our love and our youth. And now one by one they have faded forever out of our lives."

"I know," replies the peasant woman. "But remember it's for France. I, too, am sad and sit here alone and think and think until I nearly go mad. And all the time out there *(pointing)* I hear the big guns and realize that any minute my husband may have fallen, too. But it's the loneliness most of all that is killing me. If I only had someone to talk to, even a cat would be welcome here!"

"Yes," the old man answers, "it's a time of loneliness, dear. Loneliness in a crowd, loneliness in a nation, but most of all, loneliness in one's heart."

Soon the old man leaves but warns the peasant woman to watch out for German soldiers and to hide her wedding band, since "war is time for plunder."

Shortly after he leaves and she has resumed her knitting, a badly injured German soldier, his face covered with blood, throws the door open and sinks into a chair. He begs for food. "For pity sake. For your womanly pity," he implores. "Is there no more compassion in the world, has every feeling, every drop been emptied from the cup of life by this terrible thing called war?" He explains that the reason he entered her cottage was because he had looked through a window while hiding behind a tree and saw her lonely face. "Do you love your husband?" he asks.

Perhaps echoing the words of her older sister who had been divorced once and was currently in a second unhappy marriage, Mercedes had her peasant woman reply, "Like most women my marriage was made for me. My husband was not the man I had dreamed of."

As the play progresses, the soldier relates how he had killed a French soldier by plunging a knife into his heart and then begins coaxing her to be intimate with him. He takes a ring from his pocket and places it in the palm of his hand. The peasant woman, recognizing the ring as her husband's, realizes the German soldier had killed him and stolen it. "You swine," she screams. Just as the soldier grabs a chair and raises it in the air to strike her, she grabs a knife off the sideboard and plunges the knife into his breast. The stage directions call for the soldier to stagger and fall *"dead across the tiny streak of moonlight from window."* She drops the knife to the floor and pro-claims, "A French woman does not mind being alone even with a corpse to avenge her husband and for the sake of France."

There is no evidence of the play's ever being produced. It reveals for the first time, however, her interest in strong-willed female characters and in questioning the tradition of marriage. Besides being overly melodramatic in its plot, the dialogue does not seem like that of peasants and is often stilted. For instance, the peasant woman's first line when she addresses the old man reads, "Pierre! My, how you did frighten me. Where did you come from and how were you so noiseless?" Nevertheless, in this first play, Mercedes shows skill in establishing a realistic conflict and in drafting a perceptive story.

Later that year, on November 4, 1916, she had another play copyrighted at the Library of Congress, her first full-length drama—*They That Walk Enchained.*[4] The action focuses on Romola Charrington at her country home in Devonshire, England, in 1911. When she was only seventeen, Romola had met and subsequently married the wealthy Robert Chancillor. About a year or two after the birth of their son David, she discovered that her husband had been unfaithful to her. When she sued for divorce, however, she lost custody because he claimed she had been promiscuous. When he was ten years old, David wrote her a cruel letter saying he hated her and never wished to see her again. When the play opens, it is fifteen years after the divorce and David, who has lost his way motorcycling in the country, stops at Romola's home to ask for travel directions. He does not know this woman is his mother. When David discovers who she is and realizes that all the past accusations were false, he "throws himself at her feet," crying, "Mother, forgive me."

Later, Robert Chancillor appears and also begs forgiveness. He has always loved her and pleads with her for a reconciliation. She refuses. "Do you know what I am?" she asks. "I am one of those who walk enchained. One of those who are dragged into the courts against their will, who are marred and scarred by divorce and chained with a heavy weight they never more can cast off."

When they hear David approaching, Robert hides in her boudoir, but he has left his gloves on Romola's desk. David, who has put his mother on a pedestal, sees them and yells out, "You lied to me. . . . You have had a lover in here. . . . You base woman. . . . vile woman." He runs from the room and kills himself with a gun.

We will never know whether Mercedes's friend Bessie Marbury read the play or tried to find a producer. We do know, however, that producer and director John D. Williams, remembered today as the first to produce one of Eugene O'Neill's plays on Broadway, was interested in the script. Paul Kennedy, a friend of Mercedes's who worked for the Foreign Press Service, had sent the script to Williams for his evaluation and received this encouraging reply: "While I am not sure that this piece is right, practically speaking, for the stage—in that the writer's theme is sounded but not fully developed in

Act III—I am nevertheless very taken with the constructive skill, freshness of situations, and dramatic power, as a whole, revealed by the work. Therefore, I should like very much, whenever you say, to meet Miss de Acosta."[5]

Unfortunately, we do not know what transpired at that meeting, only that the play was never produced or published. If Mercedes ever submitted it to the Provincetown Theatre or Washington Square Players, it probably was rejected, not only because of the heavily melodramatic dialogue and stage business but also because it did not seem as modern and as poignant as the new plays by O'Neill and Glaspell. Nevertheless, the script reveals Mercedes's early attempts at writing a three-act play based loosely on her own family history. With themes of adultery, marriage, divorce, estrangement of a son, and suicide, the story of Romola Charrington reflects both the experiences of her older sister, Rita, as well as Mercedes's own viewpoints at the time.

Inspired by both Nazimova's thrilling performance in *War Brides* and their romance, Mercedes's next stab at playwriting was more fruitful. She coauthored with Stuart Benson a short, one-act play that appeared in the *Outlook* magazine.[6] In *For France* (1917), Mercedes depicts a woman who has lost her husband and two sons in the war effort and now learns her third son has been drafted. "I cannot give you up!" she cries. "This devouring to the last shred all that we love! Devouring! Devouring! And never satisfied!"[7] Although there is no record of the play's being produced, the published script reveals Mercedes's writing talent as well as her interest in women's issues and political activism.

The timing was certainly appropriate. Although the war had erupted three years earlier with the assassination of Archduke Ferdinand and his wife in Sarajevo, America's entry was not declared until 1917. From the outset, however, the country was vitally affected. The federal government as well as private enterprise had commercial and financial relations with all the warring countries of Europe. Cultural ties—language, literature, laws, customs—were also strong. As early as 1914, our munitions exports totaled forty million dollars, a figure that tripled during the following two years. In 1916 President Woodrow Wilson initiated a program of military preparedness in an attempt to get the country ready for war. Massive military parades, as well as Congressional acts, focused attention on the war. When the Committee on Public Information was established in 1917, the government began mobilizing public opinion. More than one hundred million pieces of literary propaganda flooded the mails; seventy-five thousand "four-minute-men" swept into movie houses and public gatherings to rally support for the war effort.

Mercedes could certainly appreciate how her sister had become involved. Rita was a vice president for the American branch of the Union des Arts, whose original purpose was to help needy artists but who also established soup kitchens during the war. She also served on a committee for the War Babies' Cradle, an organization devoted to helping mothers and children in northern France and Belgium who lacked food, clothing, fuel, and medical attention.

But writing *For France* was not the first evidence of Mercedes's interest in contesting the expected role of women in society and in following in her sister's footsteps. A few years earlier, while studying to be a nurse's aide, she would start writing at midnight and continue until the "early hours of the morning. My mother sometimes saw my light and was angry with me for staying up so late. . . . Like most mothers then she thought a woman's career was in the home and marriage—a view I did not share. I believed, without a shred of humor, in every form of independence for women and I was already an enrolled worker for Women's Suffrage."[8] She went on to become a captain for the women's suffrage movement and "canvassed every house and[,] verbally armed with every reason why women should have the vote, rang each doorbell."[9] Because of her mother's attitude, however, she had kept her writing and her poems "a dead secret" for several years. She did not show them to her good friend, Bessie Marbury, or even to her sister.

Mercedes's first book of poems, *Moods,* appeared in 1919 bearing her name as author. In prose poems divided into sections with such labels as Love, Disgust, Joy, Despair, Hurt Feelings, Weariness, and Peace, she explores further her mysterious desire for sexual intimacy, most probably for women. One is called "Twilight Dreams":

As I open the long windows and step out upon
the terrace, the presence of the mysterious
hour is upon me . . .
. . . .
A vast and deep silence has come over everything;
and I, with all else, find myself holding my
breath as I steal back into the room and sink
    into a chair.
Leaning languidly I half close my eyes,
while
far off I smell the salt and sadness of the sea . . .
Weirdly and ghostlike you creep in and, in my
twilight dreams, you come to me![10]

A critic for *Vogue* praised the poems for their "definite charm, the charm of freshness, of youth facing immensities and frankly recording its reactions to them, even of youth serenely assured of the vast importance of its ego. They are like the quick sketches of an artist; the inspiration is there; the idea is clearly expressed. . ."[11] Their haunting quality prompted Charles Hanson Towne to declare that Mercedes's poetry "bears promise of even finer achievement. . . . She may go far."[12]

The following year, she shifted from serious writing when she teamed with Deems Taylor and wrote the book and lyrics for the musical *What Next! A Musical Indiscretion in Three Unwarranted Acts,* a comic tale of a fraudulent duke who steals a pearl necklace and is apprehended by rookie detectives.[13] A couple of years earlier, Mercedes had met Hope Williams at a party hosted by Mrs. John Jacob Astor. She notes in *Here Lies the Heart,* "We were introduced and 'clicked' at once." When Mercedes told Bessie that Hope was keen on pursuing an acting career, the astute agent replied, "Why don't you write a play for Hope? I will help you produce it," and she offered the use of her Princess Theatre.[14]

Beginning with *Nobody Home* and *Very Good, Eddie* in 1915, Bessie had been collaborating with Guy Bolton, P. G. Wodehouse, and Jerome Kern in producing musicals at the tiny, 299-seat, Princess Theatre on West Thirty-ninth Street. As Richard Kislan has described them, they were "intimate, simple, adult, intelligent, economical, small-cast musical[s]." Where comedy in the typical Broadway musical was created by hired comedians, "the Princess shows aimed for humor that flowed directly from believably funny characters put into logical succession of laughable situations."[15] With lighthearted stories that were well written, contained brisk dialogue, and fit the songs to the action and the characters, the Princess productions are considered the forerunner of the modern book American musical. Unlike the Viennese operettas with their exotic, faraway settings that had been so popular, these were modern stories with believable characters caught in comic situations.

The plot line of *What Next!* was simple. The young debutante Daphne is told that she must marry the Duke of Kingsberry rather than the man she loves, Edgar Clayton. Although Daphne argues that "a marriage based on anything but love, is bound to end in unhappiness," her mother insists: "You can learn to love the Duke if you try hard enough." The Duke, who is overdressed in riding clothes and walks with a "tremendous swank," is a charlatan in disguise and plots to steal Daphne's pearl necklace during the house party that evening. In the end, the Duke is discovered and Daphne is allowed to marry Edgar.

Mercedes describes one scene in an early draft of her autobiography:

There was one song in the play: "My Composite Girl" which WAS extremely catchy. It was a song somewhat on the lines of "A Pretty Girl Is Like a Melody." . . . Hope made her entrance in the first act as a slavey. She appeared carrying a tray with some bottles on it at the top of a stairway, and as she took the first step down she fell, and landed, by some inspired method in a sitting position on the tray at the bottom of the stairs! At each performance I prayed that she wouldn't break her neck, the audience rocked with laughter, and from then on to the final curtain she had only to walk across the stage or begin a line to be wildly applauded.[16]

The main part of act 2 focused on a melodrama that was being performed for the house guests by a touring theater troupe. In the play-within-the-play, which was called *The Mystery of the Missing Necklace,* Mercedes had written a burlesque of a death scene from Zoë Akins's *Déclassé,* a play that was running on Broadway and starring Ethel Barrymore, whose character says to her lover in the tear-jerking finale:

You came to find me, my dear. . . . What else? It's so wonderful. . . . Hold my hand. . . . We're drifting away together. Oh to be in England— now that April's here—Only it isn't April—is it? (She clings to him convulsively, staring straight ahead of her.) Just you—and my young great-great-grandmother, in her big hat—there—across the river. And the gay music! Everything else—is—going. It's like the theatre—when they turn out the lights before the curtain rises—on the next act. . . . (Her head falls forward. The last shudder tears her breath from her lips.)

Playing the role of Ethel Barrymore, Grace Bristed sang "I Want to Die as They Do in the Drama." The lyrics and stage action are not provided in the typewritten script, but one can easily imagine the number was a showstopper.

Like the other Princess musicals, *What Next!* had comedy and dialogue and songs that were integral to the plot and reflected the characters. For instance, the busybody Mrs. de Voe, who exposes the Duke, sings "Shopping on the Avenue."

I've had such a very, very busy day,
Darting all about in such a dizzy way,
I've been everywhere in town, I'd like to have you know,
Great shops, small shops, dark shops, sunny shops,

Low shops, tall shops, dull shops, funny shops,
Looking here and stopping there, and always on the go.
And I've lost all thought of the things I've bought,
Of the things I've ordered and the things I've sought;
But I'll say, all the same,
It's a very charming game.

The completely amateur cast played to capacity audiences for a limited, two-week engagement at the Princess Theatre—all proceeds donated to the Girls' Protective League and the New York Probation and Protective Association. The catchy songs, clever dancing, and twenty specialty acts prompted a *New York Herald* reviewer to call it "one of the snappiest and most unusual diversions in the record of new musical comedy." Another critic claimed that the daring costumes "out-Ziegfelded 'Flo' Ziegfeld. . . . Who bothers about a plot when one can look at such pretty chorus girls?"[17] At the time, Hope Williams received a number of professional offers and went on to star in Philip Barry's comedy *Holiday* (1928). At first glance, this diversion of Mercedes's with such lightweight material might seem bizarre, but it undoubtedly afforded her the opportunity to see and work backstage with beautiful young women, as well as the opportunity to develop her budding friendship with Hope Williams.

The confusion she felt about her female romances and the sense of freedom she enjoyed with her writing continued. However, on May 11, 1920, to maintain at least a semblance of propriety and to please her mother, who used to say, "I would die in peace if I knew you were happily married,"[18] Mercedes married Abram Poole, a handsome and wealthy portrait painter. Brother-in-law to a former editor of the *New Republic,* Abram's artistic and literary interests clearly appealed to the twenty-seven-year-old Mercedes. He had graduated from Princeton University in 1904 and had studied painting in Germany, in Italy, and at the Beaux Arts in Paris. He had become a trustee of the Chicago Art Institute and had received the prestigious Grand Prix of Rome and Munich in 1909.

The couple first met at a party soon after World War I. Abram had just returned from France and was wearing his uniform "with dash and chic."[19] They danced all evening and soon began to see each other regularly. When Abram first proposed marriage, however, Mercedes balked: "I couldn't make up my mind so quickly. As a matter of fact I was in a strange turmoil about world affairs, my own writing, suffrage, sex, and my inner spiritual development. Marriage at the moment seemed irrelevant in comparison to these. I was in a vague mood and treated Abram accordingly."[20]

When Mercedes asked for Bessie's opinion, she was probably surprised. "I firmly believe that every woman should marry if this is humanly possible for her," Bessie insisted.

> Her one indisputable field of usefulness is in the bearing and raising of children. This is the end for which God intended her. I wish that before any girl decides against matrimony on general principles, she would consult me before it is too late because this is a subject upon which my advice would be of benefit, as I know what I have missed.
>
> If a woman through her own conceit registers against marriage in favor of some problematical career she will find, provided she lives long enough, that all through life she is at best only a misfit.[21]

Such a statement by an avowed lesbian such as Bessie might seem odd, but actually the sentiment was quite common at the time. To conceal their own transgressions, they often bitterly condemned in public the love between women.

Even from the beginning, Mercedes's marriage was hardly a conventional one. Rather than traditional white, she wore an afternoon frock of pale gray lace and no hat. The *New York Times* registered surprise that "there was no giving in marriage" and was "the simplest possible ceremony."[22] There was no best man, no ushers. Although the ceremony was held at her mother's home and performed by Rev. Patrick Daly of St. Patrick's Cathedral, it was the reverse of Rita's society-page wedding of 1895. This one was very small, attended by relatives and a few close friends, and followed by a small reception. Mercedes objected to having music during the ceremony and refused to renounce her surname for his. A few years later, in fact, it was reported in the *New York Sun* that Mercedes was elected into membership in the Lucy Stone League, an organization espousing a woman's right to keep her name when she married.[23] Although they planned to spend the wedding night at the Hotel Vanderbilt, Mercedes spent the night at home with her mother. It was even rumored that she took a young girlfriend with her on their honeymoon.[24]

Undoubtedly, running through the bride's thoughts was her parents' facade of a marriage and the two failed marriages of her sister, Rita. Citing incompatibility, Rita had initiated divorce proceedings from Philip Lydig in 1914 but delayed pressing the case until after the war. When the decree was finalized on July 24, 1919, it was just eight months prior to Mercedes's announcing her engagement to Abram.[25] And Rita had already begun another relationship that would soon create more sensational headlines. Their mother was upset because it was with another Protestant. Rita did not conceal from her family "that she was deeply interested in him and was even considering marrying him."[26]

In spite of her reservations and fears about marriage and her understanding of Rita's difficulties, Mercedes married, but it hardly meant the end of her "strange turmoil." Her struggle was not a unique one for a woman at that time. Historian J. K. Curry has noted that a contemporary of Mercedes's, playwright Rachel Crothers, "identified as a woman who had chosen a career instead of marriage and family. Through the years of Crothers's career, journalists readily accepted the idea that a woman's choice between career and family was an either/or decision."[27] But Mercedes felt she had to choose a different path. Even though it may only have been to please her family and to serve as a convenient cover for her lesbian desires, she consented to a marriage. Nevertheless, she refused to abandon her career and continued to write.

The same year as her marriage, in fact, Mercedes published her first novel, *Wind Chaff,* about a young American girl, Paula Wayne, whom she describes as "a strange child, oddly quiet and reserved . . . unlike other children" (11). Although it is fiction, like many writers of fiction, Mercedes used much of her own background and experience in telling the story. Like Mercedes, Paula has hair that is short, straight, and very black. Her skin color is a strange whiteness that at certain times "took on a look of almost ethereal illumination" (13). When she was fifteen years old, her father decided to send her away to a boarding school in France. She objected, but he insisted, "The greatest quality a woman can have is obedience. . . . When young, she must obey her father, or whoever guards her, and when she marries, she, of course, must obey her husband implicitly" (25). Although Paula submitted to his decision, she vowed, "I will not be conquered. I *hate* and *loathe* obedience" (28).

The school, in an old chateau outside Paris, is run by an imposing, tall, thin, older Contessa who dressed in black and usually wore a Spanish mantilla over her white hair. The Contessa has two sons and four daughters, the youngest of whom is named Catalina, the same as the young girl Mercedes befriended when she attended a French boarding school.

While at the school, Paula suffers from intense melancholy. She often defies the Contessa, climbing out of her bedroom window at night and running into the nearby village. When one of the unmarried chambermaids is about to lose her position at the school because she has become pregnant, Paula demands that the Contessa protect and shelter the woman rather than discharge her. Eventually, Paula learns from the chambermaid that she has murdered the man who raped her. Paula cries out, "Is this what life does to women?" (100).

Paula is constantly pursued. She receives love letters from several of the girls at the school. When she is sent to the tower for two weeks for refusing to disclose the author of one of them, one of the Contessa's sons, Phillipe, sneaks into the room, bars the door, throws her onto a bed, and kisses her. Just as he is about to rape her, an employee of the Contessa, Conrad Tread, breaks into the room and saves her. Her fascination with and yearning for her savior grow, and she often finds herself wishing to reach out and touch him.

While dining with a friend in Paris a few months after the attempted rape, Paula notices at a nearby table an American woman of "rare and extraordinary beauty. . . . There was something almost fragrant about her, like an exotic, delicate plant" (141–42). Mercedes writes that Paula "found herself thinking constantly of this woman, weaving a romance about her, building dreams around her, endowing her with all sorts of sublime qualities, and allowing herself to be dominated by the thought of her. She was desperately alone and lonely, and, somehow, this woman seemed to answer an idealistic craving in her nature" (146). This "idealistic craving" in Paula's nature, her weaving a romance, and building dreams around a beautiful woman are the same drives that also obsessed Mercedes.

Later, after Paula has returned to America, she learns that Conrad Tread is visiting her "dream woman" in New York City and fears that they have developed an intimate relationship. As she contemplates this possibility, Paula, like Mercedes at that age, struggles with her sexual desires. Sitting before a mirror, "[s]he peered into her own eyes, 'What is the matter with me?' she said aloud. Hot tears came to her eyes as she thought of Conrad and Faith together, and then an unreasonable desire arose in her to hurt one of them. 'Which one?' she said. 'Am I jealous, and if so, of which one?'" (188).

Although they become estranged, when Paula discovers that her dream woman, whose name is Faith, is dying, Paula rushes to her bed and cries out, "'Faith, Faith, my darling. . . . Speak to me, *speak* to me! It's Paula, Paula, who loves you, Paula who . . .' her voice was muffled as she leaned over and kissed Faith frantically, then dropped to the floor unconscious."[28] Once she learns that Conrad has loved her all along and that he had never loved Faith, Paula sets off to visit him in Siberia where he is involved in the Russian Revolution. Before she arrives, however, he is assassinated before a firing squad. The novel ends as Paula kneels over his grave. "A sense of exhilaration came to her, while her body tingled as if a wild wind storm had swept against her and had now ceased. The chaff had been carried away in the wind—the wheat remained—the worthless was separated from that which was true. A great desire came to her to go on and fight and beat life at its own game. She held out her hands, and then slowly walked back, feeling that Faith and Conrad were leading her" (255).

Since Mercedes dedicated the book to her mother, a woman who was opposed to her daughter's writing career, it seems likely that it was, at least in part, her strategy to confess to her mother her own same-sex desires. Although one reviewer called it "an illuminating commentary on modern society," the general consensus was that the book "bears every appearance of being a talented sketch, but it has not been worked over into a picture. . . If Miss de Acosta will put more thought upon her motivations and a little more hard labor into her next novel, it will be well worth reading."[29]

During the winter of 1920, Mercedes spent several weeks volunteering at the Provincetown Theatre and observing rehearsals for Eugene O'Neill's *The Emperor Jones*.[30] In her spare time, she was working on her third full-length play, *The Moon Flower*.[31] The play is set at the country home of an English family that is now living in a house overlooking the rugged mountains and walls of Segovia, Spain. Nineteen-year-old Dawn Holloway is strangely ill, hardly speaks, and yearns for a moon flower in the haunted garden of their home, which she believes will make her well.

Unannounced, a mysterious local faith healer suddenly appears and claims he can heal the young girl. Since he happens to be Dawn's real father from an early affair that Dawn's mother has never acknowledged to her husband, Mrs. Holloway rejects his offer for help. She admits she is more intent that he leave and therefore preserve her own reputation rather than have him attempt to cure their daughter's illness. When he refuses, she exposes his charlatan tricks to the villagers. Just as the angry, local peasants are preparing to stone him to death, he raises his hands and prays, "Just this once— give me power." According to the stage directions, at that moment the "light changes to a strange vaporous blue and a strain of weird music is heard. Just then a bright spot of light falls at Dawn's feet, and slowly in it, a moon flower springs forth. Rising from her stupor [Dawn] stoops down and plucks it and raises it to her lips. A breathless silence and tremble runs over the crowd." Everyone agrees they have witnessed a miracle.

The style of this script is certainly different from that of Mercedes's earlier plays, which are rooted in realism, perhaps because she observed rehearsals for O'Neill's *The Emperor Jones*. The moody twilight, the mountains in the distance with their deep purple and "strange quality of mystery and romance," the ominous figure of the faith healer in his black cloak and hat, the yearning for a moon flower, the miracle at the end complete with music and lights are more akin to expressionism. The tone of the play approaches that of August Strindberg's *Easter* or *Dream Play*. Although some of her themes remain—adultery, marital relationships, paternity—Mercedes was beginning to explore more substantial issues: what is truth, when should truth be told, what is the proof of love? Perhaps she was taking to heart what the critic had said about *Wind Chaff,* that she should put more thought into her characters' motivations and a little more hard labor into her work.

~5~

"Love Goes On"

Undoubtedly contributing to Mercedes's turmoil at the time of her marriage was her attraction to Eva Le Gallienne, a young, attractive, and ambitious actress who was stunning all the Broadway critics.[1] On Monday, May 3, 1920, Le Gallienne had opened to rave reviews in Arthur Richman's comedy *Not So Long Ago*. A *New York Times* critic called her "appealingly beautiful."[2] Five days later, on Saturday, May 8, just three days before Mercedes's marriage, they met for lunch at the Ritz Hotel.[3] By the time lunch was over, they had worked themselves into "a pitch of excitement." They talked about their hopes for the theater and even discussed how they might one day establish a company in honor of the great actress whom they both worshiped, Eleonora Duse. When they were asked finally to leave the table, they left for Mercedes's apartment. Mercedes recalled in an early typescript of her autobiography that Eva "was surprised when I told her that I was being married within a week and would be going to Europe with Abram for the summer."[4] Eva's attentions quickly cooled.

Her marriage was challenged from the start, and it was about this time that Mercedes wrote "Faded Petals." She probably intended this poem for her new husband to read.

> Come! Let us be friends.
> Throw off the cloak of passion
> (You wear it far too much)
> And though your slightest touch
> Has ceased to make me tremble,

There is no reason why—
We still cannot
Climb our hill together,
And, at twilight's end,
Call each other "friend."
The rose tree fades but has its spring and autumn,
And so with love.
But with a rose—
We gather its faded petals
And in a box of precious metals
We store its fragrance.
Why not with love?
And which is more beautiful—
Who can say?
A rose in bloom or the fragrance of its petals
In decay![5]

Not long after Mercedes returned from her honeymoon, Eva became the toast of Broadway when she stunned all the critics with her performance in Ferenc Molnár's *Liliom*. Nearly everyone agreed that her acting was near perfection: "She was not 'poetic'—she was poetry"; "There is a breath of the spiritual in it."[6] Besides showing interest in her acting, the media began to exploit her appearance, her petite figure, light brown hair, clear blue eyes, and melancholy expression. "Rare would be a synonym for her," raved one critic; "so would luminous."[7] Her picture was everywhere, promoting everything from theater to cosmetics to fashions. In the August 1921 issue of *Theatre Magazine,* she is seen modeling golf and riding clothes for Abercrombie and Fitch. Some well-intentioned advertising man even points out how well she wears sports clothes, especially those that are of a "mannish style."

With her fascination for Eva heightened by all the press attention, Mercedes decided to pursue a liaison, going to Eva's dressing room one night after a performance. A whirlwind of socializing followed. One of their favorite pastimes was visiting Stark Young, then editor of *New Republic* and a theater critic for the *New York Times.* They often dined at the Russian Eagle, a restaurant on Fifty-seventh Street where all the staff were Russian refugees. Illegal speakeasies and shady nightspots in Harlem were also popular. As Mercedes confessed, "I suppose it was the newly found excitement of homosexuality, which after the war was expressed openly in nightclubs and cabarets by boys dressed as women, and was, like drinking, forbidden and

subject to police raids, which made it all the more enticing."[8] On one occasion, they escorted the internationally famous ballerina Tamara Karsavina
to the restaurant. It was a memorable evening, because they were joined by
Konstantin Stanislavsky and members of his Moscow Art Theatre.

On December 5, 1921, Mercedes's mother died at the home of Rita in
Bedford Hills, New York.[9] She had been living with Mercedes and Abram
in New York but had chosen to visit Rita in the country a few weeks earlier. When her mother's health began to show "a distinct physical decline,"[10]
Mercedes went to be with her and Rita. Abram visited occasionally. Toward
the end, she spoke only in Spanish, as if she never had learned English, and
then quietly slipped into a coma. A dedication in Mercedes's next publication reads "To my Mother, who never wearied in her love for me; my best
friend; my greatest loss."[11]

In her autobiography, Mercedes claims that after her mother was buried
on Christmas Eve, she locked herself in her room for several weeks and
refused to come out or answer anyone who knocked.[12] She may have been
in mourning, as she suggests, but the funeral would not have been delayed
until Christmas Eve, and if she did lock herself in her room, it was not for
several weeks. In fact, by the time of the Christmas holidays, Mercedes was
entangled in an affair with Michael Strange, an actress married to John
Barrymore. From their first meeting, Mercedes "thought her beguiling, full
of humor, and rather like a healthy young Arab boy, as I told her. Her hair
was brown, her eyes dark, and her skin deep olive and clear. I was impressed
then and afterwards by her radiant vitality and health. . . . One had the
impression that she was in the ring cracking the whip."[13] Mercedes concluded that Michael was attracted to men who were more feminine than
masculine and who, in moral stamina, were weaker than herself. "Jack, being one of these men, plus being handsome, talented and brimming over
with charm, was irresistible to her. In spite of his virility and appearance of
masculinity, Jack was inwardly feminine and had a great feminine sensitivity, which led him toward women who had much of the masculine in them.
Or let us say it led him toward women who dominated him. . . . He had a
need to be dominated."[14] Mercedes believed "this inner conflict and ceaseless
warring between the masculine and feminine elements of his nature were
the cause of his drinking."[15]

At some point during the Christmas season, Michael Strange invited
Mercedes for dinner and to stay overnight. She had just had a major row
with Barrymore, who had stormed out of the house in a rage. Mercedes
was flattered by the invitation. As Mercedes and Michael lounged in front
of the romantic fire after their candlelight dinner, they heard a strange noise

below them. Armed with pokers and kitchen knives, they crept down the stairs and found Barrymore sprawled out in a drunken stupor. The evening was so memorable that Michael penned a poem she called "To the Youth of Mercedes." The personal references to gestures, hands, feet, eyes, and laughter like whip stings evoke impressions of their relationship.

> I have not yet any idea clear of you—
> Have you of yourself
> Save your gestures are every one—final—
> And I see you tearing off things—you
>   could muse aside
> O your feet seem planted—never resting on
>   the ground
> And I feel you determined—en garde—gaunt
>   with expectation
> When both armies—sleep—
> Unconsciously you bring people—circumstances—
> Into enormous momentum around you
> Then standing a little aghast—impatient in the center
>   as a child amazed at the continuity
> But your hands are beautiful—magnetic—
> O I feel your hands peeling pale fresh almonds
> Under plea of limpid—myriad eyes—by a
>   wall near the city of Masques.
> And your sudden laughter is like the
>   bent whip sting of a magnolia bush
>   in Northern springtime
> The Orient—the north pangs of each in either one.
> You see I have not yet any idea clear of
>   you
> Have you of yourself. Love. Michael Strange[16]

A few years later, when Mercedes was visiting the Barrymores in France, a similar drama occurred. Mercedes heard Michael yelling, "Help! Mercedes, help!" When she rushed to their bedroom she found them rolling on the floor and John was waving a knife over his wife's head. Luckily, Mercedes was able to intervene and prevent any injuries but not before John hurled a kerosene lamp at the two women, narrowly missing them and smashing it against the wall.

At the time of her mother's death, Mercedes was working on a theater project with Eva. On January 4, 1922, just one month after the funeral, Eva opened for a special matinee production of Maeterlinck's lyrical *Aglavaine and Selysette,* with a costume designed by Mercedes. The production was unsuccessful, but it cemented a relationship that lasted for five years.

A week later, Eva sent Mercedes a poem she composed that expressed her love and apprehension about their future. She felt she had been running madly for centuries, hunting in vain for someone to love. She often paused in her chase, hoping her pursuit was over. She believed her life was meaningless until she met Mercedes, whose beautiful eyes were filled with expectation and whose soul held incomprehensible rewards. Eva could hardly believe her search was finally over and that she would not have to resume her quest the next day.[17]

When Eva left New York in the early spring of 1922 for a national tour of *Liliom,* she sent Mercedes flowers and wrote two or three love letters daily, often with warm, intimate, affectionate greetings. Mercedes missed her lover and complained often in her letters to Eva that she was not eating well, not sleeping, and suffering from severe headaches and depression.

Eva, therefore, tried to convince Mercedes of her undying love.[18] She reassured Mercedes of her faithfulness, and wanted Mercedes to know that, even when they were apart, her arms were around Mercedes and holding her tightly (February 5 from Boston). Eva was intensely jealous of Abram. Just thinking about his sleeping with Mercedes and his attempting to arouse sexual desire in his wife threw Eva into the depths, a frenzy that reached deep into her soul. The sacred connection of sexual intimacy should be limited to just her and Mercedes. It should not include Abram. Eva felt much like Julie, Eva's character in *Liliom,* who says, "through everything—if I loved you—to the very end—no matter what happens, god bless you—my dearest" (April 14 from Philadelphia). Eva wrote that she felt so gloomy and desolate, unable to act on stage, and embarrassed about the performances she was giving (April 21 from Philadelphia). She wanted to prostrate herself before Mercedes and remain there through the night with her cheek pressed against Mercedes's palm. Mercedes was her enchantress, her muse, her reason for living. Eva wondered whether Mercedes's love for her was as overwhelming and fierce (April 28 from New York).

In a poem she wrote, Eva tried desperately to reassure Mercedes of how much it meant to her that they had found each other.

My soul, finally free from its exhausted wickedness,
One day fell asleep, and I wandered in life
Like a scentless flower
Lost in the obscurity of matter

One day I heard a song in my head
Faintly at first, and then louder by the hour.
I caught sight of a night star,
Growing and filling the world
With warm and heady light.
Then in a shiver my soul opened its proud and pure eyes
Shot a rapturous look to the skies
Recognized in the song the voice of your love
And saw the star reflect the promise of our life everlasting.[19]

By the middle of May, Eva had become desperately lonely for Mercedes as well as physically exhausted from the tour. She fainted during a performance in Chicago, and when she recovered, she could not walk. She was suffering from a complete nervous breakdown, and the tour was postponed. The press reported that the strain of playing Julie's repressed emotions had proved too much for her. However, in letters she wrote to Mercedes in May, Eva reveals other reasons for her collapse. Eva complained that she felt listless, blasé, and dispirited. She had sat down in her dressing room and cried uncontrollably when she realized that Mercedes was sailing to Europe for the summer, and she feared losing her. Mercedes's silence alarmed Eva. Although she admitted that her fear was irrational, Eva complained that Mercedes seemed unwilling to share her feelings openly. She wondered whether Mercedes's reserve and her concealment of her emotions behind a mask meant that her love was fading. Eva was so depressed about the course of her life and their love that she threatened suicide.[20]

Eva was also jealous. One of Mercedes's earlier romances had been with Billie McKeever. Although from an established New York family, Billie was unconventional and often balked at her parents' social expectations. Mercedes wrote that "she would come to our house and hide in Abram's studio and beg us not to give her away or tell anyone where she was. She was wild, untamed, and had a delicious fey quality." Eva, fearing Mercedes's strong attraction to McKeever, begged Mercedes to remember their love.[21]

Eva registered her fears in another poem she sent to Mercedes.

I dare cast an eye on life
All the misery it could ever bring down on me
Will not matter in the least
For you love me and possess me.
I dare cast an eye on poverty
For matter is harmless
And your hand touched me

And your lips consoled me for myself.
I dare cast an eye on death
That seems at times to stare at me
With eager, fathomless eyes
Since the voice of your love
Promised me immortality.
But I dare not cast an eye on your betrayal
Once I face it I will live no more,
Neither will I die:
I will endlessly wander the earth, cold and terrible,
Holding in my bloody hands
My tortured heart, ripped from my chest.
I will throw it away from me into the boundless sea
My soul will be gone
And I will forevermore detest the sun.[22]

On June 4, Mercedes sailed for Europe with her husband, along with a packet of love letters from Eva to be opened on each day of the journey. They exchanged rings as tokens of their love and swore everlasting fidelity. Two days later, Eva sailed for England, reassuring Mercedes that she would lock away in a box any letters she received so that her mother would not see them. Mercedes offered to pay Eva's hotel and some other expenses, but Eva declined the offer.[23] Eva's mood had changed. She and Mercedes would simply have to get married, she proclaimed. She would sacrifice everything to fulfill that dream. Her intense desire for Mercedes had become an obsession.[24]

In two more books of poetry, *Archways of Life* (1921) and *Streets and Shadows* (1922), Mercedes reveals the personal thoughts and anxieties she was having during her relationship with Eva. In "Soiled Hands" she recalls the thrill of sitting in a darkened theater with her lover:

After everyone had left,
It was always so wonderful sitting in the dark
theatre with you.
There was a mystery about it,
As though the echo of many plays
Still lingered in the folds of the curtain,
While phantom figures crouched low in the chairs,
Beating suppressed applause with vapor hands.
Do you remember how we always sat silently?
I would shut my eyes to feel your closeness nearer.

Then slowly and like a ritual
I would take your hand,
And you would laugh a little and say,
"My hands are awfully sticky"—or
"I can't seem to keep my hands clean in this theatre,"
As if that mattered . . . as if that mattered. . . .[25]

Even in a public place, the darkness seemed to provide her the necessary shield from prying eyes. Her overwhelming yearning to commit to a woman was consummate, a feeling she expressed in her poem "Surrender":

I will offer all my love
    Recklessly, without rest,
And give myself completely
    Upon my darling's breast—
Our pulses shall beat as one pulse,
    And in that sacred breath
I shall feel the touch of Life
    Yet know the truth of Death![26]

A woman living in shadows, Mercedes was ceaselessly tormented by her need to hide her feelings:

Today is your birthday.
Many people will come to you with offerings,
While I,
Who seemingly know you so slightly,
Yet who truly know you so well,
Must stand aside with empty hands.
If love could make this day perfect,
My love would weave for you
A web enmeshed with all your desires.
On your pathway
I would fling stars for pebbles
And tear down the moon
So that you might wear
The radiance of its silver
In your hair.
But instead—
I stand outside like a wall
And quite powerless
I send no gift at all.[27]

Her poem "Good-bye on the Boat" reflects how Mercedes felt when they had parted at the wharf before their separation in June. She had been overcome by the agony of hiding their love and trying to appear "indifferent before the others."

> Early morning—
> Rising.
> A dead, hopeless feeling about my heart.
> Going out—cold air on my face—
> Crossing the ferry with others
> And at the boat
> Finding you in the crowd.
> Hundreds of faces—
> Pushing humanity—
> Staggering porters
> Burdened with heavy luggage
> Groping up the gangway.
> Voices everywhere—
> An onrush of meaningless—empty words.
> Confused orders—repeated directions.
> You and I standing in it all
> Helpless—hopeless—
> Trying to seem indifferent before the others,
> And like the rest saying
> Trivial—futile things.
> A shrill whistle—
> I calmly saying
> "I think we had better go."
> Kissing you lightly—coldly—
> And with the others leaving you.
> Going off the pier
> My throat closed with pain—
> Eyes dim—staggering just a little.
> Then standing in the front of the ferry
> Trying not to seem crushed—
> With the confusion past
> The hideous realization
> That you have really gone
> Comes over me—
> The desperate regret

For all the trivial things I said,
And because I did not kiss you
The way I wanted.[28]

And yet, strangely, Mercedes was incapable of submitting herself totally to Eva, which she explains in another poem she called "Unpossessed."

Never shall I be all subdued,
Nor the real secret of me understood;
Passionately and violently my body may be possessed,
But my spirit
Always a virgin,
Will wander on forever
Unpossessed![29]

Because many of the poems were so revealing of her own personal torment, it might follow that her plays and novels would be as profound. Such was not the case. Reviewers praised her for her directness and simplicity but criticized her for not understanding "the value of nuance." Once again, her efforts were labeled "more a promise than a fulfillment."[30]

The lovers eventually reunited in Paris, where they stayed for several nights in adjoining rooms at the Hôtel Foyot. Every night Eva rushed to her hotel window as soon as she heard Mercedes whistle outside. With a signal from her lover, Eva would then sneak into Mercedes's room and quietly slide into her bed and into her embrace.[31] Mercedes's husband must have been either terribly naive or remarkably open-minded not to have noticed their behavior. After a brief stopover in Venice, they traveled to Budapest, where they were met by Molnár, a brass band, and banners. Mercedes wanted Eva to accompany her and Abram to Constantinople, but Eva refused. Once again, Eva said that she dreaded thinking of Mercedes making love to Abram. She could not bring herself to even discuss it.[32] Her distaste for Abram was so intense, she could not join them on the trip and returned to London.

Mercedes was going through both a delicate and awkward balancing act with her lover on one side and her husband on the other. In her poem "We Three," Mercedes laments her situation.

There is something that from between us has
    slipped away and left me chill,
Something that by its loss has made the world
    less warm

And made me feel as though the sun rising o'er
    the purple dew-touched hill,
Finds its rays cold as it touches the face of dawn.

Although we kiss and meet the same each day,
You speak my name and I yours and we clasp
    hands,
Yet from somewhere, I do not know which
    way,
Stealing between us a lurking figure stands. . . .[33]

Soon after leaving Budapest, Eva, annoyed over Mercedes's accusation that Eva did not want to accompany her to Constantinople, lashed out, charging that Mercedes no longer loved her or desired her. A few weeks later, in reference to an unpleasant letter she had received from Mercedes, Eva questioned whether their love was really worth all the misery they caused each other. Mercedes's thoughts of suicide depressed Eva so much that she told Mercedes that such ideas were selfish and malicious. Surely, Mercedes would not be cruel enough to do that to her.[34]

Toward the end of the summer, Eva wrote to Mercedes from London that her mother and three old friends had been held spellbound as she read to them Mercedes's new play, *Jehanne d'Arc*. When Eva showed them a picture of Mercedes, Eva was certain they thought Mercedes was a man. In fact, she almost told them it was her husband.[35] At Eva's invitation, Mercedes joined her lover in London during the first half of September.

Regardless of their reunion, Mercedes was becoming increasingly negative. She wrote Eva from Paris that there was nothing for her to return to in New York, and she doubted her lover's faithfulness.[36] After their first telephone conversation since Mercedes's return to New York, Eva complained that Mercedes seemed so aloof, so icy on the telephone that it made Eva feel unloved and unwanted, and prevented her from expressing her love.[37] Eva, who was once again touring with *Liliom,* argued that onstage every night when she recited Julie's line "I love you," her inspiration was her love for Mercedes.[38]

Since Mercedes was married, their relationship always had to be hidden. When Eva stole back to New York during breaks in the tour or on weekends, they met secretly in Eva's apartment. Their separation and their need for secrecy frustrated Eva to the depths of her soul. She yearned to proclaim their love to the heavens. She dreamed constantly of marrying Mercedes, of being her bride.[39] Eva was bothered that she and Mercedes were forced to meet so clandestinely like two strangers.[40]

In spite of their difficulties, they embarked on a major theater venture—
to produce *Jehanne d'Arc*.[41] Director Arthur Hopkins had already rejected
the script, complaining that Eva's restrained acting style would spoil the
play.[42] The Shuberts had expressed some interest but ultimately declined,
since they felt the cost of production would be staggering.[43] Producer Sam
Harris also turned it down, but when he asked whether Mercedes had any
other vehicles for Eva, she quickly finished another play, *Sandro Botticelli,* a
fictional account of a beautiful woman who poses for Botticelli's famous
The Birth of Venus.[44]

Sandro Botticelli opens in a corner of a garden in the park near the villa
of Lorenzo dei Medici in Fiesole, just outside Florence. It is the spring of
1476. The story focuses on Simonetta Vespuccia, who is considered "the most
beautiful and the fairest woman here—beloved by everyone. It seems almost impossible that so many men could love her and so many women praise
her." Although there is gossip that she is the mistress of Giuliano dei Medici,
she also has the reputation for seeming "too cold, too indifferent to have
ever had a lover." Before she makes her first entrance, gentlemen of the
Medici court refer to her "dazzling beauty. . . . A beauty like hers seems almost a dangerous thing." "Yes," someone replies, "it is like the beauty of an
exquisitely sharp knife. The hilt may be jeweled, but if one comes too close,
the blade draws blood."

Soon after Simonetta and several other ladies of the court enter, Lorenzo
calls for singers and musicians to entertain them. During the music, Sandro
Botticelli "never removes his eyes from the face of Simonetta." As the music
ends and they begin to discuss beauty and the paintings of Leonardo da Vinci,
who is one of the guests, Lorenzo asks Sandro, "How about beautiful women
then? Do you claim because of their beauty they can do no wrong?"

Looking at Simonetta, Sandro answers, "Their beauty has already for-
given them, long before they were born. Let them contribute to beauty, all
who wish to live eternally."

Smitten by the handsome Sandro, once they are alone in the garden,
Simonetta promises to visit his studio the next afternoon "wrapped in a
cloak—underneath that cloak I will be nude. I will be wrapped in a cloak
which I will cast off. . . . You will paint the beauty of my body. You will paint
a glorious picture that will last forever, so that I too may contribute to the
beauty of life. . . . No other man has seen the beauty of my body before, no
other man shall ever see it again."

When the curtain rises on act 2, Sandro is preparing his studio for her
arrival, moving furniture, arranging flowers, checking the lighting. Simonetta
enters "wrapped in a flame-color cloak which drapes her body to the

ground, but which shows her lines nevertheless": "A few weeks ago I thought no man could ever awaken love in me and then the night I went to Lorenzo dei Medici's . . . I could always tell when you were looking at me even if I was not looking at you. It was like feeling the warmth of the sun before its rays actually reach you." She repeats her promise to pose nude for him, but "not today." "Today it must only be love," she says passionately. Although Sandro is in love with her, the artist in him prevails, and as she strips in his studio, he forgets his passion and starts to work feverishly on his canvas. As she says later to her maid, "I was burning for him to make love to me—oh the humiliation of it—the humiliation of it. . . . I wanted to give myself to him. I wanted him to caress my beauty; I wanted him to touch my breasts; I wanted him to cover my body with kisses." Feeling rejected and exploited, the enraged maiden runs from the studio into the pouring rain, becomes ill, and dies three days later. During this time, Sandro has done nothing but work on his painting of Simonetta as Venus. When he learns of her death, "the cloth falls off the painting to the floor; an extraordinary light from the window falls on it. Botticelli's great masterpiece . . . is revealed." "My prayer has been answered," Sandro says. "Simonetta is not dead. . . . She will live forever."

During an intermission, theatergoers chattered curiously about the scene that was to follow—how ever would Eva appear nude in act 2? Actually, she simply dropped her cape while concealing her bare body with her long hair and a high-backed chair. Ironically, the painting of *The Birth of Venus* used in the final scene of the play was created by Abram Poole, Mercedes's husband and Eva's nemesis.

In the play, Mercedes had again created a drama that depicted women's issues. On opening night, her former love interest, Hope Williams, sent her flowers with the message, "All my love and prayers for tonight darling." And Jesse Lynch Williams, who had received a Pulitzer Prize for *Why Marry?* a few years earlier, sent her a telegram, reading, "Your play is beautiful. I wish you great success."[45] Nevertheless, the critics were not kind. The dialogue was called artificial, stilted, and "so flowery . . . that it resembles a seed catalogue." Eva was criticized for her inability to portray feminine passion.[46]

Mercedes by now was becoming increasingly disillusioned with Broadway: "In New York at this time, if an artist rose from the gutter the critics were all out to give him a break, but if he had background and wealth it was assumed from the start that he was an untalented idiot. Usually the critics either demolished him without fair criticism or completely ignored him."[47] With the passage of time, however, Mercedes recognized the play's weakness. "I can't understand now how any of us could ever have thought it would have the ghost of a chance on Broadway," she sighed. "It is a slight and uncommercial play with a certain charm and poetic quality. I think the story could have been adapted for a fine opera."[48] Though it ran only briefly, it became Mercedes's second play published during her lifetime.

Another play she completed in 1923 was *Jacob Slovak.*[49] Mercedes's personal view of a woman marginalized because of her same-sex desires fueled her writing with conviction and understanding. The title character, young Jewish Jacob Slovak, experiences prejudice in a little New England town. He has been hired as a shop clerk because his employer thinks "the sharpness of Jews" will somehow help him compete with other stores. But when Jacob falls in love with Myra, the boss's daughter, the conservative Protestants of the town turn on him. They argue, "It's dangerous to have these foreigners about." He finally leaves after Myra refuses to renounce her family and town to marry him.

The final act takes place two months later. Jacob has returned and now begs Myra once again to run away with him. She is pregnant with Jacob's child but is set on marrying a friend of the family who believes he is the father. She says that after the marriage she will persuade her husband to hire Jacob so that "we—you can be close to me again." With suppressed anger, he yells out, "Do you think I would let another man bring up my child? . . . No, my child is a Jew. . . . Call in the whole village. . . . Tell them you are carrying a Jew child in your womb!" Myra screams back, "I hate you—you dirty Jew!" Jacob pulls out a revolver and kills Myra. As the family rushes in to see what has happened and subdues Jacob, he manages to grab a large bread knife from the table and plunges it into his heart.

The final pages of the script reinforce the town's anti-Semitism. When the local minister instructs the sheriff to make sure Jacob's body is not put in the church, a servant girl remarks, "Wasn't—wasn't Jesus a Jew?" "Jesus?" the minister replies, "Oh, that was over two thousand years ago. Times have changed since then."

Setting the play in New England, the site of traditional American values, and ending it with such a damning and obvious indictment of the church and of the smug, provincial, intolerant villagers, Mercedes illustrates her personal views of Americans who rejected her own uniqueness. There is no record that she sought an immediate production of the play, even though the female lead was undoubtedly intended to be played by her lover, Eva Le Gallienne. After all, they had just received devastating reviews for *Sandro Botticelli,* and they were looking for some time to heal.

The summer of 1923, Mercedes and Eva returned to Europe. Just before sailing, they learned that Eleonora Duse was rehearsing in Paris for a comeback tour. The morning they arrived in Paris, therefore, they stood opposite the Hotel Regina where Duse was staying. As they looked up at her window, they felt they had witnessed a miracle—sitting there on a balcony, wrapped in a blanket, was Duse herself. Mercedes whispered, "We should kneel."[50]

Part of the time, they looked like gypsies, as they embarked on a walking trip through Brittany. Through a mutual friend, they managed to get tickets to Duse's first performance in London. Mercedes remembered that when the curtain descended, "no one applauded. Many people were weeping and the audience filed silently out."[51] Back in Paris, they attended the famous Le Monocle and Magic City, both music hall promenades that specialized in transvestite dances. One Friday evening, they even attended a soiree hosted by the infamous lesbian Natalie Barney.

By the time they were both back in New York, Mercedes suspected that Eva had broken their mutual vow of fidelity and accused her of having an affair with her own former attraction, actress Michael Strange.[52] She expressed her sorrow in a poem entitled "Lost Ideal":

> To have returned and found you changed.
> To have left you trembling from my touch—
> With smouldering fires in your eyes—
> Now to find your flame
> Burning at another's altar.
> Yet how strange—
> With this change
> No storm of jealousy rages me.
> Only a sad regret—
> That in all your words of fidelity
> Sworn so true—
> In our friendship now—
> So strained—so new—
> The truth stabs me—
> I am a finer thing than you![53]

Mercedes was still smarting from the negative criticism leveled at *Sandro Botticelli*. In fact, she felt it would be the last play she would try to stage. Regardless of the challenges in their relationship, Eva tried to encourage her lover's playwriting, telling her their failure was an indication of what they had to do the next time. Citing Mercedes's bravery in trying to overcome all the challenges and animosity of ignorant people, Eva encouraged her to use the criticism as a catalyst for improvement. She was resolved that she and Mercedes could produce great work together. They needed to continue, she maintained, in order to make life bearable.[54]

Duse had begun her performances in New York, so Mercedes went to see her "faint with excitement."[55] During their ensuing conversation, Duse quickly turned to Mercedes and said with an impatient gesture of her hand, "Why don't you write a play for me? I need a play from the soul of a poet. I need a play in which I can depict a universal character. I can no longer play characters with personal loves or personal problems." Mercedes moved to the window and watched the snowflakes drift to the ground. The association of whiteness with purity sprang to her mind and led her to think of the Virgin Mary. She turned from the window and replied, "I would like to write a drama about the passion of Mary." Duse rose and struck her hands together in a gesture of exaltation. "Mary is the character I must play," she cried. "Go home and write it. Quickly! Quickly! Agir! Agir! Il faut agir!" Mercedes worked on it feverishly for forty-eight hours and then had a friend translate it into Italian.

The play opens with Mary deciding that she will go to Pontius Pilate and offer him her life in exchange for that of her son's. But when she is refused an audience, she sobs wildly that people "cannot understand someone superior to themselves. . . . they despise superiority; resent independence and fearlessness." Coming from a wealthy, elitist background herself, Mercedes knew the hazards. Hadn't she just said as much when she challenged the critics who panned her work?

Eventually, Mary is smuggled into Jesus' prison cell where she is unsuccessful in begging him to flee for his life. In an exchange that could easily be that of a mother and her lesbian daughter, Mary buries her face in her hands and asks, "Will you still persist in making me suffer so? You are the only thing I have in the world; the only one I love—yet you are the only person I do not understand, the only one who wounds me deeply." As he is crucified, Mary "suddenly becomes the wildly enraged mother fighting for her child. . . . She is like a tortured, cornered animal, fighting her last fight with her back against the wall." In the final scene, she sits outside the sepulcher and prays for the time when people will recognize how her son embraced "compassion, tolerance, understanding and forgiveness." As a woman who was living a complicated life with both a husband and a female lover, Mercedes was undoubtedly expressing her own dreams.

Once it was completed, Duse read the play aloud to Mercedes. One moment in particular stood out. When Duse as Mary answered Pilate's question as to her identity by saying simply, "the Mother of Jesus," Mercedes felt "cold with emotion."

Instead of stressing the line and dramatizing it, she simply threw it away. She understated it. In this understatement she became, not only the Mother of Jesus but the mother of the whole suffering world. Never at any time in my life have I heard a line so read. Never at any time in my life do I expect to hear it. . . . And I believe it was not even Duse who spoke the words to me. I believe when she said these words, they suddenly became a great Universal Maternal Utterance, as she, in saying them, became the great Universal Mother. She pronounced these words as simply as the dew falls upon a flower. They were doubly marked on her manuscript.[56]

Then Duse remarked, "I will tour the whole world with this play. After playing it I will never act again. This is the play I have always dreamed of. Only a poet could have conceived the idea and written it. We will call it *The Mother of Christ*."[57] Suddenly, to Mercedes's embarrassment, Duse bent over her hand and kissed it.[58]

Mercedes and Eva attended Duse's premiere in New York of Ibsen's *Lady from the Sea* at the Metropolitan Opera House, and they tried to keep track of her successes as she embarked on her American tour. What horror, when they learned that in Pittsburgh on April 21, 1924, Duse died. Odd as it may seem, Mercedes and Eva, rather than any other official dignitaries, made the arrangements for her body to lie in state in Saint Joseph's Chapel of the Dominican Catholic Church on Lexington Avenue. They kept vigil and prayed beside the coffin. On May 1, they attended a solemn requiem mass for Duse at the Church of St. Vincent Ferrer, and watched as the black ship carrying her body glided out of the pier for Italy. For nearly half a century, until she herself died in 1968, Mercedes treasured a large, dark brown palm leaf that she had retrieved from Duse's coffin.[59] In a single stroke, the tragic death of Duse shattered plans for Mercedes's play.

For the next many months, while Eva was performing in Molnár's *The Swan,* she and Mercedes struggled to find backers for productions that would star Eva in both *Jehanne d'Arc* and *The Mother of Christ*. After one of their minipreviews, Elsie de Wolfe gushed a brief thank you "so much, Miss d'Acosta, for a delightful and unusual evening last night . . . and Mrs. Anne Vanderbilt very enthusiastic also!"[60] Eva approached Boston banker Joseph P. Kennedy and her father's old friend, Otto Kahn.

During the summer of 1924, while the Actor's Equity strike closed all Broadway theaters, Mercedes and Eva worked at Jasper Deeter's Hedgerow Theatre near Philadelphia. Eva starred for the first time in Ibsen's *The Master Builder* and persuaded Deeter to cast Mercedes in the role of the young and naive Kaja. Even though they were playing to sold-out houses, after less than two weeks, Eva announced they would be leaving the company. She complained of "disrespect and lack of courtesy" backstage, but the real reason for their abandoning the production was their desire for a vacation together.

Even though Mercedes's husband was out of town and she and Eva were finally able to live together when the actress was in New York, their relationship was deteriorating. A jealous Mercedes not only resented Eva's having a love affair with her costar, Basil Rathbone, but also accused her of having an affair with a Russian actress. During an engagement in Chicago, Eva complained about an alarming letter she had received from Mercedes that made her shudder and nearly collapse. Mercedes had accused her of having an affair with another woman. Eva attacked Mercedes for persistently misinterpreting her thoughts. She had not lied when she denied having an affair. Mercedes admitted that part of her love for Eva had died when she heard the rumors. Eva could not comprehend, after all the years of their relationship, how Mercedes could be so jealous and untrusting. Sometimes she wondered whether she should just end it all.[61]

Nevertheless, Eva continued to support Mercedes's plays and tried to get financial backers while she was performing in Chicago. Eva once again tried to inspire her lover, who was doubting her own talent as a playwright. Eva wanted her to know how much she counted on her, how much she regarded her ability, and how thrilled she would be if she became an instrument in sharing Mercedes's beautiful work with the world.[62] Just two months later, she wrote that thoughts of embodying Mercedes's character of Jehanne made her shudder. She feared she could never live up to the task, could never portray the beauty her lover had created. Eva feared failure. She feared she was not only unqualified for the role but also undeserving.[63]

Mercedes's personal life informed her writing of Joan's character. Unlike all her previous plays, which have realistic settings, this one is more evocative. It calls for "a glorious blue cyclorama" and a stage built architecturally with planes and levels. In the first scene, Joan begs her uncle for help "to escape this marriage that my mother and father are planning for me." A peasant woman praises her for "remaining unburdened by the low domestic things of life; free from slavery and the breeding of children."

Throughout the script, however, Joan is jeered and spat upon for dressing in men's clothes and cutting her hair like a man's. She is told that her unnatural behavior defames herself before Heaven. Voices in the crowd call her "a woman trying to be a man" and "a sexless woman." During her trial, Archbishop Cauchon insists, "The devil is your accomplice. You wear men's clothes as only a harlot would.... You have sinned against God, your mother, the Church and all men. You have been a traitor to your country and a disgrace to the name of womanhood." At one point, Joan argues, "We are each one of us chained to something. Each one of us in a different way. I have my battles, too."[64]

Eventually, Firmin Gémier, director of the Théâtre de l'Odéon in Paris, was interested in producing both *Jehanne d'Arc* and *The Mother of Christ* under the auspices of the Ministry of Beaux-Arts, but only if Mercedes could find some American backers. The very wealthy Mrs. Harold McCormick of Chicago initially showed interest, but in November 1924, when she met Mercedes and Eva and learned that the two women were lovers and that Mercedes was married, she quickly withdrew her support. There was no way that she would link her name with such disreputable people. Understandably, they were outraged over the provincial and narrow thinking that was preventing their dream. Eva wrote to Mercedes that she wearied of the gossip, rumor, and innuendo circulating about their relationship. It all seemed so petty and banal, and crushed her morale.[65] At virtually the last hour, a new benefactor, Alice De Lamar, saved them. A reclusive lesbian with homes in Paris, Palm Beach, and Connecticut, she had inherited ten million dollars from her father, who had amassed a fortune from gold and copper mining. If they could persuade De Lamar to love the project, Eva wrote, everything else would work out beautifully.[66] Luckily, they were successful.

As they left for Paris in late March 1925, Mercedes was bubbling with anticipation, for they had solid financial backing, a theater, and as designer, Norman Bel Geddes, who had achieved great notoriety a year earlier when he converted New York's Century Theatre into a cavernous Gothic cathedral for Max Reinhardt's production of *The Miracle.*

Complications pursued them endlessly. Since the Théâtre de l'Odéon, which they had been promised rent-free, was too small for Bel Geddes's sets, they had to go elsewhere, reluctantly settling on the Théâtre de la Porte-Saint-Martin, which cost them seven thousand dollars for thirty days. Mercedes and Eva had raised a total of twelve thousand dollars before leaving New York, thinking that would be sufficient. Suddenly, more than half their funds were depleted, and they had to ask De Lamar for another twenty-eight thousand dollars. In desperation, they also contacted Maurice Speiser, a wealthy lawyer and the manager of Philadelphia's Little Theatre, who was vacationing in Paris. He had championed Jacques Copeau's visit to Philadelphia several years earlier and had helped Eugene O'Neill achieve a production of *The Hairy Ape* in Munich in 1922. "This is a S.O.S. for you," Mercedes pleaded. "Could you come to the theatre some time this afternoon or this evening as it is so important that I should talk to you." In a second letter, she begged even more strongly: "Forgive this second appeal but we need your help terribly. Can you possibly come to the theatre to-morrow morning at 11:30. We are in a terrible hole—want your help and advice—Please come!"[67] There is no record of his meeting with Mercedes nor of his assisting them financially.

Adding to their despair was their agreement to rent the Porte-Saint-Martin, which meant they were obliged to use that theater's permanent company of actors. When it came to extras, Bel Geddes insisted on hiring a minimum of 150, a third of whom were Russian immigrants who spoke neither French nor English. Mercedes wrote about still another problem they experienced: "To add to our many troubles we had to 'police' him [Bel Geddes] . . . and spend much of our time and devitalized nerves in sober-ing him up. . . . Our young American genius discovers sex, night life, vie de Bohème and Paris!"[68]

When they finally opened on June 12, 1925, the theater world was bus-tling with excitement. American newspapers in such far-flung corners as Walla Walla, Washington; Grand Forks, North Dakota; and Duluth, Minne-sota, proclaimed the opening. *Theatre Magazine* ran photos of the sets along with detailed descriptions.[69] The French press had capitalized on the nov-elty of an American author and actress presenting, in French, a play about one of the French heroes. Front-page headlines of the Paris edition of the *Chicago Tribune* read, "Eva Le Gallienne to Play *Jehanne d'Arc*."[70] Opening night dignitaries included Elsie de Wolfe, Elsa Maxwell, Arthur Rubenstein, Mrs. Vincent Astor, Condé Nast, the Cole Porters, Ivor Novello, Dorothy Parker, Zoë Akins, and Constance Collier.

The excitement was short-lived. Even prior to rehearsals, Bel Geddes had complained to Mercedes about the script: "[Y]our play is episodic and undramatic. We all know the story, so there has to be a special reason for writing a play. Why did you write yours? What contribution have you made? . . . I have the utmost confidence that the spirit of Jeanne will radiate through Eva, but I do not feel the same spirit radiating from your play. . . . Unless your play is right, Eva's effort and mine won't help it."[71] His opinion was not the only negative one. Eva had shown the script to her old flame Alla Nazimova, who questioned whether the play was worthy of Eva's talents. What was Eva's reaction to this observation? She wrote to Mercedes that Nazimova had "behaved like a thorough cad."[72]

Hoping to compensate for what he thought was uninspired writing, Bel Geddes conceived the production as a spectacle, emphasizing lighting, sound, and movement of the actors. He designed a single, architectural setting with multilevel platforms. By means of banners, costumes, and properties, he transformed the stage into the Dauphin's throne room, Rheims Cathedral, the battle of Compeigne, and a Rouen marketplace. As Joan's moods shifted, the lighting and the mood changed around her. The French critics were impressed with the spectacle and pageantry, but they were unanimous that Bel Geddes had exaggerated his role as designer. A critic for *Le Matin* concluded, "It is a 'great show' for the eyes, and nothing at all for the brain and spirit."[73] The contribution of Mercedes suffered from all the dazzle. Sometimes ten minutes would pass before a word of dialogue was spoken. One French critic was so overwhelmed by the visual display that his only comment on the script and Eva's acting was that Eva spoke "French without the slightest accent."[74] Although plans to add *The Mother of Christ* to the theater's repertory were quickly dropped, the press reported that *Jehanne d'Arc* would move to London in August and to Broadway in the fall of the year. Neither plan materialized.

Motives for dropping the project were complex—lackluster reviews, the exorbitant cost of production, and Bel Geddes's focus on other, more promising productions. Certainly another reason was a conflict between Mercedes and Eva that had been growing for many months. After *Jehanne d'Arc* closed in Paris, Eva went off to visit Alice De Lamar at her Italian villa, leaving Mercedes to attend Natalie Barney's Paris salon. There she befriended Janet Flanner, a renowned American expatriate living in Paris, who, like several other women, was enamored of Mercedes and composed a poem for her. This one, however, was written in the shape of a large tulip:

> Her shoes were those of ladies who used to be heeded.
> She ate daintily, consuming a sweetened crumb like a singer taking a
>   high note.
> She ate flesh talking of flowers and flesh.
> Her appetites were few and they in her head, living there in grandeur
>   like political prisoners who had changed, not broken laws.
> Her hat was that of Revolution and there in colors: a pacifist, she
>   wore it in black.
> Her shoulders were slight miracles of tailoring and God.
> Her waist was thinned like a finger long embraced by a ring.
> Her hair was lignous, black, like a combed bush: her ears reddened
>   like the berries.
> She had a small white body, like a small marble park, in which her
>   eyes lived as brown nightingales.
> She despised distance and belittled the world by moving about it
>   quickly on large boats and small feet.

She used London as commonly as the Queen, walked in Venice and in
Paris was beloved.[75]

Although Eva argued that she had never loved anyone other than Mercedes, she did not deny having affairs with other women. She even encouraged Mercedes to seek an alternative physical outlet. As Mercedes and Eva
sailed back to New York on board the *Majestic* after the closing of *Jehanne
d'Arc*, fellow passenger Noel Coward complained that during the entire trip
the two women "alternated between intellectual gloom and feverish gai-
ety—and wore black indiscriminately, for both moods."[76]

By the time the ship docked in New York, their relationship had ended.
Also on board the *Majestic* was the object of Eva's next romantic involvement, scene designer Gladys E. Calthrop. Even though Mercedes objected,
Eva spent considerable time with Gladys and argued that it was impossible
for her to be faithful to just one woman. Many of Mercedes's friends were
concerned for her welfare over this demise. Dancer Tamara Karsavina wrote
that news of the split upset her dreadfully: "I cannot bear to think of you
lonely <u>and</u> unhappy. . . . I can hardly believe Eva left you. . . . It seems so
cruel. . . . It haunts me."[77] Eva wrote to her mother that Mercedes made
her "feel a brute & a heartless inhuman wretch" and that "nothing in my
life has ever been more baffling to me . . . more difficult to grasp" than the
relationship with Mercedes.[78]

During the next few months, while Eva was working on matinee productions of Ibsen's *The Master Builder* and *John Gabriel Borkman,* Mercedes
spent long weekends with actress Jeanne Eagels at Eagels's place in Ossining-
on-the Hudson, trying to help the actress "control her sad habits" of drinking
and drugs.[79] They took long walks in the country and shared their frustrations over loneliness and lovers.

Mercedes had her own opinion about why she and Eva split. Looking
back at their breakup more than thirty years later, Mercedes reflected, "I
learned many lessons from it [the production of *Jehanne d'Arc*] and it served
a number of purposes. Not the least being, that a circumstance during its
run opened the way for Eva to have her Civic Repertory Theatre and made
this project financially possible for her."[80] Closer bonds with wealthy Alice
De Lamar and scene designer Gladys Calthrop showed more promise for
achieving Eva's goals than continuing her relationship with Mercedes. Her
letters to her mother were probably more of an attempt to justify her own
ambitious behavior than to reveal the real reason for their breakup.

The last letter Mercedes received from Eva was dated March 1, 1926.
Eva admitted she was at a loss for words. She regretted the breakup of their

relationship. She had not wanted to hurt Mercedes. It was not easy making the decision to part ways. And though she knew it had been hard on Mercedes, she needed to say that it had been brutal for her as well. Eva then ended the letter very warmly, wishing Mercedes well in the future and reassuring Mercedes that her affection and adoration would remain forever.[81]

A few years earlier, Mercedes had published a poem titled "Change." Perhaps it had predicted her current emotional state.

Some one for whom I had a great passion
Now sleeps in this room with some one else—
There are traces of me in many objects—
The books I gave and fingered are lying
    on the shelf,
And an old picture whose land I lived in and
whose hills I sped,
Is still hanging facing my old bed.
So times change—
But love goes on—
Like a bird that is dead
Yet whose song,
Lives on forever.[82]

Ricardo de Acosta, Mercedes's father. Courtesy Rosenbach Museum & Library, Philadelphia, Pa.

Micaela Hernandez de Alba y de Alba, Mercedes's mother. Courtesy Rosenbach Museum & Library, Philadelphia, Pa.

Ethel Barrymore. The inscription reads, "To Mercedes with love from Ethel Barrymore, 1909." Courtesy Rosenbach Museum & Library, Philadelphia, Pa.

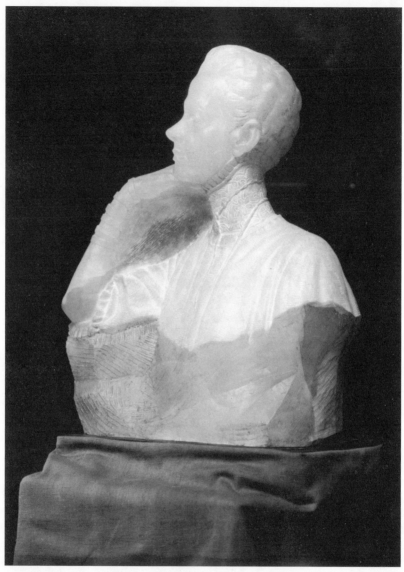

Bust of Rita Lydig, Mercedes's older sister, sculpted in alabaster by Malvina Hoffman and on exhibit at the Rosenbach Museum. Courtesy Rosenbach Museum & Library, Philadelphia, Pa.

Isadora Duncan. The inscription below the photo reads, "Mercedes, Lead me with your little strong hands and I will follow you to the top of a mountain, to the end of the world, whichever you wish. Isadora June 25, 1926." Courtesy Rosenbach Museum & Library, Philadelphia, Pa.

Alla Nazimova. The inscription reads, "To Mercedes, Alla." Courtesy Rosenbach Museum & Library, Philadelphia, Pa.

Mercedes *(left)* and Hope Williams, circa 1917. Courtesy Rosenbach Museum & Library, Philadelphia, Pa.

Michael Strange, circa 1921. The inscription reads, "For Mercedes—
    Forgive this impassioned nothing
        in this glance—
    This goes at any rate
        with much love to you.
                Michael Strange"

Abram Poole, Mercedes's husband. Courtesy Rosenbach Museum & Library, Philadelphia, Pa.

Portrait of Mercedes painted by Abram Poole, circa 1923. Author's collection.

Another portrait of Mercedes painted by Poole, circa 1923. Author's collection.

Eva Le Gallienne and Basil Sydney in Mercedes's play *Sandro Botticelli*, 1923. Courtesy Rosenbach Museum & Library, Philadelphia, Pa.

Eleonora Duse, circa 1923. Courtesy Rosenbach Museum & Library, Philadelphia, Pa.

Painting by Maurice Stern after a painting by Bastien Lapage, with Eva Le Gallienne portraying Jehanne d'Arc. The figure of Jehanne ascends in the background. The inscription indicates that Le Gallienne autographed it and presented it to Mercedes as a sign of her love. Courtesy Rosenbach Museum & Library, Philadelphia, Pa.

Mercedes photographed by Arnold Genthe in the 1920s. Courtesy Rosenbach Museum & Library, Philadelphia, Pa.

Tamara Karsavina in one of her roles. Courtesy Rosenbach Museum & Library, Philadelphia, Pa.

Greta Garbo photographed by Mercedes at Silver Lake, 1931. Courtesy Rosenbach
Museum & Library, Philadelphia, Pa.

Garbo photographed by Mercedes at Silver Lake, 1931. Courtesy Rosenbach Museum
& Library, Philadelphia, Pa.

Marlene Dietrich in Paris in 1933. Courtesy Rosenbach Museum & Library, Philadelphia, Pa.

Composite of photos of Marlene Dietrich that Mercedes had framed in black velvet. Courtesy Rosenbach Museum & Library, Philadelphia, Pa.

Ona Munson. The inscription reads, "To Mercedes, With Love, Ona Belle Watling." Ona had played the role of Belle Watling in the film *Gone with the Wind*. Courtesy Rosenbach Museum & Library, Philadelphia, Pa.

Cecil Beaton. The inscription in the bottom margin reads, "With love from Cecil, to Mercedes." Courtesy Rosenbach Museum & Library, Philadelphia, Pa.

A 1943 watercolor of Mercedes, artist unknown. Courtesy Rosenbach Museum & Library, Philadelphia, Pa.

Poppy Kirk. Author's collection.

Ram Gopal performing Śiva in a *Kathakali* dance at London's Royal Festival Hall, 1956.
Courtesy Rosenbach Museum & Library, Philadelphia, Pa.

Ram Gopal with the author, November 4, 2001, in Norbury, England. Between them is a photograph of Mercedes she gave to Gopal. The inscription reads, "For Ram . . . whose true self will always shine. Alba, 1959." Author's collection.

Mercedes's Bible, with photos of Greta Garbo and verses from the book of Matthew. Courtesy Rosenbach Museum & Library, Philadelphia, Pa.

6

"Bound to Blunder"

I n June 1926 Mercedes was back in Europe, undoubtedly looking for some kind of diversion from her misery. On the night she arrived in Paris, she ran into a man who said, "I know you are a friend of Isadora Duncan's. I hear she has behaved so badly that everyone has abandoned her. I am told that she is in a hotel on the Left Bank, practically starving." Almost immediately, Mercedes hailed a taxi and sped off to find her. To Mercedes's delight, Duncan greeted her at the door with "Archangel! . . . I think you are an archangel. How did you find me?"[1]

In no time at all, an intimate romance resumed between them. Duncan penned a poem to Mercedes that overflowed with sexual images:

Beneath a forehead
Broad and Bright
Shine eyes
Clear wells
of sight—
A slender body, hands, soft and white
To be the service of my delight . . .
Two sprouting breasts
Grand and sweet
Invite my hungry
Mouth to eat—
From whence two nipples firm and pink

persuade my thirsty soul to drink
And lower still a secret place
Where I'd fain hide my loving face.
Arch Angel from another sphere
God-send to light my pathway
Here.
I kneel in Adoration.
Dear,
My kisses like a swarm
of bees
Would find their way
Between thy knees—
And suck the honey of thy lips
Embracing thy too slender hips.[2]

Another message from Duncan to Mercedes is addressed to "Adorée":

I have played with your flames and been horribly burned. I thought
I knew already every mortal suffering, but now I see the worst was
still in store for me—I suffer <u>fearfully</u>—but I accept it because the
source is so <u>beautiful</u>. . . . But how to live with this passion in my veins
. . . I beg you not to make fun of me. I may die from it. I'm horrified
to realize that only now have I known love for <u>the first time</u>. Don't
laugh . . . a little word . . . if there is any pity in your heart for me.
Respect my secret—I am tortured and ready to cry Mercy. Isadora.[3]

Perhaps Duncan was remembering their liaison when she later wrote, "I
believe the highest love is purely spiritual flame which is not necessarily
dependent on sex."[4] An ironic statement, indeed, given the sensual poem
she had written to Mercedes.

The late summer months must have been particularly troubling for
Mercedes, who had returned to New York. Eva had been touring around
the country in Ibsen's *The Master Builder* and picking up kudos at every stop,
not only for her performance but also for her plans to establish her repertory theater in New York. By the end of the summer, headlines announced
she had won pledges of support amounting to sixty-eight thousand dollars
from eight thousand subscribers, including influential philanthropist Otto
Kahn and, predictably, Alice De Lamar.

Perhaps those announcements are what distracted Mercedes on September 20, 1926. She was charged with assault and with violation of a motor
vehicle code. The car she was driving knocked down a policeman who was

directing traffic at Fifty-seventh Street and Sixth Avenue, and she was chased by the policeman in a taxicab to Madison Avenue, where she was finally apprehended and arrested. She claimed she was unaware that she had struck him. "She was booked at the station under her maiden name, but explained that she was married." She had no driver's license but said she had just taken her test and the license had not yet been sent to her. She was released on five hundred dollars bail. When she was accompanied in court a few days later by Abram and her lawyer, she was fined only fifteen dollars. As she awaited the calling of her case in West Side Court, she displayed "a growing impatience." "I ought to get some local color out of this," she quipped, glancing at a stream of prisoners. A month later, she was cleared of "culpable negligence," and the court said the arrest should never have been made. The evidence showed she had been negligent in her driving but that the degree of the evidence did not show culpable negligence.[5] Of course, we will never know for sure why she was driving so recklessly. But it is certainly possible that she was depressed and emotionally distraught. Eva was making daily headlines, and Mercedes, who longed to be part of the theater, had been abandoned. Eva's theater gave its premiere performance on October 25, 1926, just five days before Mercedes was exonerated.

Mercedes threw herself into her work. First, she tried to find a producer for a revision of a play she had completed ten years earlier, *They That Walk Enchained*.[6] Although she had never found a producer for the original play, she still felt its basic idea was sound. After many conversations with Eugene O'Neill, however, she rewrote several scenes that added more shocking drama. She believed the revision, now called *World Without End,* was a vast improvement.

In the original, Romola Charrington had been accused unjustly of promiscuity. Now, however, she confesses that when she had learned of her husband's infidelities, she retaliated and nurtured an affair with one of their mutual friends who wrote her love letters and even stayed overnight in their home. During the divorce proceedings, their butler testified against Romola.

Another revision was Mercedes's creation of a more vivid sensual relationship between Romola and her son, David. Act 3 begins with an extremely intimate scene between them. He sits at his mother's feet. As she strokes his hair, he takes her fingers and kisses them. He throws his arms around her. Six lines later, he kisses her shoulder, her arm, and her hand as he exclaims, "I must keep kissing you." Later, when David unexpectedly returns, he sees more than a pair of men's gloves on her desk. His father, Romola's ex-husband, is in the room. When his mother confesses that she has always loved his father, David cries out, "Is it true that you care for him in spite of the many times you told me that I was your whole life?" Jealous and confused, he bolts through the door and commits suicide. Romola's dream for happiness has ended, "but life will go on the same, world without end."

Mercedes's alterations—the divorce proceedings, the letters, the incestuous suggestion, the motivation for David's suicide—raise many questions. When her sister Rita divorced Stokes in 1900, their servants had testified about his infidelities. Was Mercedes using elements from that divorce that nobody had known about? Had Rita paid servants to testify? Had Rita written letters to her son that were never answered? What prompted Mercedes to depict such an unusually intimate, physical relationship between mother and son? Was there any similarity between David's suicide and that of Mercedes's brother, Hennie, in 1911? Because Mercedes had tapped into so many of her family's circumstances for the plot, it must have been all the more discouraging when she failed to interest any producers.

She then tried to interest backers in another script she had completed a year earlier, *The Better Life*.[7] With overtones of the nineteenth-century classic *Camille, Anna Christie,* and a dash of Shaw's *Pygmalion,* Mercedes fashioned a play about a prostitute with a heart of gold. The setting for act 1 is a rough, sordid cabaret frequented mostly by seamen. Mark Ashley, a wealthy idealist, has come to the bar with a distinguished lady friend he wants to introduce to Maggie, a woman he hopes to marry. Even though she is a local prostitute, Mercedes describes her as "arresting . . . something wistful and tremendously appealing about her. She is frail and seems delicate." The role undoubtedly was intended for Eva Le Gallienne, who had played the same kind of fragile character in *Liliom*. When Mark finally proposes marriage, Maggie agrees, confessing, "with people like you, people higher up, it may be easier to find . . . maybe a better life—maybe God."

Reality soon sets in. Maggie and Mark have married, and during an extravagant party at his parent's estate on Long Island, Maggie learns that Mark's sister is having an affair with one of Maggie's former customers at the cabaret. The sister is engaged to be married to another man, but she "is only marrying that stupid boy for money." Maggie decides to return to her former life "away from this pretense and falseness . . . where thieves are thieves, where prostitutes are prostitutes." The final scene takes place in Maggie's small, dingy boarding room. She is dying of consumption. Mark, who had rejected her three months earlier, now has decided to join her. She dies in his arms.

In some ways, the play was an advance for Mercedes. Never before had she written seedy, rough, low-life characters. She continued exploring her themes of marriage, unfulfilled love, family, and the submissive role of women in society. However, she now added two more motifs that are prevalent in American literature—the need to belong and the strong element of class conflict. Maggie concludes she does not belong to any class, and Mark discovers too late that he has been trying to belong to the wrong class.

Although the settings described in the script appear realistic and accurately described, the dialogue sometimes sounds forced, untrue. Mercedes had never lived nor associated in these low-life hovels, so she had little opportunity to feel the language and the rhythm of their speech. Yet even though Eugene O'Neill had lived among sailors and had visited brothels and seafront bars before writing *Anna Christie,* critics leveled the same charges against his dialogue. Perhaps the most preposterous element is Mark Ashley's escorting his upper-class lady friend to this bar and house of prostitution. She would probably never have set foot in the establishment, and Mark would probably never have asked her. Maybe Mercedes was trying to write an emotional, last-act death scene for her lover, the kind of scene all actresses love to play, and perhaps the right actress could play it convincingly, but in the writing it appears overly melodramatic. No producer was interested.

A couple of years later, Mercedes prepared some slight changes in the script, now calling it *Illusion.*[8] For instance, Mark Ashley, now called Hunt Ashley, addresses up front the absurdity of having his fashionable lady friend accompany him to this seedy bar. "What other woman," he acknowledges, "would have chucked all her plans the way you did, and leap on a train going in an entirely different direction and then be met by a wild man like myself, and before you hardly have a chance to clean up, be brought down to a dump like this? And you haven't even murmured a word of protest!" By having Hunt acknowledge the implausibility, Mercedes added to the scene's credibility. She transposed other scenes, added a lengthy encounter between Maggie and one of her clients, and altered some of the dialogue. Still, no producer offered a contract.

Mercedes was more hopeful about a brand new script she was working on, *The Dark Light.*[9] Set in a remote spot on the west coast of Norway, near Stavern, the play revolves around the sibling rivalry of a set of twins, Svanhild and Ivar, who are both poets. Mercedes describes Svanhild as "curiously startling looking. . . . [She] gives an impression of great physical strength. She seems very boyish. . . . There is something untamed and wild about her." Her brother Ivar, on the other hand, appears to be much like Mercedes's own brother, Hennie, the one who had committed suicide. Ivar "is slender and very delicate looking. His features are beautiful and poetic but almost too sensitive. . . . There is also something very sad about him—an elusive melancholy note. . . . His hands are white, slender, and nervous."

Ivar's fiancée, Turid, is reminiscent of Ibsen's Thea in *Hedda Gabler*. Small, beautiful, and timid, she defied her father, ran away with Ivar, and has inspired Ivar's recent poetry, which she keeps in her handbag. Overwhelmed by Svanhild's generosity, Turid gives her the poems to study and critique. When Svanhild later confesses her dislike for the poems and advises Turid to destroy them before they are published and damage Ivar's reputation, Turid takes the envelope of poems and flings them into the fireplace. Ivar shrieks with rage and hatred when he learns that his work has been destroyed. "Those poems were my soul. The depths of me. Get out of my life!" he screams at Turid.

After Svanhild and Ivar are left alone, she presents him with his poems. Not knowing it, Turid had burned an envelope of blank paper. The poems "are beautiful—so beautiful," Svanhild admits. The stage directions then read that "Svanhild drops her arms to her side and lowers her head. For a full second they look at each other. When Ivar speaks again, his voice is hardly audible" as he says, "love you." Ecstatic, Svanhild replies, "And I love you—love you—have always loved you." They then kiss on the lips "deeply, violently, passionately—clinging to one another."

Ashamed that he loves his own sister and that his love poems were meant for her and not really for Turid, Ivar wishes he had the courage to kill himself. But instead, finally triumphant in achieving the love of her brother, Svanhild rushes out of the room, throws herself from the top of a neighboring lighthouse, and is killed instantly.

The sensational plot involved sibling tensions, unrequited love, incest, closeted desire, and suicide, but it also revealed Mercedes's impressions about art and the writing of poetry. She was convinced that the play would sell. Because scene designer Gertrude Newell and John Barrymore were interested in producing it, she held several readings to entice backers and even auditioned some actors. Once again, nothing came of her efforts.

She also completed the writing of a novel, "The Arrow of Longing."[10] The story opens in a small mountain town in Wyoming in 1917. Michael is born out of wedlock to a working-class woman who has high aspirations for her son. Early on, she tells him, "You must do with life what he [Michelangelo, who is Michael's namesake] did with stone. Break and mould it into a great form—a form of your own. Use life itself as your stone—work on it, and from and out of it, make something beautiful. . . . Make chances for yourself."

The owner of the factory where Michael's mother works is Benjamin Free. Because Michael learns to play the violin and shows great promise, his teacher takes him to the Benjamin Free home in hopes that Free will pay for violin lessons. Eventually, Michael falls in love with Benjamin Free's daughter who is named America. When Michael's mother dies, America arrives at the cemetery as the funeral ends and finds Michael alone in a rainstorm. She comforts him, takes him home, undresses him. "She crawled in beside him and with the nearness of him he was suddenly her lover. . . . He was the wounded weak one; needing her strength and sympathy to be poured into him. It was she now who gathered him in her arms. Arms that grew strong with the power of love." We then flash forward four years. Michael has arrived in New York City and tries to see America, who lives there, but she is in Europe. Mercedes, in describing Michael's despair and loneliness, revealed the depth of her own desolation.

> Most people who cling to friends or family or someone they love, rarely reach that poignant moment of utter aloneness, when like a blade of fire it burns into one's heart with the realization that there is not another creature in one's life that one can count, or lean upon. Such aloneness is more than being lonely. Loneliness in a way, is a certain state of expectation; one is lonely because one feels out of things and wishes to be in them—one is lonely because one needs and wants companionship. Unconsciously one is expectant, and ready to welcome anything or anyone that will diminish or destroy that loneliness. Contrary to loneliness, aloneness has no expectation. It is a state of exaltation, in which having no one but oneself and some divine inner power to count upon, one is suddenly utterly fearless of life, having nothing to gain or lose from any other human being. . . . There is no doubt it [exaltation] has been the state of the spirit of many great poets; perhaps it is truly necessary for any great creative expression.

Alone in New York, Michael meets Cira and has a one-night stand with her. She normally has sex with women only, not men. "You see, to the world at large I am one of those abhorred people—a lover of women," she explains.

By the time he is twenty-eight years old, Michael is among the first ranks of composers and is known internationally. He meets Monica while in Venice and marries her. They move to Paris where, he eventually discovers, America is living and has become a successful sculptress. He feels trapped in his marriage to Monica, even though he had always warned her that he longed for America and would leave her if he ever saw America again. When Michael asks America to marry him and tells her that he is already married to Monica, she refuses. It is not his marriage that upsets her but that he had not waited for her and that he did not believe they would meet up again: "It has made me see that the unreality of you was the thing that was important in my life—not the reality. . . . I think now the you I believed in was someone I fashioned in my own brain."

Monica, in the meantime, thinks she is losing Michael and goes to plead with America to leave Michael alone. The two women fall in love. The story ends with Monica committing suicide so as to free both Michael and America. America explains that "it was Monica's child-like idea of nobleness. . . . Death is better than life."

The sensational themes of hopeless love, loneliness, rejection, lesbianism, and suicide were perhaps too daring in 1926. Although the same themes may have helped to thrust Radclyffe Hall's *The Well of Loneliness* into an international spotlight two years later, right then they did not help sell the manuscript to publishers.

Mercedes was encouraged when actress friend Jeanne Eagels expressed interest in starring in a production of *The Mother of Christ*. But when the actress presented the script to producer Sam Harris, he thought Eagels "was too identified with the character of Sadie Thompson in *Rain* for the public to accept her as the Virgin Mary." Eagels was so interested, however, that she talked to Monty Bell at Paramount Pictures and persuaded him to make Mercedes an offer. She did not accept it. She wanted the play produced in the theater before shown on the silver screen.[11] This decision was probably a major blunder, for it could have paved the way for her introduction to Hollywood. In the 1920s, however, New York theater folk still snubbed their noses at this new form of entertainment.

Mercedes decided to return to a play she had been working on for several years, *Jacob Slovak*. Since 1923, when she had completed the script, Mercedes had been exploring possible productions. She had approached Norman Bel Geddes about designing it, but he refused. He explained in a letter to Le Gallienne:

> It was so nice of you to write me that long-ago letter about my terrible ideas for "Jacob Slovak." I think that either you are wrong, or else did not comprehend my point of view toward the play. The play certainly is not of a local character and yet it is not broad enough to treat in a direct stylized manner. It is, in my estimation (which, being the case, is undoubtedly wrong) that the play is too much half-way and that Mercedes should draw it one way or another.
>
>   Why do you write me a letter and underscore "You must not compromise"? Why should you misconstrue anything that I have said as a desire on my part to compromise? Some of my judgements may be wrong but the theatre is too vital to me, and my life will be too

short to waste time compromising. . . . I do not think "Jacob Slovak" is a strong enough play for me to do as a first production and I tell you this in the face of the fact that Mercedes has someone who will finance it. Is this compromise? Force et confiance! Norman Bel Geddes[12]

Mercedes took his advice and revised her script, opening it first at the Brooklyn Theatre in March 1927 with the title *Closed Doors* and starring Florence Eldridge and Jose Ruben. Under the direction of Edward Goodman and produced by Joseph P. Bickerton Jr., it was such a success that they transferred it to the Greenwich Village Theatre six months later.[13] Though Eldridge and Ruben reprised their roles, James Light now directed and Cleon Throckmorton designed. When it opened as *Jacob Slovak* on October 5, 1927, Mercedes thought she had finally proven herself as a successful playwright. "Perfectly cast, perfectly acted and perfectly directed," wrote one critic. The *New York Times* called it "an honest and interesting play . . . with fine emotional and touching scenes," and a critic for the *New York World* praised Mercedes's originality and conviction and described the play as an "interesting study of prejudice and desire under the eternal elms." *Billboard* thought it was "strong meat. . . . an excellently written play presented with real skill and understanding."[14] Just ten days after the off-Broadway tryout, the Shubert brothers moved *Jacob Slovak* to a Broadway house.

Her revisions certainly improved the script.[15] One major change is the relationship between Jacob and Myra, the shopkeeper's daughter whom Jacob wants to marry. In the original, Jacob's treatment of her when she came to his lodging bordered on sexual harassment and maybe even acquaintance rape. She had not been a willing partner. But now, fearful of his desire for her, he blurts out, "Go home, Myra, I can't stand having you here any longer—you're driving me mad—go home." But instead, she stays and does not refuse nor push him away as in the earlier version. Whereas in the original version Myra had pushed him away from her and threatened to spit on him, now she reveals her desire for him and how she is struggling with her decision to reject his proposal of marriage or renounce her family and town.

The final act takes place three months later. Jacob, who now has a respectable position playing in a symphony orchestra, has returned for Myra. But when she insists that though she is pregnant with his child she still cannot run away with him, Jacob replies, "And are you going to bring my child up the way you've been brought up? Taught lies and hypocrisy." Though tempted, Jacob cannot reveal to the town that the baby she is carrying is his. Before he leaves, he warns Myra, "I'll come back over and over again in your child. . . . Another man may bring up that child, but it will be my child and my race."

Myra hesitates as he exits, "as though she were agonizing within herself whether to call after Jacob or not. Then slowly she sinks on the chair and buries her head in her hands." Certainly, this is a more poignant ending than the original in which Jacob killed Myra and then himself.

Although the production drew additional critical praise when it moved uptown, it closed after only a handful of performances. The public was confused when Lee Shubert, without ever consulting Mercedes, changed the title to *Conflict* and then refused to advertise the change. When the Shuberts were sued by another author who claimed the new title was his, the production was withdrawn. Mercedes was overwhelmed, since all signs suggested that the play was going to settle into a successful run that would have meant boosting her credibility as a playwright. Ironically, the Shubert Archive has no record of the play, of the production, or of any correspondence with Mercedes. No photographs exist.

A few weeks after *Jacob Slovak* closed, Mercedes returned to Paris where she began assisting Isadora Duncan in completing her memoirs. Many days, Mercedes locked Isadora "in her room and only let her out when she slid a number of finished pages under the door."[16] But when the autobiography finally appeared after Duncan's tragic death, Mercedes was accused of writing parts of the book herself. In a letter to the internationally renowned scene designer Edward Gordon Craig, she argued that Isadora was the sole author.

> You are quite wrong about it [the book] because she <u>did</u> write it and every word of it. I was with her myself when she wrote many chapters before my eyes—and many after that I have in her handwriting—and she read me month to month what she had written until it was finished—over a year before she died. I placed the book myself with Bobi & Liverwright [*sic*] by giving them the first eleven chapters and they sent Isadora twenty-five hundred dollars advance which was a great God-send for her at that moment.[17]

Craig could not believe that Duncan, his former lover, could have written such a personal account that identified many people by name. It was "utterly cruel in its thoughtlessness of others," he charged. "We shall have a lot of trouble trying to make sensible people like this book by Isadora because she lets [the] fool talk over much." He claimed that several London publishers had described the book as "decidedly libelous." To him it was vulgar.[18]

Mercedes fought back: "I disagree with you as to it being vulgar—I do not think there is a single vulgar thing in it, but only <u>great</u> beauty, honesty and much sadness." Perhaps hoping to calm her adversary, Mercedes sent him copies of her plays *Jacob Slovak* and *The Mother of Christ*. She told him that she had originally written *The Mother of Christ* for Duse and that a production of *Jacob Slovak* was scheduled for London.

She could not refrain from boasting to Craig that the internationally famous actor Alexander Moissi had expressed interest in performing *Slovak* in Germany and that Max Reinhardt was considering a production of *The Mother of Christ* in Salzburg.[19] To have had either of them endorse her writing was a major coup. Moissi had starred as Everyman in Reinhardt's first Salzburg Festival and was known for his complex, psychological interpretations. Only a few years earlier, in 1924, Reinhardt had overwhelmed Broadway theatergoers with his production of *The Miracle*. When the Reinhardt company toured the United States during the 1927–1928 season, audiences were captivated with Moissi's portrayals of Oberon in *A Midsummer Night's Dream*, a tramp in Tolstoy's *He's to Blame for Everything*, a servant in Schiller's *Love and Intrigue*, and Fedja in Tolstoy's *The Living Corpse*, so she was delighted that these two geniuses were interested in her scripts. Unfortunately, nothing materialized.

Mercedes obviously never saw what Craig scribbled in the margins of her letters to him: "The whole thing [Duncan's autobiography] was a low trick & this woman blabs—not knowing one can easily see where she lies." "You cannot write a play for Duse to play . . . you are bound to blunder."

Although the contribution Mercedes made in actually writing Duncan's autobiography will forever be in doubt, there is no question of her importance in getting it published. Mercedes took the manuscript personally to Boni and Liveright, where her friend T. R. Smith was editor-in-chief. He subsequently offered Duncan a contract. When the book was finally published in late 1927, the *New York Herald-Tribune* hailed it as "a great document, revealing the truth of her life as she understood it, without reticence or apology or compromise." And when it was reissued in paperback in 1995, the publishers advertised it as "the uninhibited autobiography of the woman who founded modern dance."[20] Clearly, Mercedes was instrumental both in the tone of the book and in its becoming a standard holding by most libraries.

After returning to New York in August 1927, Mercedes accepted an invitation to join Bessie Marbury at her lakeside cottage in Kennebec County, Maine. It was an ideal, rustic retreat with walls paneled in natural bark and most of the furniture constructed from tree branches and animal hides. Just the right, tranquil spot for Mercedes after the disappointments of *Jehanne de Arc* and her breakup with Eva. By this time in her life, Bessie's weight and ailments pretty much dictated that she remain at home and invite guests for company. Joining Mercedes were playwright John Van Druten, the

Eugene O'Neills, and Carlotta Monterey. There must have been exciting conversations with Van Druten, who later became famous for such Broadway hits as *I Remember Mama; I Am a Camera;* and *Bell, Book, and Candle;* and with O'Neill, who had just wowed the Broadway critics with *Desire under the Elms,* a sensational story of greed, incest, and infanticide. One can only guess what lessons Mercedes learned about playwriting from these accomplished peers.

Mercedes recalled that it was a strange house party. She noticed early on that Carlotta was the kind of woman who would make most men shy, and Gene was no exception. He behaved like a nervous schoolboy whenever she looked at him. One afternoon Carlotta and Gene went out swimming and boating together. Two years later, they were married.

Mercedes's hopes for *Jacob Slovak* were renewed when a London production was announced for the Arts Theatre Club. John Gielgud and Ralph Richardson would star in their first production together.[21] Mercedes was excited that Gielgud would be starring, for she had recently been thrilled by his performance in Alfred Neumann's *The Patriot* on Broadway. He had returned to London to play Oswald in Ibsen's *Ghosts* with Mrs. Patrick Campbell but also had agreed to star in Mercedes's play.

Using the new title of *Prejudice,* Arthur K. Phillips directed, and Gladys E. Calthrop, the woman who had come between Mercedes and Eva after *Jehanne d'Arc,* designed the production. The critics were certainly enthusiastic when the play opened on June 17, 1928. The *Daily Sketch* called it "a remarkable and powerful religious play," and the *Evening Standard* stressed that Mercedes had "a sense of character and of writing for the stage, and she avoids mincing matters, sometimes to the verge of brutal frankness." Other critics said it was "a moving play . . . finely acted" and that it went "far to restore one's faith in the London theatre."[22]

There were questions, however, about the play's relevance. Mercedes's script was compared with another American drama about prejudice that was running in London, *Show Boat,* starring Paul Robeson. Reviewers questioned why she had portrayed Americans "as hostile to the Jew as to the negro." They recognized that racial prejudice was present in America and England, but they denied the existence of anti-Semitism: "Jew-baiting in this country belongs . . . to the past."[23] In 1928, just a few years before the Holocaust, English audiences would not acknowledge that persecution of Jews existed. John Gielgud gave one of the best performances of his early career though he remembered little about the production or audience reaction years later, only that Mercedes was "always very strikingly dressed in tricorn hats and becoming cloaks."[24]

While she was in London, Mercedes renewed her intimate friendship with the acclaimed Russian ballet dancer Tamara Karsavina. She had always been attracted to dancers and the way they expressed art through their bodies. When Mercedes had seen Karsavina dance in Paris in *Le Spectre de la Rose* and *Petrouchka* a few years earlier, she had been "haunted by her beauty."

> In these two ballets I was deeply moved by a curious, touching quality which she projected when she danced. When later I came to know her well I could see that this quality was part of her—the very fabric of her deeply mystic and Russian soul.... Great facial beauty, extreme grace, perfect technique and supreme artistry.... No ballet dancer today can remotely approach her mastery of body control, her arm movements, her elevations and the spiritual as well as physical beauty she projected across the footlights.[25]

They had met in the early 1920s while Karsavina was on a ballet tour of the United States, and they had become immediate friends. When Mercedes went to Paris after her breakup with Eva Le Gallienne, Karsavina sent her a telegram: "My fond thoughts bless you please think of me as your devoted loving, thamar." Even though Karsavina was married, the two women were constant companions while Mercedes was in London for *Jacob Slovak*. After Mercedes's departure, Karsavina sent another telegram: "Mercedes Darling, I was glad to hear from you. I miss you here and feel I got even more attached to you than before."[26]

Soon after *Prejudice* opened in London, Mercedes sailed for Paris with Gladys Calthrop, joining torch singer Libby Holman and actor Clifton Webb as they toured Bavaria. Mercedes became so enthralled by Libby that she fluctuated for several weeks between affairs with both Libby and Gladys. Her infatuation with Libby did not last long, however, probably because Libby, though very talented, was "drug-drenched and highly promiscuous."[27] When Eva Le Gallienne learned that Gladys had gone off to Italy with Mercedes, she wrote to her mother in London, "surely [Gladys] couldn't be such a fool." About a month later, she wrote to her mother again: "I simply feel that it is a question of time before she [Gladys] sees the light.... I haven't written to M. for 2 years—& to G. I scarcely ever write.... I wish they would all go & live in East India—in some far jungle!"[28]

When Mercedes returned to New York, she resumed her writing. At first, she completed a series of essays.[29] "On Great Men Recognizing Greatness" describes poets Byron and Shelley as "singers and passionate slaves of beauty. They had the good fortune to find in each other, not only a mental beauty, but also a rare physical beauty."

An explicit affirmation of same-sex desire appears in an essay simply called "Walt Whitman": "He proclaims sex in all things; the man to the woman, the man to the man, the woman to the woman.... He proclaims sex not disgustingly or lewdly, but frankly, openly, truthfully. He proclaims all parts of the human body beautiful, to him the body is in the soul and the soul in the body." Because the essays contained such radical thinking for the time, especially from a female author, she was never able to find a publisher.

She did find a publisher, however, for her novel *Until the Day Break*.[30] Using the same technique she had used in several plays, Mercedes begins with two men chatting and establishing the central focus of the book, a debate about the role of women. Mark Strong claims that "the entirely feminine woman is never intellectually companionable.... She does not wear well either—one wearies of her caprices." His older friend disagrees, "In my day we wanted women women, men men—and we succeeded in getting them" (2–3). Several years later, Mark is talking with a young woman, Victoria, who is wrestling with whether to marry. She does not fully understand why she does not want to marry. "It's something in me, something struggling for expression that I don't understand," she explains (24). "No woman need marry today for want of something better to do," he insists (25). Victoria questions his advice. "Women of my class, or all classes for that matter, ... have been taught no profession.... They are not content to be domestic, being conscious that there are bigger and more interesting fields in life—at the same time they are not equipped or trained for a greater scope of any kind ... they only know they do not *want* to do what they are doing" (27). Although she marries Gordon Frost, Victoria longs for a career. "I *must* have something in my life" (38), she pleads and announces that she wishes to become an actress like her mother before her. She realizes she has a wild, revolutionary side to her temperament "that despises convention, that loathes discipline, and struggles only for freedom" (54).

Like Mercedes, Victoria eventually rejects a life of domesticity, moves away from her husband, sails to Paris, and embarks on a career in the theater. After a frustrating rehearsal, she admits to a friend that she feels ostracized by the rest of the company. "Where do I belong? ... I don't seem to fit anywhere," she cries (145). Sitting late one night along the Seine she meets Orlanda, a woman who confesses her desire for other women:

> I have had more emotion through women; they give me that sense of beauty.... As for worrying about the sex end of it, that seems to me unimportant. In America I suffered much. They are not old enough to comprehend these things. It is perhaps their youth, which does not

recognize that real love is real love, no matter whom it is for.... It is curious, the world does not blame people for having black or blond hair. They are just born that way and it is accepted. But for something deeper; something *more* 'you' than colour of hair or eyes, one is condemned. They do not realize that God made each one for some ultimate reason; with his own salvation to work out, a pattern to follow and unfold, as his own spirit sees it. (170–86)

Orlanda, though in love with Victoria, realizes that she is intent on an acting career and suggests that she move to Chartres and study under the great actor Raphael. The student and teacher eventually fall in love, but because he will not break his vow of celibacy, they struggle with hiding their feelings. After she finally makes her debut in Madrid and becomes an overnight sensation, she agrees to an engagement on Broadway. When she learns, however, that her mentor and the man she loved has committed suicide, Victoria decides to renounce the stage and spend the rest of her life with Orlanda. "She is lonely and I know now we need each other," she says. "I think I even need her more than she needs me. We will make our life together" (310).

Bessie Marbury remarked that "this love story is so imbued with the ideal that it raises sex into that realm so often described as the odor of perfume."[31] At least two reviewers agreed with Bessie. A *New York Times* critic appreciated Mercedes's portrayal of a "very, very different young lady who rebels at the monotony, the pallid routine of her conventional life." And Anne Kulique Kramer, writing for the *American Hebrew,* thought the story was "convincingly told with power and beauty. It is a book that only an extremely sensitive woman artist could have written." Others were not so positive. A reviewer for the *Tatler* complained that the book was "one of the most glorious excursions into the improbable that I have ever read." Describing Mercedes's writing as "peculiar," Neil Lyons in his column for *Bookman,* likened it to the "irksome iteration of a hen who has laid an egg."[32]

The year Mercedes published *Until the Day Break*—1928—saw another novel that portrayed same-sex desire but became much more controversial. In *The Well of Loneliness,* when author Radclyffe Hall depicted lesbians as "more or less healthy people leading more or less normal lives," she brought "female homosexuality out of the closet."[33] Because the public had considered lesbians as perverts and degenerates, they were outraged at this new, sympathetic portrayal and condemned and censored the book.

Just two years earlier, Broadway had been introduced to lesbianism in *The Captive.* Though hailed as a masterpiece when it was produced in Europe, New York reaction was quite the opposite and echoed the country's homophobia. Brooks Atkinson of the *New York Times* despised the "revolting theme," the "loathsome possibility" of a "twisted relationship with another woman." Other reviewers were equally damning:"a cancerous growth,""gangrenous horrors of sexual perversion," "a decadent woman." George Jean Nathan fumed that the play was corrupt and evil and "a documentary in favor of sexual degeneracy."[34] When the production was finally closed by a police raid after four months, stars Helen Menken and Basil Rathbone were arrested. Not surprisingly, Mercedes "saw the play over and over."[35]

Mercedes's mentor and old friend Bessie Marbury was the play's agent and led a group of civil libertarians in its defense. Fearing state censorship, she advocated having all plays submitted for licensing to one person who would have the authority to prohibit productions or demand rewrites. In the end, the state legislature passed a bill in relation to plays "depicting or dealing with the subject of sex degeneracy or sex perversion." The appearance of homosexual characters or discussion of homosexuality was forbidden. The affront to people such as Bessie and Mercedes who were keenly involved in the performing arts was damning. *The Captive* was hailed as a masterpiece in Paris, Vienna, and Berlin and was being produced all over the world, but it could not even be allowed a showing in New York.

On December 13, 1928, Mercedes attended a Christmas party that consisted of "several Lesbians and arty young men."[36] Among them was Cecil Beaton. Born in London in 1904, Beaton had dabbled with photography while he was still a student at Cambridge University and by 1928 had established a successful business. He traveled to New York in 1929 and the following year was hired as a photographer by *Vogue* magazine. Beaton and Mercedes left the party together, and two days later he accompanied her to an exhibition of sculptures by her friend Malvina Hoffman. By the end of the day, Beaton had concluded, "Mercedes was charming, talking jerkily in a hollow voice. She is very mannish but charming, kind, clever & interesting & I know she will be one of my greatest friends in New York."[37] The very next day, Beaton invited her to his apartment to see some of his photographs that he was preparing for a book.

> It was a lovely evening & Mercedes delighted me by being so wildly enthusiastic. . . . Her criticisms were very apt. . . . She doesn't mind contradicting me flat. She never curries favor. . . . She talked superhumanly, enthusiastically about her work & a play which may be coming on soon which she thinks is a very wonderful play & with which she had had bad luck because it was written for Duse. . . . But

now it appears she has found the right person & the play, the first to deal with the Mother of Christ after the Crucifixion, will either be a terrible failure or a triumphant success. This funny, thin, hawklike little woman stayed talking in quick starts & jerks until very late.[38]

Unfortunately, there is no record of whom Mercedes was planning to play the role of Mary. *The Mother of Christ* never made it to the stage.

The last stage play Mercedes ever wrote, *Himself,* was a departure from her previous scripts, perhaps in response to the moral mandates being foisted on playwrights.[39] A fantastic farce adapted from a French play by Alfred Savoir called *Lui,* it is the story of Hans Elhing, a man who has been sentenced to an insane asylum for thinking he is God. He escapes from the institution and winds up attending a meeting of the International Congress of Free Thought being held at a hotel high in the Swiss Alps. After much animated debate, the membership has just voted to suppress God: "unanimous—minus one vote." During an unusually heavy rainstorm and avalanche, Hans announces that because he is God, he voted against the motion, and then he informs the hotel management and guests that he has the power to change the weather, but he prefers to remain neutral.

A character simply called Princess, who has left her husband and children, runs in and out of scenes, searching longingly for her lover. She contemplates suicide and says, "Why not? It's terrible suffering to love without it returned. One loses all control, all patience. . . . Love is a thing which seems to elude everyone," she cries. "People love in spite of themselves. Real love must forget oneself. It means loving the beloved's hair, the warmth of his body, even the water in his bath and the nails on his toes. Love, it is not creating, it's quite the contrary, it's sinking, disappearing in someone else; it's to die smothered." Given Mercedes's problems with relationships, the image of the Princess resonated with her own.

Everyone in the play wants better weather—the hotel management so the clients can ski and use their bobsleds and the clients so they can take the funicular down the mountain. Even though they do not believe in God, they all turn to Hans as "a political necessity," hoping that he will solve their problems. He answers, "It's curious and humiliating. . . . I am bored always being called in the last moment." In the end, just as Hans is about to be whisked back to the insane asylum, he tells the Princess, "Think. If what I claim is true, if I am God, where else would I be, but in a lunatic asylum. The fact that they have locked me up is already a point in my favor."

Once again, Mercedes's attempts for a Broadway production failed. She had not managed to land clear rights to the play from the French original, and the Theatre Guild produced it in another translation. She surely wondered whether she would ever again see one of her plays staged. She had to have questioned her talent as a playwright.

Certainly adding to Mercedes's misery and gloom during these years were the reversals suffered by her sister Rita. They often made front-page headlines. On August 5, 1921, just two years after her divorce from Philip Lydig, Rita announced her engagement to the Reverend Percy Grant, rector of the Episcopal Church of the Ascension at Fifth Avenue and Tenth Street. Annoyed with his church's official opposition to his engagement, Rev. Grant charged from the pulpit that "the Episcopal Church was not a live church" and argued that women should be permitted to become vestrymen and even ministers. He also complained that the church had "busied itself this summer wrangling about a medieval attitude toward divorce."[40]

A year later, headlines on page one of the New York Times read, "Dr. Grant Assails Episcopal Church Canon on Divorce." In his Sunday sermon, he protested the obstacles being placed in the way of his marriage to Rita and charged that the church was attempting to usurp the power of the state. "You cannot make the Bible a handbook for modern lawmakers," he argued. "Puritan New England attempted to do that. . . . The liberal needs of an age break through and discard the ideas of the past."[41] Regardless of his claims, the church's House of Deputies, meeting in Portland, Oregon, three weeks later, concurred that the only reason to accept divorce would be for infidelity, and anyone who disobeyed church policy "cuts him or herself off from receiving Holy Communion." One of the deputies at the meeting was quoted as saying, "That puts a stop to the aspirations of the Rev. Percy Stickney Grant to marry a divorcee."[42] Not long after, the New York Times ran another front-page headline: "Mrs. Rita De A. Lydig and Dr. Percy Grant Break Engagement; Couple Act Because of Bishop Manning's Refusal to Permit Church Wedding."[43]

Two years later, as she was writing a book that she later called Tragic Mansions, Rita offered her own view of marriage in an interview with the New York Times. "Marriage without love is a suicide pact. It is death—spiritual and moral and often physical death—for both husband and wife. In any fashionable marriage that is made without love there are bound to be resistances and revolts and hatreds that become murderous in their tendency even when they do not actually achieve murder in fact. . . . The fashionable marriage, without love, leads to relations that have no constancy and to divorce after divorce."[44]

When readers of the New York Times opened their newspapers on the morning of April 7, 1927, they were shocked at what they saw on the front page. Rita had filed a petition for bankruptcy, with liabilities amounting to

$94,352. Because she had failed to defend herself against a suit brought by Callot Soeurs of Paris for "wearing apparel sold to her between April and November, 1923" a judgment was filed against her in the New York Supreme Court. Forty-two creditors were listed, including old friend Elsie de Wolfe.[45] Against her doctor's orders, Rita appeared at the hearing to testify that she had no income and no assets beyond the effects listed in her petition. The pallor of her face was set off by a costume of unrelieved black. News accounts reported, "A tricorne hat with drooping plumes at front and back, and a long coat, with a cape effect, gave her an air of smartness despite its sombreness." In her written statement, Rita explained, "I have become involved in debt as a result of several years of illness, many expensive surgical operations, frequent periods of months at a time in hospitals, and my consequent inability to look after my affairs properly."[46]

A few weeks later, most of her rare art objects were auctioned off to pay her debts—Zuloaga's *Portrait of a Philosopher,* a sixteenth-century bronze statue, a Queen Anne coffee pot, six George III candlesticks, a set of eighteenth-century Chippendale mahogany dining chairs, rare books, and a Minton service of gold-decorated china with 301 pieces. But since the sale brought in only fifty thousand dollars, she was forced to promise that all the profits from her new book, *Tragic Mansions,* would go to her creditors. Unfortunately, Rita's forthright and relentless descriptions of the reigning American millionaires, the fashionable rich, offended readers and stifled sales. In the end, she settled her debts by paying forty cents on the dollar.[47]

The hunt for hidden assets, however, lasted for several months and was frequent fodder for the press—that she had been receiving forty thousand dollars annually for fifteen years from four persons, that she was receiving three thousand dollars a month from an anonymous benefactor, that she owned two chinchilla coats valued at thirty thousand dollars each and a chest of silver valued at ten thousand dollars, that she received a monthly check of three thousand dollars from the estate of W. K. Vanderbilt, and that she was living at the Hotel Drake with three servants. One report even quoted an ex-butler who claimed she was spending thousands of dollars every month on morphine.[48]

Although Rita may have tried to hide some of her assets and was undoubtedly trying to maintain her luxurious lifestyle, it was certainly true that she had been suffering from poor health. In March 1925, when she underwent emergency surgery at Harbor Sanitarium for an intestinal disorder, her sister, Mrs. Aida Root, had been called to the hospital. They thought Rita was dying. In August and December of the same year, she underwent further surgery.[49] After the lawsuit, her health continued to deteriorate. For a brief period, she was under the care of specialists in Paris and seemed to improve, but in June 1929 she admitted herself to a New York hospital because of a nervous disorder. Four months later, on October 19, 1929, she died in her apartment at the Gotham Hotel. Newspapers reported that she had died of "pernicious anemia," but her death certificate, which listed her age as fifty-four, recorded the cause of death as nontraumatic hemorrhage into the cerebrum that had been prompted after five years of general arteriosclerosis.[50]

Her death was actually due to a condition she had contracted many years earlier. While driving in a Hempstead cart on an estate she had rented in Westbury, Long Island, Rita and her sister Aida had a disastrous accident. The horse that Rita was driving ran away and fell against an embankment, at the same time kicking the dashboard to pieces so that both passengers plunged out of the cart and landed on the ground beneath his feet. As the horse struggled to rise, it stepped on them and left them seriously injured along the road. Aida nearly died as a result of the accident. She had to undergo several major operations, with the removal, finally, of one kidney. At the time of the accident, Rita appeared to be only slightly injured, but it was just this injury that created internal complications which eventually led to her death.[51]

Mercedes was at her sister's side when she died. It was a terrible loss. "It is true we were sisters," she wrote thirty years later. "But by choice, foremost we were friends and after nearly a lifetime of evaluating her, I think I can say without any kind of prejudice that I have never met any other woman of her quality."[52]

To recover from her loss, Mercedes initiated a series of late-night kitchen suppers. Theater notables such as Katharine Cornell, Jeanne Eagels, Alla Nazimova, Elsie Ferguson, Laurette Taylor, Constance Collier, Noel Coward, Margalo Gilmore, Clifton Webb, Alfred Lunt, and Lynn Fontanne would drop by her and Abram's new house on Beekman Place to unwind, drink, and dine until dawn.

The closing years of the decade had been extremely devastating for Mercedes. She had witnessed the humiliating financial decline and agonizing death of her beloved sister. Although she had shown great promise in the early 1920s with her novels and poetry, publishers no longer seemed interested in her writing. The temper of the times had changed from when she had begun her playwriting career. Two of her plays, *Sandro Botticelli* and *Jehanne d'Arc*, had failed to spark either critics or audiences. Only *Jacob Slovak* had created much enthusiasm. Several of her scripts—*The Mother of Christ, The Dark Light, World Without End, The Better Life, Illusion, Himself*—were never produced. The public outrage against lesbian themes convinced Mercedes that she could never again write as openly as she had in earlier times.

To add to the strain, she was married to a man she did not love and she had lost a lover of five years. It must have been painful to receive this note from Edward Gordon Craig: "I recall your visit to my house with that young warrior Miss Le Gallienne, who has . . . since then captured fortress after fortress in New York."[53] Eva's new Civic Repertory Theatre had garnered front-page headlines across the country and had earned her a place on the *Nation* magazine's roll of honor for 1927 along with Eugene O'Neill, Ernest Hemingway, and Max Reinhardt. Mercedes's career, by contrast, was in a major decline.

$\sim 7 \sim$

"My Beloved"

few months after the London opening of *Prejudice,* Mercedes had received a despairing letter from Bessie Marbury, who was disappointed
that Mercedes had used another agent to sell her play in London. "Do
you have to slip away without seeing me. . . . Is anything the matter? If
you are happy and interested elsewhere it is quite alright—only I want
you to know I am always thinking about you. Affectionately, Elisabeth."[1]
As soon as Mercedes returned from Europe, she renewed their intimate
friendship. A few years later, having become interested in filmmaking
through her relationship with Jeanne Eagels, she was begging Bessie to
market her *Jehanne d'Arc* script in Hollywood. She failed.

However, Bessie telephoned her in late 1930 with great news: "RKO
wants a story for Pola Negri. I have suggested you might write it. If they accept
you it will mean going to Hollywood. I know you are unhappy over Rita's
death. Hollywood will give you new life."[2] Born in Poland, Negri had first
made a hit with American audiences when she starred in Ernst Lubitsch's 1919
German film *Madame Du Barry,* renamed *Passion* in its American release.
During the next ten years in films such as *Hotel Imperial, Woman from Moscow,*
and *Way of Lost Souls,* her image had been sealed as a sexy vamp—strong,
earthy, passionate, full of fire. Mercedes was thrilled that she might have the
opportunity to write for this distinguished celebrity, considered a rival to
Gloria Swanson and known as a lover to Rudolph Valentino.

Invigorated by her new prospects, Mercedes quickly began work on her
first film script, *East River.*[3] The film was to open with views of famous rivers:

the Seine in Paris, Thames in London, Danube in Vienna, Whanghu-Pu in Shanghai, and ending with the East River in New York City. After a long shot of the East River, the camera was to track downtown and then dissolve to a close-up of Nadia, a poor, idealistic Russian immigrant played by Negri. When she is harassed by a man who wants to marry her, she fights back and winds up being thrown in jail for disturbing the peace.

As she is being released from prison, she meets Larry Reynolds, another prisoner who is being released. He is a college graduate and dreams of becoming a musical composer but is alcoholic. They walk to a speakeasy under the Brooklyn Bridge where she is recognized and welcomed by everyone. She says she might be somebody if she only had money and the right chances. Larry collapses. She takes him to her apartment where they quickly fall in love and decide to marry. Even though he comes home drunk the day before the wedding, she forgives him and proceeds with their plans. The first part ends with a huge wedding party.

The second part opens in Larry's family home on Eighty-sixth Street. It is sumptuous, with fifty-eight rooms, butlers, and servants. His sister Judy is throwing a huge Gatsby-like party. Larry plays the piano while Nadia sings "Debronzyaka," a song about a Russian peasant girl who is dragged to a party by the Emperor's son and leaps from a palace window to her death in the icy Neva River. Predictably, Larry gets drunk, and Nadia leaves the home in despair, walking in the rain along the river until she reaches her little apartment.

The next scene is of Nadia lying facedown on her bed the next morning. Larry enters, insisting he will never drink again, and she forgives him. We then see scenes that indicate he has reformed, for he is working on a new opera, *East River,* which will star Nadia. He finishes the opera, and guests are invited to hear it. Nadia feels triumphant in reforming her husband, and she now seems accepted as a "miracle worker" by Larry's mother. At the party, Larry learns that his sister's new boyfriend is the same man whom Nadia had pushed into the river. Infuriated because he thinks that the man is still after Nadia, Larry takes a drink and storms out of the room. He will settle matters with the boyfriend! The scene ends with Nadia calling Larry's mother a wicked woman and accusing her of worshiping happiness: "your religion of being happy for all to do as they like" has made Larry unfit to live among humans.

Cut to a wild party on a ship about to sail for Italy. Among the drunken crowd of people pursuing one another from cabin to cabin are Judy and her boyfriend. Nadia boards the ship and flirts with the boyfriend, hoping he will tell her where she might find Larry. As the ship sets sail, she runs off in time but drops her bag, which the boyfriend picks up. Dissolve to a scene under a bridge where the boyfriend shows Larry a key from the bag and claims that Nadia gave it to him. To prove his point, the boyfriend says he will go to her room. If he blinks a green light from the room, Larry will know that Nadia has refused his overtures. If he blinks a red light, it will mean she has agreed. The boyfriend then sneaks into her apartment and threatens Nadia. She grabs the light, they struggle, he falls into the river, and she blinks the green light. An hour later, Larry returns safely to her arms. Overly melodramatic? Perhaps. It was eventually rejected as a vehicle for Negri but was at least good enough to land Mercedes a contract.

Negri and the studio brass at RKO met with Mercedes in New York and decided she should leave straightaway for Hollywood. Before she left, however, she joined Hope Williams, Tallulah Bankhead, and dancer Marjorie Moss for a final weekend fling with Clifton Webb at his country house on Long Island. Her husband Abram had written her a very touching message only days earlier on their wedding anniversary. Addressing it "Baby," he writes, "Thanks for eleven wonderful years and I hope many more with a little love added."[4] Regardless of his feelings and what it might mean for their marriage, Mercedes would move West.

To some observers, it must have seemed a foolhardy decision. Because of public indignation over the scandals involving such stars as "Fatty" Arbuckle, Charlie Chaplin, and Rudolph Valentino, the industry had only recently adopted the Motion Picture Production Code in 1930. A negative, restrictive code of censorship, it imposed an official morality for all films. There would be no scenes of drug trafficking or use, nudity, or any "bad" acts unless they were balanced by some element of "good" in the story—evil and good were never to be confused. It prohibited depictions of interracial sex, abortion, incest, and homosexuality. Dozens upon dozens of words were considered improper, including the word *sex* itself.

Regardless of the restrictions, the possibilities in Hollywood were more attractive than the promises of Broadway. The peak of 280 productions in New York during the 1927–1928 season plummeted with the onslaught of the Great Depression. In 1920 there were fifteen hundred theaters throughout the country available for live theater, but by 1930 this figure had plunged to only five hundred. Trends in the film industry were quite the opposite. At the end of 1928, Hollywood had only sixteen recording machines being used for the new "talkies," but by the end of 1929 there were 116. Nearly half of the movie theaters in the country were equipped for sound. The public may have been experiencing economic disaster, but they were going to the movies on Friday nights.

Mercedes writes that Hollywood "was considered a wild and, in a manner of speaking, a morally 'lost' place. The whole world thought of it as a place of mad night life, riotous living, orgies . . . uncontrolled extravagances, unbridled love affairs and—in a word—SIN."[5] Though a New Yorker by birth and background, she hoped that in Hollywood she would find a more accepting and artistic community.

Shortly after her arrival in Hollywood in June 1931, Mercedes managed to land an invitation to tea at the home of Salka Viertel in Santa Monica. Born at the turn of the century into a middle-class Jewish family in Austria, Salka had made her way to Vienna and had become an actress. Discovered by Max Reinhardt, she married writer-director Berthold Viertel, founded a theater company in Germany after World War I, and ultimately moved in 1929 to Hollywood, where she joined the story department of Metro Goldwyn Mayer. She and Mercedes had several mutual friends, particularly Hope Williams and Eleanora von Mendelssohn, the great-niece of composer Felix Mendelssohn and goddaughter of Eleonora Duse. Salka and Eleanora had performed together a few years earlier with the Max Reinhardt company in Germany.

As they all chatted away over lunch, the doorbell suddenly rang and in walked Greta Garbo. In her autobiography, Mercedes describes Garbo's physical appearance—her feet, her hands, her hair—and the clothes she wore. But her descriptions in earlier drafts of the book are much more intriguing. She compared Garbo to her mother and to her sister Rita. "There is some element which emanated from Rita which also emanates from Greta, a sort of despotic attitude—a tendency to overrule everyone while at the same time having in this attitude a certain tenderness and consideration. . . . Greta's high-handedness is like Rita's and also a certain aspect of her humour, as well as her tristesse."[6] In another draft, she was even more revealing.

> What struck me the most about Greta when I first saw her was her resemblance to both Rita and my mother. I was not prepared for this and it nearly bowled me over. No doubt, a psychologist would say that I had at some time created a "woman image" in my subconscious and all women who charmed me I had to reconcile to this image, but in this case it was definitely not so. Greta looks, and looked that day, <u>physically</u> like Rita and my mother, yet in type they could not have been more different. . . . But between Greta and Rita there is more than a physical likeness—there is, what I would call, a psychic one.[7]

Regardless of her denial, an argument could certainly be made that Mercedes had indeed created a "woman image" in her subconscious.

In her examination of "women-committed women," historian Leila J. Rupp discovered two distinct types: women who lived like couples in long-term domestic relationships and women who developed an "intense devotion to a charismatic leader." Many times the devotion was one-sided, from an awestruck follower whose adoration evolved into hero worship.[8] As Mercedes pursued Garbo for thirty years, she was reconciling Garbo to her "woman image." Mercedes could never recall what they talked about that afternoon, claiming she was "too overwhelmed to record the conversation." However, she always remembered what Salka said after Garbo left: "Greta liked you and she likes few people."[9] Indeed, Mercedes was awestruck and quickly succumbed to hero worship. Thus began her lifelong infatuation with Greta Garbo.

Two days later, Salka called again; Garbo wanted Mercedes to join them for breakfast. This time, Mercedes was attracted to Garbo's legs. In a passage missing from her published autobiography, she wrote, "They were not tan or the sunburned color which is commonly seen, but the skin had taken on a golden hue and a flock of tiny hairs growing on her legs were golden too. Her legs are classical. She has not the typical Follies girl legs or the American man's dream of what a woman's legs should be. They have the shape that can be seen in many Greek statues."[10] After breakfast, Salka suggested that the two other women walk to her neighbor's unoccupied house overlooking the sea. Once there, the Pacific Ocean in view, they pushed back the rug in the living room, listened to old records, and danced, waltzing to "Good Night, Sweetheart" and tangoing to "Schöne Gigolo." But when Garbo invited Mercedes home for lunch, she had to refuse. She had already accepted an invitation from Pola Negri. Halfway through the luncheon, Mercedes received a telephone call from Garbo, begging her to leave and join her. When she arrived, Garbo was waiting for her in the driveway, dressed in a black Chinese silk dressing gown and men's bedroom slippers. She looked tired and depressed. Sitting under the shade of eucalyptus trees, Garbo complained of her grueling work schedule on the film *Susan Lenox*. "Let's just sit and not speak at all," she whispered. And so they sat silently as "the sun grew fiery red and slowly sank behind the hedge." Garbo broke the silence: "Now you must go home."[11]

One biographer of Garbo supplied a different ending for the evening. In Antoni Gronowicz's account, Mercedes talked about meditation and her vegetarian diet and said, "I'd like to stay with you longer and show you the proper attitude toward life." Mercedes stayed the night. "I knew she was almost as excited as I was," Garbo told Gronowicz. "She possessed vivacity, charm, and a great knowledge of love. She had excited me in everything she did."[12]

Mercedes decided that she wanted to host a party to celebrate her first screen writing assignment. She invited Alla Nazimova, Katharine Cornell, Laurette Taylor, Constance Collier, Diana Wynyard, and her new interest, Garbo. But when Garbo telephoned to say she had come down with a cold, Mercedes abandoned her guests and sped to Garbo's house with bags of oranges and lemons to make a drink that she swore would cure the cold.[13]

A few weeks later, Garbo confided to Mercedes that she was going to be away for six weeks. She had rented a little cottage on a lake in the Sierra Nevadas owned by actor Wallace Beery and wanted to be alone. It was a memorable day. No sooner had Mercedes returned home from Garbo's when she learned that *East River,* her film for Pola Negri, was being shelved. She would receive her salary until the end of her contract, but the future looked bleak. Two days later, Garbo telephoned. She had decided to return for Mercedes. "I am about three hundred miles away and I am motoring steadily, so I will get to your house sometime late this afternoon. Can you come to the island?" Garbo spent the night with Mercedes, and late the next afternoon they set off for their idyllic retreat, crossing the scorching Mojave Desert, stopping two nights at small hotels, and reaching the fourteen-mile-long Silver Lake the third day. Beery's little island and rustic log cabin were visible half a mile from shore. They climbed into a boat, and Garbo took up the oars.

"We must be baptized at once," Garbo cried as they docked the boat. She threw off her clothes, dove into the icy water, and swam like a fish. That evening, she poached mountain trout and brewed strong, Swedish coffee for the two of them. "How to describe the next six enchanted weeks?" Mercedes mused. "In all this time there was not a second of disharmony between Greta and me or in nature around us....There in the Sierra Nevadas she used to climb ahead of me, and with her hair blown back, her face turned to the wind and sun, she would leap from rock to rock on her bare Hellenic feet. I would see her above me, her face and body outlined against the sky, looking like some radiant, elemental, glorious god and goddess melted into one."[14]

Once again, Mercedes's penchant for the theatrical colored the truth. In her biography *Greta Garbo: A Life Apart,* author Karen Swenson explains that Garbo's photography schedule for *Susan Lenox* was not completed until July 11, and the *Hollywood Reporter* of July 27 noted that she was due back in town that day. Wallace Beery had arranged for Garbo to use his cabin for

three weeks, not six.[15] Considering the time to travel to and from Silver
Lake, the six weeks were probably more like two or three. Furthermore, the
island where the log cabin once stood is close to the mainland, not a half
mile from shore. Nevertheless, the time together bonded the two women
and strengthened Mercedes's already passionate infatuation.

Back in Hollywood, she turned to poetry to express her feelings, publishing one of her compositions in the prestigious *Poetry* magazine founded
by Harriet Monroe.

> In this vast wild land, you have
>   Lived so in my brain,
> That surely the image of you
>   Must lie
> Engraven by my thoughts forever on
>   These rocks, this plain;
> Drawn like a sword of stars across
>   This sky.[16]

Writing in lavender ink, the color traditionally associated with lesbianism,
Mercedes began to create a book of poems dedicated to Garbo that she
continued adding to over the next thirteen years. The first selection, "To
Greta," was written shortly after they returned from Silver Lake.

> Take my beloved, these poems that
>   are only small things
> For the memory of moments that
>   for me had wings.
> For the sake of a house on a lake, your
>   laughter, your sighs,
> And for the Heaven and Hell I have
>   seen in your eyes.
> For the sake of my Love, strong as
>   Truth, deep as the sea,
> And for a White Flame in you
>   that reaching out lit me.[17]

For the first six weeks after they returned to Hollywood, Garbo was
involved with retakes for *Susan Lenox*. Whenever she was free, she and
Mercedes were together, walking in the nearby hills, picnicking on the beach
in Malibu, swimming in the sea, riding horses in the countryside, playing
sets of tennis. They were living near each other in Brentwood, so Garbo
would often visit. Since moving to Hollywood, Mercedes had lived with

John Colton, her old friend from New York who had written the screen-play for *Rain* and the play *Shanghai Gesture*. But his frequent entertaining of speakeasy proprietors, underworld characters, and rough "cowboys" from the gay clubs convinced her of the need to move. She was ecstatic when she found an available house directly next door to Garbo on Rockingham Road. The two women were then seen together constantly, photographed for a newspaper one time striding down Hollywood Boulevard dressed in pants.

Besides occupying all of Garbo's leisure time, Mercedes also attended her filming of *Mata Hari*. On one occasion, she accompanied Garbo for a cos-tume fitting with Adrian. It was supposedly Mercedes who suggested to the designer that for her final scene Garbo wear a long black cape and brush her hair straight back. The result was very much like the portrait of Mercedes that Abram had painted years earlier. Maybe it was the constant compan-ionship with Mercedes that made the film Garbo's first "to communicate a coded message to gay and lesbian audiences."[18]

The unrelenting attention Mercedes lavished on Garbo took its toll on their relationship. More and more frequently the press hinted at Garbo's gender-bending sexuality—her dressing in masculine tweeds and slouch hats, her buying men's suits for herself, shopping for clothes at the Army-Navy Store, associating with her "gal pal" Mercedes. Referring to Garbo, one article proclaimed, "The most talked-about woman in Hollywood is the woman no wife fears."[19] By Christmas, Garbo, perhaps concerned by all the gossip and Mercedes's possessiveness, took off for New York to stay at the Hotel St. Moritz with Salka Viertel, leaving Mercedes behind. Since Salka lived with her husband, she provided a convenient cover for Garbo. Through Mercedes's connections, Garbo managed to take in Broadway performances by several of Mercedes's friends—Alla Nazimova in *Mourning Becomes Electra,* Eva Le Gallienne in *Camille,* Katharine Cornell in *The Barretts of Wimpole Street*. In spite of her reservations, Garbo did see fit to at least send Mercedes a Christmas card and flowers.[20]

Early in 1932, Mercedes presented to Irving Thalberg, production chief for MGM, a screenplay she had written for Garbo that she called *Desperate*.[21] Garbo was to play the role of Erik, a young woman who is caught between trying to satisfy the demands and interests of both of her divorced parents. Frustrated with the struggle to please both of them, she rebels. Quoting a line from Nietzche's *Thus Spake Zarathustra,* she says she will "learn to live des-perately." In a series of short episodes, Erik is seen living a fast life—in a high-speed motorboat contest off the coast of Monte Carlo, on a hunting trip in England, drinking with sailors at a bar in Marseilles, gambling in Berlin, drinking absinthe at a bar in Paris, pawning her jewelry in Italy.

One night at a bar in Harlem, a friend of hers becomes involved in a drunken brawl and is killed. Fearful that she may be implicated as an accomplice, she disguises herself as a boy, putting on a man's suit and shoes, slicking back her hair, and pulling a hat down over her eyes. Except for one brief scene, the last half of the film shows Erik as a "beautiful, pale, Shelley-like boy." Mercedes explains that "in making herself into a boy, shedding her skin as it were, she dissolves her whole identity."

In the final sequence, Erik has fled to Wyoming, mistaken for a boy and dressed as a "pretty new cowboy." After a man she falls in love with finally realizes Erik's true identity and learns that she loves him, he rushes into a rodeo ring where Erik is riding the meanest stallion. He manages to control the horse as they ride out of the ring together. A final long shot shows them standing on a hillside overlooking the ranch as they embrace.

According to Mercedes, Thalberg stopped the project when he learned that Garbo would be dressed as a boy for half the film: "We have been building Garbo up for years as a great glamorous actress, and now you come along and try to put her into pants and make a monkey out of her. . . . The story is out."[22] But there had to be more than the scenario that Mercedes offers. Garbo had already worn men's clothes—white shirts and trousers—in *The Single Standard* just two years earlier. Thalberg probably did not approve of the overall story line, but Mercedes only heard what she wanted to hear— or only told what she wanted people to believe.

On April 29, 1932, Garbo's *Grand Hotel* opened to rave notices. Just a month later, after seven years in the United States, she announced she was returning to Sweden for an extended vacation. But before she left, Mercedes's friendship proved to be a salvation for her. On Friday afternoon, June 3, First National Bank of Beverly Hills was declared insolvent, and on Monday it closed its doors.[23] Garbo had lost an undisclosed fortune. Mercedes claimed that she helped Garbo sneak into the bank and remove her securities that were locked in a safety-deposit box. Also, on June 16 she wired a telegram to President Hoover: "Please forgive me for bothering you at this moment when you have so much on hand but much is at stake. As you no doubt know the First National Bank of Beverly Hills closed last week in which the film star Greta Garbo had all her money. I consider much grave dishonesty surrounds her. She is a child and incapable of taking care of herself. I have wired the Swedish ambassador Mr. Bostrom to protect her and hope you will communicate and advise him."[24] Mercedes was concerned that if MGM learned of Garbo's financial difficulties it would be disastrous, as they were negotiating a new contract. She insisted that Garbo move in with her to save rent money. She even hired a carpenter to build gates to the estate so as to shield Garbo from prying eyes. It all worked. With a new contract and check for one hundred thousand dollars from MGM, Garbo boarded a train for New York, planning to sail for Sweden as soon as possible.

Accounts differ as to whether Mercedes boarded the train with Garbo or followed later. In any case, before too long they were seen together walking along Fifth Avenue. One evening in their hotel room, Garbo wept as she related to Mercedes how the late director Mauritz Stiller "had been in absolute control of her life" and how his memory still haunted her. Mercedes proceeded to extract from her luggage small statues of the Virgin Mary, Saint Teresa, Saint Francis of Assisi, and Buddha. She placed the statues in the corners of the room, lit candles, knelt in the middle of the room, and stripped. "Come here, kneel beside me, and get undressed," she urged. "Let the fragrant smoke and my prayers touch your naked body and protect you." The two naked women knelt and addressed each of the saints. Garbo fell into a deep trance and slept. When she awoke, Mercedes and she were lying together in bed.[25]

Mercedes yearned to accompany Garbo to Sweden, but Garbo refused. She did not want the press hounding her and making her explain the relationship. Mercedes fumed, "I am sure you're afraid of being accused of having sapphic inclinations." "You're right!" Garbo snapped back.[26]

The only evidence of Garbo's apology for her curt reply was flowers she sent to Mercedes along with a comic strip from a newspaper. In the cartoon, two Bowery boy types are leaning against a brick wall. One says, "She didn't thank ya, did she, Skippy?" And Skippy answers, "Well, we ain't speakin—that's why." The initials "G.G." are written in ink in the lower left corner.[27] Certainly a strange way for Garbo to make amends with her intimate friend, but at least it was some kind of communication.

Mercedes was still under contract to MGM at the time and was working for Thalberg on a script about Rasputin, the Russian religious mystic and faith healer. One day Thalberg instructed her to include a violent and dramatic sequence in which Rasputin tries to seduce Princess Irene Yussupov. Mercedes protested, arguing that since Rasputin and the Princess had never met, such a scene would distort history. It would be "absolutely inauthentic and probably libelous." Thalberg reportedly rose from his chair and stormed out of the room screaming, "I don't need you to tell me a lot of nonsense about what is libelous or what is not. I want this sequence in and that is all there is to it."

Mercedes immediately wrote to Prince Agoutinsky, who had introduced her years earlier to the princess, telling him of Thalberg's demand. She received an immediate reply. If even the character of Princess Irene appeared in the film, the family would sue. When Mercedes showed the cable to Thalberg, he flew into a rage. How dare she consult with anyone about the picture. "You had absolutely no right to do such a thing without my permission," he charged. He then picked up his telephone and asked for her contract to be delivered to his office, then ripped it to shreds and flung it into a wastebasket in front of her.

Anita Loos, author of *Gentlemen Prefer Blondes,* was living in Los Angeles at the time and reported to her good friend Cecil Beaton: "The Garbo-Mercedes business has been too amazing. They had terrific battles, and Garbo left without saying goodbye. Then Mercedes flew to NY to see her and Garbo wouldn't. Mercedes flew back despondent—lost her job with MGM and is in the most awful state. Also says she is broke—can't get a break and it's too terrible. The story is as long as the dictionary—but much more amazing."[28] She must have felt especially vindicated when *Rasputin and the Empress* finally premiered in late 1932. It was an international hit, but when it opened in London, Prince Yussupov filed a four-million-dollar lawsuit against the studio. Mercedes offered written testimony that the Prince had instructed her to eliminate all mention of his wife and that she had shared this information with Irving Thalberg. When the suit was finally settled, the princess was granted $750,000 and Mercedes won her job back along with a hefty raise.[29]

During those long months of separation from "her beloved," Mercedes expressed her painful loss in two more poems.[30]

-1-

I tread my way alone
Where our way wound.
Deserted road, but still
Most sacred ground
Where your feet tread.

Still the same brush
(The branches tore your knee)
Still the same shadow cast
From our dark drooping tree.

Still the same place.
Did I say "Same"?
What stupid words
That seek a name!

All words are empty now,
Only pain and acheing fear
Remain in desolation,
Since you walk no longer here.
Hollywood 1932
Greta is in Sweden

-2-
I said;
Forever and forever, I must follow
you.
I cannot stay a second in
this place
Without the sight of your
belovéd face.

But now I stay.
Ground, that felt you pass
Lies quiet under tread
While sadly I wander home
With sleeplessness to bed.

Wide my eyes,
And brain grown dark,
And wrent sheets
For acheing hands,
And dry sockets of hurt
and pain,
And lips parched-fevered
with your name.

And silence! Ah, thank God
for this!
Silence like a sentinel stands
at hand.
While suddenly, all life
stops still . . . . .
As I hear your heart in a
Nordic land!
Hollywood 1932. Greta is in Sweden

With her beloved in Sweden, Mercedes walked alone the deserted roads they had walked together. Her hands ached for her lover, and her lips scorched from repeating her name. She wandered sleeplessly, knowing that she had committed herself to following Garbo forever, yet not really understanding those feelings. What Mercedes wrote in her autobiography about Garbo's suddenly disappearing to New York was quite an understatement: "After she left, Hollywood seemed empty to me."[31]

~8~

"State of Slavery"

Hollywood may have seemed empty to Mercedes with Garbo thousands of miles away in Sweden, but not for long. At a grand party hosted by Irving Thalberg, she met the subject of her next love affair—screen goddess Marlene Dietrich. The day after the party, an infatuated Dietrich wrote her husband, Rudi Sieber, about their meeting. "I met a writer, Spanish, very attractive, named Mercedes de Acosta. They say Garbo's crazy about her. For me, she was a relief from this narrow Hollywood mentality. Here they should build all the churches in the shape of a box office."[1] A day later, Dietrich penned another letter to her husband whom she affectionately addressed as Papilein.

> I saw Mercedes de Acosta again. Apparently Garbo gives her a hard time, not just by playing around—which by the way is why she is in the hospital with gonorrhea—also she is the kind of person who counts every cube of sugar to make sure the maid isn't stealing, or eating too well. I am sorry for Mercedes. Her face was white and thin and she seemed sad and lonely—as I am—and not well. I was attracted to her and brought an armful of tuberoses to her house. I told her I would cook marvelous things for her and get her well and strong.[2]

Dietrich had arrived in Hollywood only two years earlier but had already become a sensation for her androgynous performances. In *Morocco* and *Blonde Venus,* she had worn top hat and tails. In *Shanghai Express,* she had visited a lesbian night club. Clearly, her persona had been established as an

113

intelligent, independent, yet tantalizing femme fatale. As Kenneth Tynan described her years later, "She has sex, but no particular gender. Her ways are mannish: the characters she played loved power and wore slacks. . . . They were also quite undomesticated. Dietrich's masculinity appeals to women, and her sexuality to men."[3] Mercedes was no doubt enchanted by this new goddess of the silver screen.

In one of her many messages to Mercedes penned in French, Dietrich warned that as soon as Mercedes tired of her, she would descend into her tomb and not even inconvenience her with shedding a tear.[4] Disliking Hollywood, Dietrich had contemplated returning to her native Germany, but now she claimed, "It will be hard to leave Hollywood now that I know you."[5] Two weeks later, she invited Mercedes to join her at her beach house: "Please come the ocean is more beautiful than ever the sun is waiting for you and I am waiting."[6]

In October, she included some buttons in a letter to Mercedes that she signed with a kiss. The next month, she mailed her a dressing gown and some handkerchiefs from the men's department of Bullock's. Addressing the card inserted with the package to "Mon amour!," Dietrich wrote, "Beautiful one—I adore you forever—and I kiss your hands."[7] The presents continued to arrive—scarves, pajamas, slacks, sweaters. Until she sold her papers to the Rosenbach Museum in 1961, Mercedes kept several gifts from Dietrich: one yellow anklet bearing a lipstick smudge at the edge of the heel, a small pink and black nylon neck scarf containing eight black circles with the name "marlene" printed through the center of each circle, a single seamless nylon stocking. On one occasion when Dietrich knew she would be late in arriving at a dinner party hosted by Mercedes, she sent the following: "My Love. . . . please do eat and go to bed and wait for me there."[8] Although Dietrich was married, it did not prevent her from showering Mercedes daily with dozens of roses or carnations or rare orchids. "The house became a sort of permanent Chelsea flower show, a madhouse of flowers," Mercedes complained. "I was walking on flowers, falling on flowers, and sleeping on flowers. I finally wept, flew into a rage, and sent Anna [her maid] off to the hospital with every damn flower in the house."[9]

In fact, Dietrich's thoughtfulness became so worrisome to the usually overly impassioned Mercedes that she complained of Dietrich's declaration of everlasting love. "Don't say 'always,'" she begged, "for in love it is blasphemy. One never knows if from now on one truly loves or if one is making oaths and one simply forgets them. Don't say always, for in love nothing binds you."[10] Mercedes and Le Gallienne had made similar vows a decade earlier, so she knew they were unrealistic.

Mercedes, smarting from being treated so coolly by Garbo, was smitten. First Garbo and now Dietrich—two women who were said to "epitomize the glamour of sin."[11] Signing her name "White Prince" or "Raphael," Mercedes wrote almost daily messages to her new heartthrob, addressing them to "Golden One," "Wonderful One," "Darling One." In one she oozed, "It is one week today since your beautiful Naughty hand opened a white rose. Last night was even more wonderful and each time I see you it grows more wonderful and exciting. You with your exquisite white pansy face— and before you go to bed will you ring me so that I can just hear your voice."[12]

Continually astounded by all the attention, Mercedes composed a small love poem for her "Golden One":

For Marlene,
Your face is lit by moonlight
breaking through your skin
soft, pale, radiant.
No suntan for you glow
For you are the essence of
the stars and the moon and
the mystery of the night.[13]

Still another time, she promised, "I will bring anyone you want to your bed! And that is not because I love you little but because I love you so much! My Beautiful One!"[14]

On January 22, 1933, Mercedes learned that her old friend Bessie Marbury had died. She had been ill for some time, suffering from chronic hypertension. Following minor surgery to relieve pressure on her veins, she lapsed into a coma and died of heart failure. While her body lay in state in her drawing room, the world paid its respects. President-elect Franklin Delano Roosevelt sent his regards. Leaders of the Democratic Party praised her "leadership," "wise consul," and "genius." On the floor of the Congress, Representative Mary T. Norton of New Jersey noted, "The Democratic women of New York and of the nation have lost not only an able friend and leader but one of whose inspiration, vision, and loyalty we shall sadly miss."[15] More than twenty thousand people lined the streets for her funeral two days later. In attendance were governors from six states, several mayors, and New York Supreme Court Justice William Harman Black, as well as publisher Condé Nast, theater producers Daniel Frohman and Gilbert Miller, and playwright Noel Coward. Mercedes, however, caught up in the drama of her own life in Hollywood, did not attend.

Through the spring months of 1933, she was often with Dietrich, who included Mercedes at her lavish banquets and swimming parties at her Santa Monica beach house. They attended tennis matches. Sometimes Mercedes would accompany her to the Paramount studio and watch her filming *The Scarlet Empress*. In May 1933, Dietrich left for Europe. She mailed Mercedes dozens of letters and telegrams while she was gone, always signing off with love and kisses and saying, "I kiss your beautiful hands and your heart."

The passionate affair lasted little more than a year. Mercedes's cloying emotionalism had damaged her relationship with Garbo, and now it was having the same effect on Dietrich. When Dietrich's mentor and director, Josef von Sternberg, ended their business partnership, Mercedes took responsibility. "I am angered that anyone can hurt or wound you," she wept. "I only know that I would like to keep my arms around you to protect you from any pain. I pray that I was no way the cause of this thing—that Mr. von Sternberg did not know about me. To lose such a friend as Mr. von Sternberg and harm your work just for loving me would indeed be paying too large a price. Beautiful, thrilling Firebird—Do not forget your wings that belong only to you that do not need anyone else to carry you high, up high!"[16] When Dietrich received the letter, she was annoyed that Mercedes could think she played that sort of a role in her life. But the ultimate irritation for Dietrich was hearing Mercedes drone on about Garbo.

Even after her split with Dietrich had become certain, Mercedes continued her outpourings.

> To try and explain my real feeling for Greta would be impossible since I really do not understand myself. I do know that I have built up in my emotions a person that does not exist. My mind sees the real person—a Swedish servant girl with a face touched by God—only interested in money, her health, sex, food and sleep. And yet her face tricks my mind and my spirit builds her up into something that fights with my brain. I do love her but I only love the person I have created and not the person who is real.
>
> Until I was seventeen I was a real religious fanatic. Then I met Duse and until I met Greta, gave her the same fanaticism until I transferred it to Greta. And during those periods of fanaticism they have not prevented me from being in love with other people—which seems to take another side of my nature. It was so with you. I was passionately in love with you. I could still be if I allowed myself. Many times when I am away from you I desire you terribly and always when I am with you. I know you have felt my desire because I have known you when

you felt it.... Perhaps this letter will mean nothing to you. But I shall always cherish the days and nights that you did love me and your beautiful efforts to drag me out of my "indigo" moods. . . . Darling One, I kiss you all over—everywhere. And I kiss your spirit as well as your beautiful body.[17]

She may have known on some intellectual level that the relationship was over, but she was still heartbroken when Dietrich fell in love with actor Brian Aherne.

While Garbo was in Sweden, she made a few feeble attempts to keep in touch with Mercedes—a Christmas telegram, a brief note with a check for $850 to reimburse Mercedes for some purchases she had made, a telegram on March 2, 1933, saying that she was returning soon.[18] But Mercedes, though supposedly in love with Dietrich, felt abandoned by Garbo, her "beloved," and penned yet another melancholy poem to her.

I will go back to my own land.
Land of Spain. Sad, tragic land.
Place of warm hearts, dark eyes
    and hair.
I shall wander lonely there.
Alien to my own blood and kind,
I shall not find
Your eyes or the gold of your
    skin burnt fair.
But at the end,
Cold lands swept by wind
    and snow,
Is where my heart will
    die, I know [19]

In April, one month before Dietrich sailed for Germany, Garbo returned from Sweden. Even though Mercedes alleged that Garbo had sent her a telegram from her ship, the SS *Annie Johnson,* announcing her arrival, evidence does not support the claim.[20] Instead, Garbo wired her old friend and Mercedes's rival, Salka Viertel. She asked Salka, not Mercedes, to help her sneak past the press when she docked on April 30 in the port of San Diego. "Dearest," she wrote, "It's such a peculiar wanderer who comes to you. The only thing that matters is that you're here. Otherwise—I don't know what."[21] Salka met her at the port and drove her to Los Angeles. And, to Mercedes's dismay, Garbo moved in to live with Salka and her husband.

The Viertels enjoyed an open marriage, allowing each of them to pursue other relationships but at the same time preserving their own. Just one week before she received the telegram from Garbo, Salka had written to her husband in Germany, "Dearest Berthold, in spite of temporary infatuations which have nothing to do with our belonging to each other, *you* are the love of my life." He replied, "Salka you will never regret that you have confided in me so completely. Nothing better and more beautiful could have happened between us. . . . Cable me, phone me, and never give up loving me. Do you hear, never! As for me, only death can cure my addiction to you."[22] In spite of, indeed, perhaps because of their decision to preserve their marriage, Garbo chose to live with them rather than with Mercedes. Salka may have doted as much as Mercedes, but at least her marriage provided some boundaries as well as a convenient cover.

Mercedes was miserable. Not only had her relationship with Dietrich deteriorated but they were now separated, with Dietrich in Europe, and her "beloved" Garbo was keeping her at arm's length. Intending to help shield her housemate from Mercedes, Salka had persuaded Thalberg to construct for Garbo a private entrance and driveway at the studio to block all uninvited guests. She wanted Mercedes out of the picture and removed from Garbo's affection.

Mercedes's only hope, she thought, was to write a screenplay for Garbo. In her autobiography, she says that she had been working on a script about Queen Christina of Sweden and showed it to Garbo when she returned from Europe. "But as things often go in the film world in Hollywood," she grumbled, "the idea was taken from me."[23]

Once again, the facts reveal a different story. As early as 1927, four years before Mercedes arrived in Hollywood, MGM had considered the story for Garbo.[24] And in 1930, when Salka was filming the German language *Anna Christie* with Garbo, the two had discussed it. Salka thought Christina's personality suited the film star: "she was eccentric, brilliant; and her masculine education and complicated sexuality made her an almost contemporary character."[25] Encouraged by Garbo, Salka wrote a screenplay with the assistance of Margaret Le Vino and negotiated a contract with Thalberg for her ninety-page script. In the end, she and Le Vino were paid seventy-five hundred dollars.[26] Once again, Salka had finessed her rival; she would be working closely on a film with Garbo and Mercedes would be kept at a distance. On July 28, 1932, the day before she sailed for Sweden, Garbo had cabled Salka from New York, thanking her for all her work on the screenplay and signing it, "Auf Wiedersehen Liebe Salka."[27] It is unlikely, therefore, that a script by Mercedes about Queen Christina was ever considered by the studios. The Salka contract was signed and early production plans were under way before Garbo ever left for Sweden.

Mercedes's deep depression was further complicated by a serious injury when she was hurled sixty feet out of her car and landed on her head. Thinking her dead, the gathered crowd covered her with a blanket and waited for the police to arrive. Although she escaped permanent disfigurement, she was hospitalized for several weeks and needed extensive plastic surgery on her face. When she heard about the accident, Dietrich telephoned from Paris and offered to pay the hospital expenses. Later, she asked, "How are my scars?" Even Garbo was moved enough to visit her in the hospital.

To Mercedes's delight, Garbo seemed to be interested in her again. About a month after the accident, she gushed in a letter to Dietrich, "Golden Beautiful One, I see the 'Other Person' [Garbo] all the time who is completely changed toward me—beautiful and sweet—and completely unlike last year.... I will be happy to see your beautiful little face again. Your White Prince."[28] And she was overjoyed when Garbo invited her to go along on a winter vacation to Yosemite. It would hopefully be a rerun of their first romantic retreat to Silver Lake.

Tragically for Mercedes, the trip never took place. When the day came for them to depart, Mercedes waited at length for Garbo to come by and pick her up. Finally, she drove herself over to Garbo's house and sadly discovered that her "beloved" had left without her and had gone off instead with the director of *Queen Christina,* Rouben Mamoulian.

Mercedes was more than fearful of Mamoulian's influence over the woman she worshiped. Russian-born, he had studied at the famed Vakhtangov Studio in Moscow and in 1927 became the toast of Broadway with his direction of *Porgy.* The next year he directed six plays, including Eugene O'Neill's *Marco Millions* and Karel Capek's *R. U.R.* In 1930 Garbo had seen the Theatre Guild production he had directed of *A Month in the Country* with Alla Nazimova. He was popular, talented, and known to be a lady's man. And now the Hollywood rumor mills churned out reports that he and Garbo were contemplating marriage.

Her dislike for Mamoulian did not go unnoticed. One time when he came out of Garbo's house, he found Mercedes "pacing up and down the sidewalk out front." When Garbo got into his car, she slid down in the seat to hide from Mercedes and pleaded with him to step on the gas. Mamoulian refused. "You sit up, dammit," he exploded, "and we'll drive out. I will not let you crouch in my car because of this." She sat up, they drove out, and Mercedes stood by helplessly.[29]

When thoughts of suicide returned, she managed to find an old revolver. "As I held it [the revolver] in my hand," she confessed, "I felt again the old sense that it was a way of escape."[30] Luckily, she was encouraged to seek out Sri Meher Baba, a Hindu holy man who had only recently arrived in Hollywood from India. When she first saw him, he was sitting in a Buddha position, dressed all in white. His long, black hair, thick, black moustache, and dark eyes radiated an uncanny warmth. He had taken a vow of silence, so after he embraced her, he wrote on a chalkboard, "Go, fetch me your revolver." After doing so, he then wrote, "Suicide is not the solution. It only entails rebirth with the same problems all over again," and he made her promise to never again contemplate suicide.[31]

Reinvigorated by her meeting with this man of wisdom, she met with Irving Thalberg and told him she had always dreamed of seeing Garbo "play a peasant role in which she could brush her hair straight back off her face and wear simple clothes. . . . I wanted her for once to portray a role where beautiful clothes would not stand between her and her great acting. I wanted her to do a picture close to the soil where nature would play a part."[32] After a lengthy conversation, Thalberg assigned her to write a screenplay about Joan of Arc.

During the first nine months of 1934, her "whole heart was in the script. . . . [She] worked on it passionately and intensely."[33] She became so obsessed that she began to visualize Garbo as Joan. "So complete was this transference in my mind," she explained, "that when I walked with her in the hills or on the beach I often saw her in medieval costume or in armor."[34] In March, she attended the Los Angeles opening of *Hedda Gabler,* starring her former lover and first Joan of Arc, Eva Le Gallienne. Le Gallienne later complained to her mother that Mercedes showed up backstage, "behaving as if we had seen each other, or at least corresponded with each other daily! She talked a great deal about 'Greta' this & 'Greta' that."[35] All of Mercedes's chatter about her relationship with Garbo must have been particularly upsetting to Le Gallienne at the time, for she herself was undergoing serious upheavals in her own life. She had only recently been forced to move out of her Civic Repertory Theatre in New York, and she was on the edge of losing her lover of several years, Josephine Hutchinson. To hear her former lover rave on about a film version of the story of Joan of Arc she was preparing for Garbo must have been galling.

In early summer, Mercedes moved to a house in Brentwood to be near Garbo on North Carmelina Drive. She indicates in her autobiography that she moved first and then Garbo followed. Again, this is a bit of a distortion. The snooping eyes of the *Hollywood Reporter* disclosed that Garbo moved first and that Mercedes followed by renting "a shack next to the Garbo menage."[36] If she could not live with her in the same house, she would do all in her power to live as close as possible.

On August 4, Mercedes delivered her notes and first draft for the screenplay directly to Thalberg. Her descriptions of Jehanne in the accompanying fifteen-page essay she submitted to Thalberg reveal how she viewed the character.

> Even as a child she was noted for her abounding physical energy. She was able to run faster than any boy in the village and carry weights as easily as a man.
>
> As she grew older she became inclined to silence, and spent much of her time in solitude and prayer. She repelled all attempts of the young men in her village to win her favor and only once she disobeyed her parents. This was an incident in which they attempted to force her into marriage. A young villager pretended that in Jehanne's childhood she had been promised to him in marriage by her parents. This the parents did not deny. Jehanne, however, stoutly denied it and the young man had her cited and brought before the ecclesiastical judge of Toul. It was imagined that rather than undertake the effort of speaking in her own defense and likewise disobeying her parents, she would submit to marriage. To the great astonishment of all that knew her, she went to Toul, appeared in court, and with enormous courage and clear reasoning defended her own case and won.[37]

Thalberg seemed elated with Mercedes's work, throwing his arms around her and declaring he would discuss it that day with Garbo. But only a few days later, she received word from the studio that Garbo had rejected the story. "Greta is being influenced by someone," he insisted. "She would not make this decision on her own."[38] Looking back on the situation years later, Mercedes wondered why she had never discussed the project with Garbo in the first place and why she had never confronted her when she rejected it.

Of all her disappointments in Hollywood, this one affected her the most, yet something held her back. She could not bring herself to discuss it with her "beloved." "For some time after this when I was with Greta," she wrote, "a ghost seemed to stand between us—the ghost of Jehanne d'Arc. But I never again mentioned a word to her or to anyone else about it."[39] Perhaps Thalberg's observation was correct. Garbo's next film was *Anna Karenina,* and working on the screenplay was none other than Mercedes's nemesis, Salka Viertel.

Even with this ghost standing between them, Mercedes pursued Garbo whenever possible. During a shopping trip together in Hollywood in November 1934, Garbo emerged from a shop wearing a new pair of slacks. Since she had also persuaded Dietrich to purchase slacks from the same shop, Mercedes took all the credit for this new fashion statement. "From that second on, women all over the world leapt into trousers," she boasted. "This was the beginning of the Great Women's Trouser Era! ... Every photograph that appeared of her [Garbo] sold thousands of pairs of trousers."[40]

In early 1935, Mercedes's husband of fifteen years finally announced that he wanted a divorce. He disclosed that he planned to marry Janice Fair, an attractive dancer who had performed in the *George White Scandals,* a musical revue rivaling the *Ziegfeld Follies* and *Earl Carroll Vanities.* She had also been modeling for some of Abram's paintings.[41]

Mercedes was stunned by the announcement. "That we could no longer make a success of our sexual life seemed to me no reason to separate," she argued. "I was too European to feel, as Americans do, that the moment the sex relation is over one must fly to the divorce courts."[42] Once again she felt rejected:

> It was as though my father or some close friend had written to me that he wanted me out of his life. ... I was quite willing for him to have a mistress. We had had a great row about it as he said I was immoral for suggesting such a thing. I did not think so. I thought it was only civilized and generous to suggest it and make him feel it was all right with me. ... He suggested I go out to Reno for six weeks. I firmly said I would not do this, that he could go to Reno instead of me. 'But,' he said, 'if I do, it will appear as though I were divorcing you. A man simply cannot divorce a woman. It is not done.' I answered that I did not care a damn what was done or not done and that, since he was the one who had started the whole idea, he could jolly well go and get it.[43]

Against his will, Abram became the plaintiff in the divorce and was forced to initiate the action.

The divorce was less amicable than Mercedes relates. In fact, it was stormy. Family members remember hearing a different version of what precipitated Abram's decision. It seems that one evening Abram walked into their bedroom in New York unexpectedly and discovered Mercedes with another woman. He had obviously known of his wife's sexual desires for women, but actually seeing her perform in their bedroom was just too much for him to bear. A violent outburst ensued. When Abram insisted that the other woman leave immediately, Mercedes proceeded to smash one of Abram's highly prized antique chairs.

Abram was also angry that Mercedes lived so much of the time across the continent in Hollywood and spent his money. Although she was occasionally under contract with one of the film studios, most of the time she was unemployed. Indeed, she partied, entertained, and traveled to Europe— all at his expense. Her extravagant spending had always been an issue. A few years earlier, Mercedes had returned from Europe with a heavy trunk containing hundreds of boxes of light blue stationery with her address engraved in silver. "It did not seem unusual to me to have paid a thousand dollars for it," she wrote. Abram, who had met her at the dock, thought otherwise. He "walked angrily off the pier."[44]

Once it was finally settled that they would divorce, Mercedes suggested to Abram that they save money and avoid acrimony by using the same lawyer, namely her brother-in-law, who wanted to remain in the good graces of the de Acosta family, since he planned to divorce Mercedes's sister.[45] Abram dismissed the suggestion, however. He could not see how this lawyer could represent both parties fairly.

Neither Abram nor Mercedes appeared in person before the court. Abram remained in New York, while Mercedes fled to Europe. The divorce decree signed by district judge Thomas F. Moran in Reno, Nevada, on September 19, 1935, reveals their discord. He declared "that the allegations of Plaintiff's Complaint are not sustained by the testimony and that the allegations of Defendant's Cross-Complaint are sustained by the testimony." He then ruled "that Defendant is entitled to the Judgment and Decree of this Court for an absolute divorce from the Plaintiff" and "that the written agreement between the parties, dated June 25, 1935, should be adopted, approved and confirmed by this court."[46] Unfortunately, there is no record of their specific disagreements nor of their actual June 25 agreement. Abram's son by his second wife recalls that his father was required to pay Mercedes four hundred dollars every month. In 2001 dollars, that would have provided Mercedes with just over five thousand dollars per month.[47]

The *New York Times* reported a few days after the settlement that during the divorce proceedings, Mercedes had presented a "cross-complaint charging cruelty," testifying in a deposition that Abram had become indifferent about four years earlier and had begun "to treat her curtly and sullenly."[48] Given that she had engaged in passionate romances with several women since the time of their marriage and had moved to Hollywood, her complaint seems baseless.

Because of the emotional upheavals resulting from her relationship with

Garbo and now her divorce, she had lost considerable weight and decided to visit a well-known dietician in Pasadena, Dr. Harold Bieler. He diagnosed her loss of weight as psychological and prescribed a strict vegetarian diet, especially a puree of assorted squash with onion and potatoes. It was not a difficult treatment to follow. Often as a child she had become sick and vomited after being forced to eat meat.

But she needed more than just a change of diet. At loose ends, Mercedes headed for Europe even before the divorce was settled, in part because Garbo already had sailed for Sweden. Upset over Garbo's departure, she had consulted her guru, Sri Meher Baba, who had warned that "the extreme of agonies" of her present state could "grow so terrible at times that they may lead to excesses of mad behaviours or even insanity or suicide." He advised her not to chase after Garbo.[49] Nevertheless, on June 22, 1935, she sailed on the SS *Normandie,* bound for England and then on to France. Even the *Hollywood Reporter* noticed her hasty exit with a rather cryptic comment: "Mercedes d'Acosta [*sic*] is in Europe divorcing her husband, Abram Poole— or didn't you know she had one?"[50]

Most memorable was her visit to an old Franciscan monastery near Assisi, Italy, that was built in the fifth century by a secret order of Tibetan monks.[51] The Franciscans took it over after the death of Saint Francis and remained there until the seventeenth century. Abandoned for nearly two hundred years, it was rediscovered after World War I by a former nun named Sorella Maria. Along with twelve other women, she restored the ancient building and began accepting visitors who were in need of spiritual, physical, or moral help. Mercedes was eager to visit because, as she confessed, she also "had great need of the solace it had given so many people."

After arriving at the railroad station at Assisi, she was driven six miles in an old car and then instructed to mount a tiny donkey that would take her up a steep mountain path. An hour later, she could hear the monastery bells ringing from the tower. Sorella Maria greeted her at the gate and led her into a tranquil garden where they sat in silence. When Sorella Maria finally broke the silence, she began to counsel Mercedes about all of her problems and gave her "revolutionary advice as to certain things" she should do. She was then ushered to her room, a small, square, stone cell. One deeply set, square window provided her a view of the valley. The women had built the furniture, carved the doors, created the earthen pottery. "In this cell," Mercedes marveled, "there was a tranquility—almost a tenderness—that I have never found elsewhere." She remained for several days. The evening she was leaving, Sorella Maria escorted her into the chapel and lit a little altar lamp, saying that the light would remain burning as long as she remained at the monastery. "Many times since then, when I have been unhappy or despairing," Mercedes wrote, "I have thought of this little light and it has given me courage."

During much of 1935, she was also receiving frequent advice from Sri Meher Baba. On January 16, 1935, he thanked Mercedes for agreeing to collaborate on a picture "for me and my work."

> I want you to work for me and in my cause as much and as best you can. That will help your spiritual advancement a great deal, and will, besides, bring you closer to me in love, which you so desire. And remember, dear Mercedes, I will always help you spiritually in all your aspirations for inner and higher life, which I know and deeply appreciate. As for your apprehension re: Garbo, as I already told you, she will come to the real thing, in time, I know, and you needn't at all feel anxious about that any more. This phase of her life will pass off too—it has to—and then you will find her a changed being—her real self that will express itself beautifully in the story you have written—and the world will see a real Garbo, and a real picture too.[52]

On June 6, 1935, he wrote from Bombay to his followers that he was going into seclusion in the Himalayas. "I expect you, as my best beloved and closest ones, to bear everything patiently for all the love you dearest have for me... . Love is always like that. All have to suffer, for Love. Jesus suffered all His life, for Love. . . . You know, beloveds, how I love you, and I know how deeply you darlings love me, and how keenly you feel the separation and suffer for your beloved Baba."[53] The message must have been particularly meaningful to Mercedes, who was suffering with her love for Garbo.

About a month later, on July 10, 1935, from Mount Abu in India he wrote a more personal letter to Mercedes concerning her suffering for love.

> I don't want you to be so intensely nervous, despondent and depressed, as to give up all hopes and drown yourself in sorrows to feel so miserable. . . . These difficulties and anxieties in life that one has to face are only apparent and transitory—mere passing phases that throw a temporary gloom and present a dismal aspect to everything for the time being, but like the clouds, they are all carried away by the winds of time, with the beautiful sunshine of happiness and bliss which alone exists behind all this, for ever.[54]

He encouraged Mercedes to continue working on the film of his life.

You <u>will</u> do it, and I <u>want</u> you to do it, even in spite of disappointments all around and in this very disturbed frame of mind, and even if Greta has gone away without seeing you. . . . Go to Sweden to see her, without fail. But at the present moment, my work is most important. . . . And it is quite possible that this film, if written with all the force of your soul and of the love you have for me, will bear results which will greatly enhance your future life and work. . . . So, dear Mercedes, do not brood over the clouds that are hovering over your head now and make your life gloomy.[55]

Exhilarated by her experience with Sorella Maria and encouraged by the advice of Meher Baba, Mercedes asked him if he thought she should try to visit Garbo in Sweden. He replied from Ahmednagar, India, on September 12, 1935, "Cable Greta but don't worry if unanswered." A month later he sent another cable to Mercedes: "Go Sweden. Love."[56] She took his advice. While anxiously awaiting a reply, she visited Eleanora von Mendelssohn, who lived in a castle near Salzburg, Austria. Other guests included Alice Astor, Iris Tree, Max Reinhardt, and Arturo Toscanini.

Several weeks after inviting herself to Sweden, Mercedes finally received a reply from Garbo that had first gone to Mercedes's home in California and then was forwarded to her in Paris. Garbo used the same words to greet her as Salka Viertel always used to describe Mercedes—"Black and White," which were the colors of clothes Mercedes preferred as well as the appearance Mercedes conveyed with her white skin, black hair, and ruby red lipstick.

It is clear in what Garbo writes that she did not initiate the invitation to Mercedes. In fact, Garbo's reply to Mercedes's request for a visit was cool, to say the least. She confessed that she was feeling very moody and disagreeable. Although she reluctantly agreed to meet Mercedes for dinner at Stockholm's Grand Hotel, she was quick to remind Mercedes that Mercedes had promised to leave Sweden after only one day. Garbo did not want to be obligated to her in any way.[57]

Not a particularly warm invitation, but at least the door was opened a crack for Mercedes to visit. Realizing her anxiety over meeting Garbo, Meher Baba cabled Mercedes at the Grand Hotel in Stockholm on October 19, 1935: "Cheer up, Dearest, be brave. am helping you. Love."[58]

In Stockholm, Mercedes and Garbo lounged together in the Royal Suite of the Grand Hotel, dined with the accompaniment of a soft string orchestra, toured the zoo, and attended a movie together. The next day, Garbo took her to stay at Tistad Castle with her friends, Count and Countess Wachmeister. They trudged the snow-covered hills on long walks and marched across plowed fields. One evening, after several rounds of schnapps in the library, they joined the Wachmeisters for an early Christmas dinner. Garbo presented her with a gift of a pair of stout rubber boots to better tramp the Swedish hills. Before she left Stockholm, Garbo took her to see the cold-water flat where she had been born. "I was very much moved," Mercedes wrote. "I was moved because it was her birthplace and also by the fact that she had brought me there to see it. I knew that such a gesture meant much to her. As we moved away neither of us spoke."[59]

Soon after, Meher Baba received a cable from Mercedes that she was leaving Sweden on November 2. He replied:

> Now that you have seen her, let it cheer you up to go on with the work of writing my story. . . . I know how you feel for the separation of Greta, I want you not to allow yourself to be too much taken up by that thought, for things are going to happen, as they already have, for the better. I know, for Greta and for you, both. So get yourself busy with some work, the studio work or any other that goes easy to you and keeps your mind engaged. Thinking and working on MY story would be BEST if you would just try to persevere.[60]

Mercedes "was moving in a dream within a dream."[61] She was happy. She was at peace. She believed that her relationship with Garbo had been restored. She was so enthralled that she composed three more poems for her Garbo collection.[62]

-1-

Your face is like a frail white
   violet.
Haunting wherever I go.
And your eyes are like deep
   blue violets.
Troubled by a dream of snow.
   Sweden. 1935[63]

-2-

There is holiness in ploughed land.
Waves of black earth being still.
Like a dark sea of barren
   dreams.

Yet, in this earth there is hope.
So, too, even in a dream.
And from earth and dreams
    will spring
Eternal flowering!
    Tistad 1935
    Sweden

    -3-

You, in your own land, I see
    you even now,
Watching strong oxen straining
    neath a plough.
Dark fields of mud fringed
    by brooding pine.
Far off a sea where water
    and land entwine.
Red barns, sharp winds, a
Nordic peasant's face;
A Swedish landscape
    melting into space.
While in your beauty and this
    land I see,
A deeply mystic, strange
    affinity.
    Tistad
    Sweden 1935

Although Mercedes may have thought the visit was idyllic, the truth was otherwise. Garbo's great talent for acting served her well. Soon after Mercedes left Sweden, Garbo confided in her friend Salka. "I have no lovers but I have troubles just the same. It is maybe from all the wrong done to my poor body. Mercedes has been here as you know by now. I took her to Tistad as I didn't know what else to do. She is more quiet than before but otherwise the same. She didn't see much of [Stockholm], I was afraid to let her stay there. I was a wreck after she went and I told her she must not write me. We had a sad farewell."[64]

Back in Hollywood, Mercedes could think of little else but Garbo. When she closed her eyes, she could picture so vividly the gentle hands that she yearned to have caressing her body. In one of her most personal and intimate poems, she told Garbo

I love your hands.
They make me think of sea gulls
    against the sky.
I cannot tell you why,
Except I feel their flight
    a fleeting thing,
Like the swiftness of a white
    bird on wing.
Then they make me think of mountains,
When we climbed your hands so held
    the rocks in their grasp,
I felt they had the whole great
    mountain in their clasp.
Then, too, they make me recall
    tender things.

The way I have seen them caress
    a lover.
And stretch out gently to
    greet a shower.
And once I saw you touch
    a wounded doe.
Surely the hands of Healers
    must touch so!
    Hollywood 1935[65]

With her renewed confidence in their future together, Mercedes returned to Hollywood and rented an estate on Bristol Avenue, near the homes of Joan Crawford, Barbara Stanwyck, and Jeanette MacDonald. Anticipating Garbo's moving in with her, she constructed a ten-foot-high privacy fence around the property with separate, private entrances for both her and Garbo. A huge, canopied bed with a magnificent view of the Sierra Nevada was positioned in Garbo's section of the estate.[66] In spite of all Mercedes had done, Garbo was not pleased. Because there was only a croquet lawn on the property and she wanted a tennis court and pool, she refused to move in. Eventually, she took a house nearby, greatly disappointing Mercedes.

Mercedes no doubt wondered whether she should have taken more seriously the advice offered her by Sorella Maria soon after she returned to Hollywood. "I'm worried about you. Not only because of your loneliness and your difficulties which pain me. But because of the state of slavery in which you live. Since she [Garbo] scorns all you've done for her out of the extreme generosity of your heart; since she acts so indifferent and obstinate in her silence; one must respect her way of being and what she wants. You in turn must become absolutely reserved. Otherwise, you would lack the dignity of your human conscience."[67]

Instead of heeding the advice, Mercedes quickly accepted a new assignment from Thalberg—to serve as a consultant for a screenplay of *Camille* for Garbo. She was thrilled to describe for him the earlier productions with Sarah Bernhardt, Eleonora Duse, and her former lovers Alla Nazimova and Eva Le Gallienne. All seemed to be going well until Thalberg suddenly caught pneumonia and died. Mercedes, who was out of town at the time of his death, returned to Hollywood and found herself fired. Hired in her place was Salka! When the final retakes were being shot at the end of 1936, Garbo complained to her old friend Count Wachtmeister, "We have to shoot retake after retake and are going to do some more in a couple of days. . . . Nothing new has happened apart from Mercedes wanting me to ring. But I am going to have to think about the matter first. Poor Mercedes—she has got an extraordinary ability to make people nervous. Even people who are not quite as unkind as me."[68]

Garbo may have expressed annoyance with Mercedes, but it did not prevent her from exploiting their friendship. She allowed and even encouraged Mercedes to shop for her shoes, place orders for clothes with her seamstress, and even search out a new house to rent when she returned to California. All Mercedes received in return were cool messages from her beloved, wishing Mercedes would find happiness and thanking her for doing some shopping for her.[69]

As Mercedes's frustrations accelerated, Sister Sorella Maria extended more advice. She was confused by Mercedes's attitude, because the last she had heard was that her meeting with Garbo in Stockholm had "led to a rapture of laughter—and dancing." Sensing that Mercedes suffered from a "passion of pity" for Garbo, she wrote, "Can you help her see that this accentuation of self-consciousness is destructive? . . . If your friend has no living faith, can you not help her accept her fate—and peace will come through helping the poor?"[70] And two months later, she wrote again. "I can pray that your friend Greta will come with you to Eremo—and find help and inspiration. . . . I know absolutely nothing about your friend—It was simply your 'passion of pity' which gave me a glimpse. . . . Do tell her that Sorella Maria's great light seems to bring us more and more to the <u>simplicity of service</u> as solution <u>of life's</u> problem."[71]

Certainly troubling Mercedes for most of 1937 and 1938 was Garbo's affair with the renowned classical conductor Leopold Stokowski.[72] They had met in February 1937 at a party hosted by Anita Loos, and for more than a year they were inseparable. In October, front-page headlines proclaimed "Divorce Rumor Links Garbo and Stokowski."[73] It appeared as if the conductor was divorcing his wife so that he could marry Garbo. Although Garbo denied the rumors, she left the door open for the future, claiming, "There will be no marriage for at least two years."[74] In December, they sailed together to Sweden where they stayed for more than a month. In late February, Garbo joined "Stoki" in Rome as they began a two-month tour of Europe, returning to Sweden in early May. She did not return to New York until October 7, 1938.

Mercedes was beside herself. Had she lost Garbo's affection totally? Had she lost it to a man? She had been invited by Sri Meher Baba to visit him in Cannes, France. In letter after letter to him she had expressed how dejected she would feel without Garbo, whom she would miss so terribly if she went to France. She may not have told him that she also felt she needed to be in the country so she could keep up with gossip and try to protect her interests as best she could. Baba urged her to come anyway and to stay for at least three months.[75]

Eventually, Mercedes did go, sailing on the SS *Normandie* along with Noel Coward. She realized, "At this time Baba had an influence on me." But she also realized, "I was pathetically seeking some kind of spiritual guidance and I blindly seized onto him."[76] She remained only a few days, however, catching the *Normandie* on its return trip. Indeed, she must have learned about the headlines that rumored a marriage between Garbo and Stoki. The very day of the headlines, October 20, she set sail for New York.[77]

Regardless of the loss she was feeling, as one of her poems reveals, Mercedes persisted with her devotion to Garbo and continued in her "state of slavery."

I love you because no
matter how wrong you are,
in your error you
are more right than
people who are right.
    Hollywood 1937[78]

9

"There Is No Other Way"

I n the mid-1930s, Mercedes had attended a dinner party where she met
the English mystic and philosopher Paul Brunton, who had only recently
published his book *A Search in Secret India.*[1] She was so intrigued with
him that she went out immediately, bought a copy, and began to study
his philosophy. She learned for the first time about Sri Ramana Maharshi,
a great sage in India who had become internationally renowned for both
his saintliness and his particular kind of yoga called "self inquiry" in which
a person meditates and focuses continuous attention on the feeling "I am"
in order to recognize his or her identity.[2]

Born in 1879 in a little village in southern India, Maharshi had gone at
the age of twelve to live with his uncle after his father died. At age sixteen
he had heard a family relative talk about the holy hill of Arunachala. The
very name served as a sort of magic spell on him; he knew he must some-
day visit. Soon after, he became fascinated by a book about Hindu saints
and decided to emulate their spirit of renunciation and devotion. He began meditating daily.

When he was seventeen years old, he suddenly was seized by a fear of
death, even though he was in excellent health. He felt he was dying. He
began to think of what he should do. He held his breath, closed his lips and
eyes, and lay down stretching his limbs out as if he were dead. He reasoned
that his body was dead and would be burned and reduced to ashes but that
the death of his body did not mean the death of his soul. The body may
die, he concluded, but the spirit that transcends it would not die. His fear

of death miraculously disappeared. Subsequently, he soon set off for Aruna-chala, where he became a monk, eventually living in a cave.

His fame quickly spread. Crowds came, asking him spiritual questions and requesting his advice. One early follower was the Englishman F. H. Humphrys, who had traveled to India on business. After meeting Ramana Maharshi, he described him as "a man beyond description in his expression of dignity, gentleness, self-control and calm strength of conviction." In a letter he sent to a friend back in England, he wrote, "You can imagine nothing more beautiful than his smile. . . . It is strange what a change it makes in one to have been in his Presence!"[3]

Some visitors to Arunachala used to stay for several days; others settled there. They would begin arriving as early as five o'clock in the morning when there would be the chanting of Vedic hymns. After breakfast at seven, Ramana would walk about for an hour on the holy hill. At eight, he would sit for meditation along with the visitors. Guests would sit at his feet. Nobody spoke. They would gaze into his eyes for thirty minutes or more. He would not speak to them unless they expressed some questions. Then, he would give simple, direct, short and clear replies. The midday meal would be over by eleven. After that, till two o'clock in the afternoon, there was no activity. Then the crowd would begin to arrive for more meditation and discussion, after which Ramana would go again for a stroll. That would be followed by more chanting of Vedic hymns. Supper would be over by seven-thirty.

Thomas Berry explains in his *Religions of India* that yoga

> is intensely concerned with the human condition, how man is to manage the human condition, to sustain his spiritual reality in the midst of life's turmoil, and to discipline his inner awareness until he attains liberation. . . . Yoga can be considered among the most intensely felt and highly developed of those spiritual disciplines that enable man to cope with the tragic aspects of life. . . . The human condition, unacceptable, must be transcended. . . . What Yoga proposed was a technique of spiritual development that would enable man to discover his true nature on a higher plane of existence wherein he would attain freedom from the restrictive forces that bound him to the world.[4]

Later in his book, Berry suggests, "Yoga begins with the experience of sorrow *(dukkha)*. This is the given, the point of departure, the basic, irrefutable fact of human existence, that which makes supposedly human life inhuman."[5]

Mercedes, who had certainly experienced sorrow and turmoil, was instantly drawn to Ramana Maharshi's approach to spirituality. She had moved to Hollywood seven years earlier with high hopes of becoming a screenwriter for the stars. Her dream had never materialized, and now she was virtually unemployed. Her future in the film industry looked bleak. Although she received monthly alimony from her ex-husband, she could not count on him for any kind of emotional support. She had thought her reunion with Garbo in Sweden in 1935 was a sign of future happiness, but she was mostly being ignored by the woman she loved. The messages she was receiving from both Sister Sorella Maria and from Sri Meher Baba were not helping. They both sympathized with Mercedes and the challenges she was facing, but they did not provide any concrete ideas that would help. She finally concluded that Sri Meher Baba's constant urging that she should concentrate on filming his life story was selfish and not really speaking to Mercedes's needs. Also upsetting was his insistence that she renounce her life and move to his ashram in India for five years. She desperately hungered for new, specific ways to "cope with the tragic aspects" of her life.

She purchased Ramana Maharshi's *Truth Revealed* and read it ceaselessly from cover to cover. The sections that meant the most to her she marked with a red pencil.

The mind must be used both to illuminate the path and to destroy itself, once this purpose is effected.

Know thus that the quest for this ego amounts to wholesale renunciation.

Clear away all mental dispositions, by steady and incessant meditation in the Heart.

The Fire of Consciousness is he who having consciously eliminated all the objects of the five senses, and having realised the Self, abides firmly in the One Reality. Say that he is the Wielder of the Thunderbolt, the Death of death, being Valiant Slayer of death itself.[6]

What attracted her was that Ramana Maharshi provided precise techniques she could follow, including exercises to achieve restraint, spiritual discipline, posture, breath control, concentration, and meditation. The more she read, the more she came to realize that one day she would have to visit Sri Ramana Maharshi in person.

It was to her good fortune that Mercedes attended a party in March 1938 hosted by Bernadine Szold Fritz at his estate overlooking Beverly Hills. She met Hindu dancer Ram Gopal, often described as "the Indian Nijinsky."[7] Born in south India, Ram had grown up in an educated household where he had heard countless tales of ancient Indian legends and folklore. Eventually, he concluded his dance studies and toured Burma, Malaya, Hong Kong, Singapore, and Tokyo, presenting dance recitals of ancient legends to recorded authentic Indian music. He made such a sensation when he arrived in Hollywood that the famous impresario Sol Hurok arranged a season for him in New York. In the 1950s he was featured in several Hollywood films, including *Purple Plain* with Gregory Peck and *Elephant Walk* with Elizabeth Taylor and Dana Andrews. In 1999 Queen Elizabeth II conferred upon him the Order of the British Empire.

Even at this first meeting, Mercedes and Ram discussed personal matters. She told him of her interest in Eastern religions and how she had been corresponding with Meher Baba. Ram was not impressed. He thought Baba was "a small man spiritually, and although he meant well, he was too interested in self-promotion."[8] Ram had met Ramana Maharshi, who lived only seventy miles from his home in India, and he felt confident of the man's sincerity, since his elder sister was a great devotee of his. Mercedes also confessed to her new friend that Garbo "dominates my life. In her I have found a father, a mother—everything." Ram knew as he left the party that he and Mercedes would be friends for life. "She was beautiful," he remarked, "with black short hair, wonderful eyes. She returned my aura . . . very warm."[9]

Because of her lifelong interest in dance and her newfound attraction to Ram Gopal, Mercedes booked a ticket to his performance at the Wiltshire Theater in Hollywood. She was more than captivated by his artistry. His body—so lithe, slender, smooth, and effeminate. His hands—so gentle and expressive. Witnessing Isadora Duncan and Tamara Karsavina dancing had been sensual experiences, watching them "soar away and beyond the body into that mysterious realm of rhythm through the gateway of motion."[10] Now there was Ram Gopal. He embodied all of their special, seductive magic and reflected an Oriental androgyny.[11] She was thrilled to hear him explain why he became a dancer. "My solar plexus, the pit of my stomach turned me to dance. There was something in me, a magnetic pull to dance," he confided. "I could feel terrific vibrations through my feet and my whole body would become plastic."[12] Mercedes and Ram soon became soul mates.

When Ram invited her to join him in Poland the summer of 1938 as he prepared for an engagement in Warsaw, she jumped at the opportunity, thinking she would then head for India in the autumn. Although she was disappointed in Sri Meher Baba, she knew she would always be welcome to visit him in India. Only the year before, he had written, "You must come to India next year as soon as you can, and if possible Greta to come with you. I am with you. You have my love."[13] She did ask Garbo, who was in Sweden with Stoki, to join her, but to no avail. Garbo turned down the offer.

In a brief note, Garbo pointed out that since she was soon returning to America, she would not be able to see Mercedes in Europe. Although Garbo expressed some interest in accompanying Mercedes on her travels, she declared that she needed to limit her appearances in public until she was no longer in headlines. She preferred not to discuss personal matters, since this was always a struggle for her.[14] Mercedes may have hoped to learn of some of those personal struggles, especially if they had concerned Garbo's affair with Stoki, but nothing more was mentioned.

Before arriving in Poland, Mercedes and Ram agreed to meet in Paris. "Paris will rub some of its magic off on you," she wrote. "I shall be your guide and introduce you to the right people, whose minds and arts and talents in literature, painting and music, will make you realise [sic] that Paris is the greatest of all western cities for its culture and beauty."[15] During those few days in Paris, Mercedes introduced Ram to Gertrude Stein, Alice B. Toklas, Picasso, and Carl Van Vechten.

The two of them then took a train to Poland, where they stayed for several weeks at a beautiful estate in Komorza that was owned by Ram's lover, Polish nobleman Alexander Janta. The letters that Ram later sent to Mercedes reveal the affection and intimacy they shared at the time. "I remember you so vividly," he wrote. "Your enormous dark eyes that laughed and cried, and then grew distant as you spoke to me of your thoughts and sufferings and ambitions—and we spoke of so many things of the spirit, and the beauty of Love."[16] A few months later, he wrote again.

> I see you lolling in the Sun of Komorza. And our excursions in the forest. Our trip to Warsaw which was very lovely—just you and I. And then dear Poznan! remember how we went and asked for Tea and the damned waiter served us up with Vodka! How desperate we were and didn't we swear!? And you loathed the buildings and architecture of that town didn't you—because they were so Teutonic? Those little intimate talks in Komorza in our bed rooms, exchanged confidences, the games of tennis with dozens of little blond babies dashing all over the place and throwing tennis balls everywhere—but to us! Ah—I wonder, will we ever be there again some time in this Life.[17]

They basked in the sunshine, paddled canoes down a nearby stream, strolled naked together through the gardens, and talked of Isadora Duncan and Garbo. At one point, Mercedes turned to Ram and confided, "What a pity you are not a woman because then I'd have sex with you."[18] Their intimate talks and exchanges of confidences must have strengthened Mercedes as she prepared to embark on her visit to Sri Ramana Maharshi, which she later called "the greatest experience of my life."[19]

Visiting Paris was usually a highlight for Mercedes. But during her stop-over this time on her way to India the entire city was in darkness because of the impending war. It was an unpredictable period throughout Europe. Earlier in the year, Hitler had overthrown the Austrian government and had annexed Austria into Germany. During the weeks Mercedes had been loll-ing in the sun with Ram in Poland, Hitler had demanded that the Sude-tenland, an area of Czechoslovakia populated by 3.5 million Germans, be annexed as well. Most Americans were rushing out of Paris and out of Europe. Mercedes's own hotel emptied out except for herself and Marlene Dietrich. On September 29, the Munich Pact was signed, whereby the Al-lies agreed to Hitler's demands while he pledged he would make no more claims of land. That night when Mercedes was standing in front of her bank on the Place de la Concorde in Paris, newspaper headlines proclaimed "Peace in Our Time." Even though people danced for joy in the streets, Mercedes felt uneasy and apprehensive about the future.

She had booked passage to Ceylon, accompanied by Consuelo Sides, wife of Alfredo Sides, who had worked with Mercedes many years earlier on the musical *What Next!* They intended to go directly to where Ramana Maharshi lived, but when the ship docked at Bombay, Mercedes received a message from Meher Baba, begging them to visit him at his ashram in Ahmednagar, about two hours from Bombay. It proved a mistake. Although she had been promised a room or cabin of her own, she wound up having to sleep with all the other women in a large dormitory. The heat was intense, and the women snored. The next day, she learned that Meher Baba assumed that she was planning to remain for five years. When she specified that she was leaving that day and that she really had come to India to see Ramana Maharshi and not him, he made no comment. Although he was friendly when they departed and even kissed Mercedes good-bye, she never heard from him again.

After several days of touring together around the country and visiting the Taj Mahal, Benares, the caves of Ellora and Ajanta, and finally Pondi-cherry, Mercedes set off alone to rendezvous with Ram Gopal at his fam-ily estate, Torquay Castle, in Bangalore. Once she was rested from her trav-els, she proceeded to the holy hill of Arunachala. When she first entered the darkened hall, about all she could see was Ramana Maharshi sitting in Buddha posture on a couch in the corner of the room. He was naked ex-cept for a loincloth.

As he sat there he seemed like a statue, and yet something extra-ordinary emanated from him. I had a feeling that on some invisible level I was receiving spiritual shocks from him although his gaze was not directed at me. He did not seem to be looking at anything, and yet I felt he could see and was conscious of the whole world. . . . After I had been sitting for several hours . . . he moved his head and looked directly down at me. . . . I can only say that at this second I felt my inner being raised to a new level—as if, suddenly, my state of con-sciousness was lifted to a much higher degree. . . . Perhaps in this split second I was no longer my human self but the Self.[20]

Mercedes sat in the hall with him for three days and three nights. Some-times he spoke to her, other times he was silent. To many of her questions he replied that she should not become too intellectual—just meditate. At one point, he placed his hand on her right breast and said, "Here lies the heart—the dynamic, spiritual heart. Learn to find the Self in it."[21] Finally, warning her that there was soon going to be a war breaking out, he ad-vised her to return to America. When she published her autobiography two decades later she dedicated it to "Bhagavan Ramana Maharshi, the only completely egoless, world-detached, and pure being I have ever known."

When Elsa Maxwell interviewed her a few years later and asked her about religion, she said she had started life as a Roman Catholic, but that "if I had to be anything, I would be a Buddhist." She was greatly impressed with how the Indian culture and religion empowered women so that they were more involved in politics than American women. "How secluded our women [in America] really are! How untouched by the realities! It's laziness, really," she insisted.[22] Ram Gopal remembers how Mercedes contrasted the two reli-gions: "The Roman Catholic Church wanted Mercedes to conform to their image and truth. But Buddhism allowed her to find herself. She wanted to be the truth that she found and saw, not what someone else had found."[23]

Back in Hollywood from her long sojourn in Europe and Asia, Mercedes tried to resume her relationship with Garbo. Because they were both con-firmed vegetarians, Mercedes came up with the plan to invite Garbo to accompany her for an afternoon at the home of her new friend Gayelord Hauser, a young, dashing, handsome man who had opened one of the first health food stores in Chicago and who had promised to prepare a delicious vegetable lunch.[24] He lived with his lover, equally handsome Frey Brown, high up in the hills behind Beverly Hills in a lovely home with a swim-ming pool. Mercedes thought her ploy worked; Garbo seemed enchanted. All four of them had a delightful afternoon, dining, swimming, and play-ing badminton.

Her scheme backfired, however; Garbo and Gayelord were absolutely enamored of each other. If Mercedes had feared Stoki's interference, that was nothing compared with what she now had to face. Gayelord became Garbo's most "ardent admirer, 'protector' and friend—most loving friend."[25] He became her bridge to the outside world, screening all her contacts. On one occasion when Mercedes was trying desperately to reach Garbo, he wrote to her, "The lady went through one of her 'depression weeks,' and hasn't been able to do a thing, which may explain why she has not called you again. . . . Do take my advice and not write to her address, as that is one of her 'pet peeves.'"[26] Gayelord took credit for improving Garbo's health. When they met, he wrote, "she was suffering from overtiredness and insomnia, and was in danger of anemia." But with his weaning her away from strict vegetarianism and coaxing her back to "intelligent eating . . . she quickly regained her energy. . . . Many people congratulated us both on the 'new' Garbo."[27]

Garbo visited Gayelord often. They attended parties together, went on long walks together, and even traveled together in January 1940 to New York where they were spotted lunching at the St. Regis Hotel, dining at either the posh "21" or the Cotillion Room of the Pierre, attending gallery previews at the Metropolitan Museum of Art, strolling through the streets of the city. In February, Garbo, Gayelord, and his lover drove south along the eastern seaboard, flew from Miami to Nassau, and boarded the *Southern Cross* for a Caribbean cruise. Even though Gayelord was committed to his partner, rumors began. Hedda Hopper announced, "Now that Garbo and Gayelord Hauser are motoring through the State of Maryland, those marriage rumors are again being revived."[28] Mercedes knew the rumors were false this time, but they were still grating to read. What was worse was realizing that she had made the introduction and now she was being left out in the cold.

At about the same time that she was suffering from the Garbo–Gayelord affair, she was reintroduced to Ona Munson. They had first met seven years earlier when Mercedes and Garbo dropped by the home of director Ernst Lubitsch, who was entertaining Ona. Thirteen years younger than Mercedes, she had danced in New York as a child, performed in vaudeville, and appeared on Broadway in the musical *No, No, Nanette* in 1925. She was the first person ever to sing "You're the Cream in My Coffee" in the 1928 musical *Hold Everything!* One thing in common between her and Mercedes was that both had had romantic affairs with Alla Nazimova. Ona's, however, had been only four years earlier when she played Regina to Alla's Mrs. Alving in Ibsen's *Ghosts*. At the time Mercedes and Ona met, Munson was the talk of the town for her portrayal of the voluptuous Belle Watling in *Gone with the Wind*. But what really drew them together was their mutual interest in yoga and spiritualism.

For some reason, Mercedes gives Ona rather short coverage in her published autobiography. In an earlier draft, however, she remarked that Ona "often came to my house . . . she came many weekends to stay with me. . . .When she started shooting [films for Republic Studios] she often came from the studio directly to my house and spent the night."[29]

While Garbo and Gayelord were cavorting on their cruise, Mercedes returned to New York to attend an exhibition of her sister Rita's clothes sponsored by the Museum of Costume Art, now part of the Metropolitan Museum of Art.[30] Among the items exhibited were Venetian needlepoint lace blouses with high standing collars, more than forty cream-colored and black mantillas of Chantilly lace, twenty-six pairs of ancient velvet and satin culottes, fourteen nightgowns with Milanese and Valencienne lace, three shoe trunks of Russian leather containing thirty-four pairs of shoes, antique fans, and an umbrella with the name "Rita" set in diamonds on top of the stick. Arranged by Irene Lewisohn, Aline Bernstein, and Polaire Weissman, the exhibit drew three thousand people when it opened on March 12, 1940, and police had to be called in to prevent people from touching the clothes. Frank Crowninshield, former editor of *Vanity Fair*, opened the exhibit and subsequently published a lengthy, illustrated tribute in the magazine.[31]

Mercedes received several letters from Ona while she was in New York that reveal the depth of Ona's love for her. "Darling, darling, darling—I miss you so terribly," she wrote on February 20, 1940. "It just doesn't seem right to be here [in Los Angeles] without you." She then discusses the new duplex she had just rented for herself and her mother. "We are now on different floors with completely separate quarters and entrances so that you can visit me any time of day or night without even being seen. I absolutely <u>adore</u> you!"[32] In a letter six days later, Ona reported an incident that had just occurred when she went dancing at Ciro's. Marlene Dietrich and Erich von Stroheim entered the hall and kept staring at her. "Erich's eyes really popped out and he said very loudly, '[B]ut it just can't be the same girl [as in *Gone with the Wind*].'" She ended the letter, "Your absence is a terrific void in my life & I long to hold you in my arms and pour my love into you." A few weeks later she returned to Ciro's, and this time she wrote that Marlene "turned the eyes of everyone on me until I blushed up to the roots of my hair. She stared continuously & I got so uncomfortable I had to leave." Mercedes must have expressed fear that her old flame, Marlene, was making overtures to date Ona. A few days later, Ona tried to calm her down.

"Darling I'm amazed at you even thinking such a thing as regards Marlene. I knew it was laid in my lap the very first night I saw her because she was so obvious. . . . I thought it would amuse you, not worry you." She tried to reassure Mercedes that she was "not interested in any chi-chi with Marlene or anyone else."[33] Still another time she wrote, "I kiss your dear face all over, every little crevice. Please my sweet, rest in my love because it is all there for you."[34] In a Christmas letter she wrote several years later, Ona acknowledged having "shared the deepest spiritual moment that life brings to human beings" and having "created an entity as surely as though [we] had conceived and borne a child."[35]

Their relationship, however, was fraught with problems. Mercedes doubted Munson's sincerity and faithfulness and accused her of still being interested in a woman referred to in letters as "Dorothy A". Ona argued, "Every single thread that held me [to Dorothy] has been broken. I actually don't want her as a friend. . . . How strange that you don't believe in me. . . . I have no desire for any one other than you and you can absolutely depend on that."[36] Mercedes's doubts and questions seem particularly out of place. After all, she was still pining for Garbo.

Still another thorn was the status of Mercedes's career; it was practically nonexistent. Garbo and Dietrich were at the height of their careers and Ona was turning heads, but Mercedes's was fast dimming. Ona kept comforting her and telling her to "please get that thought out of your head that you're a failure."[37]

Within a few months, their relationship was over. Ona corresponded with Mercedes for the next couple of years and always noted her continuing affection. In January 1942, for instance, she wrote, "I am glad also that you have been able to wash the bitterness away. . . . I have never changed, even in those times, in my feeling for you, and I never will."[38] Except for one birthday celebration for Ona in 1942, they did not see each other again for a decade. At one point in the mid-1940s, Ona resumed her relationship with Dorothy A.[39] A few years later, she married Russian artist and designer Eugene Berman. As she tried to explain to Mercedes back in 1941, "I think of you always with great love. . . . My only reason for not seeing you is due to circumstances in my life."[40] Circumstances, indeed. First, Ona abandoned her for another woman and then for a man. Ram Gopal saw it coming. "It's too bad," he said, "but a lot of homosexuals and lesbians come and go. Once the sex is over they are gone. This was true of Ona and Mercedes."[41]

Six months after the bombing of Pearl Harbor on December 7, 1941, Congress established the Office of War Information (OWI) to control the content and imagery of war messages. The main functions of the OWI were to undertake campaigns to enhance public understanding of the war at home and abroad; to coordinate government information activities; and to handle liaison with the press, radio, and motion pictures. In effect, the OWI was charged with selling the war. One of their decisions was to establish *Victory,* a weekly propaganda magazine.

Mercedes applied for an editorial job. One reason she was attracted to the position was that another editor was the highly respected Frances Keene. She had published translations from the original Italian of works by Cesare Pavese and Luigi Pirandello. She also had edited an anthology of writings by anti-Fascist Italians and exiles, *Neither Liberty nor Bread.*

Before hiring Mercedes, however, the FBI questioned her at length. The interviewer

> came up with a question about John Colton and dug up the time I had shared a house with him when I first went to Hollywood. He seemed disturbed that I had lived in a house with a man without being married to him. We discussed this matter at length. He then said, with rather an uneasy air, "It seems to me on looking through these pages, that you have a great many men friends who are not on the level sexually." I thought this a quaint and original way of describing homosexuality. I laughed. He continued, "This is not a laughing matter, and now that we are on the subject, how would you describe yourself, speaking, of course, purely sexually?" He blew his nose again and looked embarrassed. I was about to get angry when I remembered Rita's instructions to me when I was a child: "whenever in a difficult situation, handle it with humour." I thought quickly. Quite indifferently, I said, "Oh, I am ambidextrous and androgynous. A sort of combination of both." He leaned across the table and shouted, "You are what?" I repeated what I had said. He turned to the secretary and asked, "Can you spell these words?" She said she could not and did not even know what they meant. "Spell them for her," he commanded. "I'm afraid not," I said. "I am not here to give the government spelling lessons."[42]

Mercedes ultimately accepted the job, in part because she had no offers for work in the film industry. Like many writers who had moved to Hollywood from New York—Robert Sherwood, Elmer Rice, William Faulkner—she had been lured by money and the hope to make her mark in this new and booming medium. The "talkies" that had just begun two years earlier had forced the studio heads to hire writers who could supply dialogue. As film historians Larry Ceplair and Steven Englund point out,

"No matter that movie writing was downgraded by the eastern literati; the challenge of celluloid captured many writers' imaginations."[43]

But Mercedes had not counted on the complications from studio story departments. Unlike playwriting, screenplays were written by committees and not by individuals. Writers existed not to create and prepare original stories but to adapt properties purchased by the studios. "The writers who lasted in Hollywood," Ceplair and Englund concluded, "learned how to do their best with whatever was thrown at them while at the same time removing (as much as possible) their ego investment in the script itself.... The writer's survival in the motion picture production process demanded this ability."[44] Clearly, Mercedes did not fit this mold.

Other challenges faced her as well. Friends warned her that since most of the producers and directors were Jewish, no one would hire her because she had a German housekeeper, Anna Nehler. Although she was determined to stand by Anna, she recognized that even some of her friends were shunning her. One afternoon when she drove up to her house after shopping, she saw fire engines in front of the house and smoke pouring out of the garage. Someone, she concluded, had waited until she had driven away and then tried to torch the house with Anna inside.[45]

Because of her Spanish background, Mercedes was particularly concerned about the outcome of the Spanish Civil War, which had erupted in 1936. She was an ardent Loyalist, supporting the Republican government in its resistance to Franco and his Fascism. Even though the official policy of the United States was one of neutrality, she did not hesitate in attending the occasional "Sunday at Salka's," a literary salon hosted by Salka Viertel for left-wing artistic and literary conversation. Martin Dies, chair of what was soon to become the infamous House Committee on Un-American Activities, condemned these meetings. In August 1938 he announced that his committee would be traveling to Hollywood to investigate communistic activities in the film colony, and the following year, he referred to the motion picture industry as a "hotbed of communism."[46] Soon after, a member of the California legislature announced that he intended to launch an investigation of "Reds in the movies."[47]

Even before the United States entered the war, the film industry had been affected by political developments. Hoping to boost ticket sales at the box office, several hundred movie celebrities sought to illustrate their loyalty to the United States by attending a mass meeting in 1936 and pledging to campaign against Fascism, Nazism, Communism, "and all other dangerous isms."[48] (Could it be that they also implied lesbianism?)

What did all this mean to the studio bosses? Leo C. Rosten pointed out

European politics cannot be ignored by an industry which, as a whole, derived from thirty-five to forty percent of its revenues from abroad (before the war broke out), nor by individual producers and studios that got as high as fifty percent of their income from outside the United States. Every time a nation was crushed under the juggernaut of Berlin or Rome, Hollywood felt the blow in its pocketbook. No other American product was strangled so quickly and automatically by the conquering regimes.[49]

Mercedes could certainly see that the industry was becoming more conservative, leaving little room for such an independent thinker as herself.

But clearly another reason she accepted the editorial position with the *Victory* bulletin was because it meant being back in New York, at least temporarily, where Garbo was then living most of the time. Mercedes longed to be near her even if she could not see her in person as much as she wanted. Her former lover, Alla Nazimova, wrote her a pointed letter shortly after she arrived in New York. "Well, darling, keep busy and I hope you feel happier than when you were here and take the advise [*sic*] of an old woman: find happiness and purpose within yourself, don't rely on others to bring it to you,—it does not work in the end. Sounds trite but I found it to be true. Love. Alla."[50]

When she moved back to New York to accept the *Victory* job, she moved into a little room in the Hotel Ritz Tower.

> The manager, Charlie Macauley, was a delightful, much loved man. Many of the people in the hotel then were there only because of him—especially the theatrical people and other artists. He never pressed any artist for a bill. . . . I could only afford one room, but he gave me a lovely one on the sixteenth floor overlooking the East River when I told him I always loved to see the sun rise. He redecorated it for me and from a bedroom he made it into a bedroom–sitting room and painted it the colour I wanted, and added built-in bookcases. Ruth Chatterton was living there then and Greta took a room there at Christmas time and stayed several months. Everyone who lived there felt at home with Charlie and we spoke of the hotel as "The Old Homestead" and our "club."[51]

Since all the articles published in *Victory* were anonymous, assessing Mercedes's contribution is impossible. One exception is an essay she saved in her papers, "Robinson Jeffers: A Poet in the Classic Tradition." Mercedes recorded in longhand below the title of the article that she was the author.[52]

Several years earlier, soon after she had been dismissed by Thalberg for not cooperating on the film of Rasputin, she had driven up the coast to Jeffers's home in Carmel. In this one-page essay written in memory of that meeting, she saluted him as the "epic poet of America," one who "has more nearly approached the Greek ideals of artistic expression than any other American poet in contemporary times."

Another essay probably written by Mercedes featured her old friend Malvina Hoffman. Calling her "one of the world's most distinguished sculptors," Mercedes describes the exhibit presented in the Hall of Fame of Chicago's Natural History Museum of 101 of Hoffman's sculptures "depicting the principal racial types of mankind." A museum official was quoted as saying, "If the visitors to the hall will receive the impression that race prejudice is merely the outcome of ignorance and will leave it with their sympathy for mankind deepened and strengthened and with their interest in mankind stimulated and intensified, our efforts will have fulfilled their purpose."[53] Although these two essays may not seem to be pieces of war propaganda, they were intended to boost morale among readers and help sell the war by promoting the value of American artists.

Mercedes did not remain with the magazine very long. No evidence exists to show why she left. It could be that what she wanted to write was not seen as strong enough propaganda for selling the war; it could be that she needed a position with a higher salary; it could be that she expected some kind of byline, or at least some recognition for her contributions.

In any case, by 1943 Mercedes had jumped ship and become an associate editor for *Tomorrow* magazine.[54] The magazine's founding editor, Eileen J. Garrett, was known as one of the most respected mediums of the day, recognizing the need for scientific as well as open-minded investigation of paranormal phenomena. Because of the new position, Mercedes decided to move back to New York permanently. There was no reason to stay in Hollywood. She bought a new apartment at 471 Park Avenue where she could see the rooms in the Ritz Towers nearby where Garbo lived. She claims that in spite of the wartime blackout regulations, the two women would "signal to each other at night with lighted candles."[55] Given that the relationship between Mercedes and Garbo was strained, it seems unlikely that this romantic signaling ever took place. And even if Mercedes had wanted to, she had to know that Gayelord was probably in the room with Garbo at the time.

One of Mercedes's proudest achievements was the March 1943 issue of *Tomorrow.* Under her personal supervision, it was devoted to "looking southward" to Latin American authors and issues. As Eileen Garrett proclaimed in the editorial, "On the southern continent a democratic people are seeking to use their great potentials. . . . It is not too soon to devote our efforts towards that understanding we must have to pave the way to making ourselves intelligible each to the other."[56] The issue contains articles about Haiti, Argentina, Brazil, and Peru, as well as reviews of several new books on Latin America. In addition, Mercedes supplied a review of Dudley Fitts's *An Anthology of Contemporary Latin-American Poetry*.

She also provided the English translation for the poem "Seventh of November: Ode to a Day of Victory." Written by Chilean poet Pablo Neruda, it commemorates the fifth anniversary of the defense of Madrid during the Spanish Civil War, as well as the twenty-fourth anniversary of the foundation of the Soviet Union. A fiercely pro-Communist work, the poem reads in part:

> Seventh of November, where are you now?
> Where are your flaming petals? Comrade,
> where is your song? Arise! Lift him who has fallen.
> Where blood flows,
> across the poor flesh of men the laurel blooms
> and will create a hero.
>   And you again, Union,
> you again, sister of the peoples of the world.
> Pure and Soviet Nation, your seed returns to you
> full, like foliage bursting from the soil!
> . . . .
> I salute you, Soviet Union, with humility
> on this day; I am a writer and a poet.[57]

When this issue of *Tomorrow* first appeared, Mercedes was so pleased she sent autographed copies to Eleanor Roosevelt and Vice President Wendell L. Wilkie. A few years later, however, during the McCarthy hearings, she worried that she might be called to testify before the House Un-American Activities Committee and denied a passport because of her political leanings.[58]

Besides her new editorial position, she was hired by National Concert and Artists Corporation to present lectures around the country. Others on the circuit included Lillian Gish, Guthrie McClintic, and Lee Simonson. Two of her major lectures—"New Trends in Art and Literature" and "Friends and Celebrities"—cannot be found, but a copy of her shorter, ten-minute lecture, "The Challenge of a Changing World" has been preserved.[59] She quotes observations that Sri Ramana Maharshi made about the changing world back in 1938 when she visited him in India.

Millions of people will feel such an instantaneous change within themselves, that it will seem that their entire past life will drop away from them. They will, in a manner, be re-born. . . . There will shortly be a great world chaos in which millions of people will be killed and die. These people must die because in this present life they are not yet ready for the enormous transition this age will see. They must die in order to re-incarnate into the new Era and come back with a spiritual vision in place of the old materialistic vision.

Mercedes believed that "we are on the brink—in the doorway, so to speak, of an *absolutely* new world" and urged her audiences to be ready for the changes. She insisted that Christianity and all other religions that had sanctioned wars, bloodshed, hypocrisy, and lies must also vanish. "Surely no one who witnesses our crumbling world can fail to see that Christianity has failed. *Christianity has failed,*" she insisted, *"but Christ has not."* Audiences must have been a little taken aback by her assault on Christianity, but at least she managed to do better by her praise for Christ himself. Unfortunately, there is no evidence available concerning the success of her lectures or even how many she presented.

Once back in New York, Mercedes resumed revising one of her plays, *The Mother of Christ,* using the new title of *The Leader.* This time, however, she asked her old friend Natacha Rambova to assist her. She had known Natacha for many years, having first seen her dancing a tango with Rudolph Valentino at a benefit for Actors' Equity. After studying dance in Paris, Natacha had joined a ballet company that toured the United States. She had wound up teaching ballet in Los Angeles where she had met Alla Nazimova and subsequently designed the star's film versions of both *Camille* and *Salome.* After her divorce from Valentino, she had moved to New York where she opened a dress shop, designing all the clothes herself. For several years, Mercedes and Natacha had studied together Eastern and ancient religions, astrology, yoga, and psychic phenomena.

The contract that they signed stated they were "to share equally in any and all profits and benefits which may accrue from our play now titled The Leader—a modern abstract adaptation originally conceived and written by me from your original biblical play The Mother of Christ."[60] Unfortunately, there is no known copy of this adaptation.

They had managed to persuade Robert Edmond Jones to design the set. He felt the time was right for a religious play. After all, *The Song of Bernadette* had been a recent film success and there were reportedly eight other religious pictures being made in Hollywood. Encouraged by Jones's enthusiasm, Mercedes wrote to Igor Stravinsky, asking whether he would compose original music for the production. In their correspondence, Stravinsky must have felt that it would be difficult to cast a known actress in the role of Mary and suggested that Mercedes use some kind of a light in place of the character. Mercedes objected.

> When we raise the money we can at once look for an unknown woman, someone with great simplicity, beauty and feeling. . . . As I wish to make the part of Mary extremely human as well as divine, I feel it must be played by a woman and by no other means. The last speech of the play I am going to rewrite and bring it up to our time so that Mary can address the mothers of today who are in the audience. . . . Bobbie said the other day that he had such a longing to work on something which would "encompass beauty, inspiration and feeling" such as this would. . . . The important thing I want from you is a letter stating that you are willing to compose the music.[61]

A month later, Stravinsky replied.

> This provisional project (not definitive, as you said) that you have sent me, I will sign gladly but for only one condition: you modify your piece in regards to the role of the Holy Virgin, as I requested it of you when the question of my participation (composition music for your piece) came up. My opinion in this respect remains the same and you now must make a decision of which will determine my acceptance or refusal to compose the music. Therefore I await your decision. I kiss you.[62]

There is no record of how Mercedes and Stravinsky settled their difference of opinion, but no production ever materialized. She had sent the script to Ona, but the actress was not interested.

This failure must have been particularly frustrating, since her former lover, Eva Le Gallienne, was starring on Broadway in a successful revival of Chekhov's *The Cherry Orchard* and was making plans to establish a new classical repertory theater with Margaret Webster and Cheryl Crawford. The actress's name was recognized throughout the country. Not at all the case for Mercedes. In spite of her publications, her years in Hollywood, and her traveling on the lecture circuit, she was almost unknown.

Mercedes was hoping that by returning to New York she might somehow resume her relationship with Garbo. By the time she arrived, however, her "beloved" had begun a new liaison. In January 1942, Gayelord Hauser escorted Garbo to an exclusive dress shop owned by Valentina Schlee.

According to reports, Valentina's husband, George Schlee, walked into a fitting room where Garbo was trying on a dress and discovered her nude. It was the beginning of another love affair.[63]

Born in St. Petersburg, Russia, George had met Valentina in Sevastopol when he was in the army and fled with her to Athens as the Russian Revolution was winding down. Eventually, they married and emigrated to the United States where she opened up their exclusive dress shop at the Savoy Plaza Hotel on Fifth Avenue in 1928. Ironically, among the first people the Schlees met in New York were Mercedes and her then-husband, Abram Poole. Valentina designed a black dress with white Russian embroidery for Mercedes, and Abram painted two portraits of Valentina.[64] During the next ten years, Valentina designed dresses for such artists as Gloria Swanson, Norma Shearer, Joan Fontaine, Paulette Goddard, and Rosalind Russell and had her gowns featured in such Broadway productions as *Idiot's Delight* and *The Philadelphia Story.* In 1940 the Schlees purchased a building just off Fifth Avenue as the new home of Valentina Gowns.

Soon after he met Garbo, George initiated a ménage à trois and explained to his wife that he loved Garbo "but she will never want to get married, and anyway you and I have so much in common."[65] The threesome were often seen together at New York's finest restaurants, parties, and the theater. Garbo no longer had much time for Gayelord and had even less for Mercedes.

Although her romance with Garbo had come to a virtual standstill and she was being kept from even talking to her, Mercedes continued her love, continued reconciling Garbo to the "woman image" in her subconscious. In 1944 she penned the last poem she ever wrote for Garbo.

> You belong to me.
> Some things just belong to other
>   things;
> There is no other way.
> Why not let us then say,
> for example . . . . the salt to
>   the sea,
> A bird to the sky . . . and you
>   to me!
>   Hollywood
>   1944

Mercedes's world was fast unraveling, and the following year gravely added to her decline. Her alcoholic brother Ricardo, who had been a successful tax lawyer in New York and a friend of President Roosevelt's, died

on March 18, 1945. She "plunged into despair."[66] When she felt lonely and
depressed, she visited her sister Maria who lived in a flat nearby. And then,
ten days before Germany surrendered on May 7, 1945, Mercedes received
a letter from her sister Baba who was living in London. She said she was
thankful the war was about over and her husband Freddie would be returning soon. She was counting the days. Exactly one week later, Mercedes received a telegram from Baba: "Freddie killed yesterday."[67]

As soon as she could manage, in July 1946, Mercedes sailed for Europe,
first stopping off in London to visit her sister and then heading on to Paris.[68]
A few years earlier, she had nothing to keep her in Hollywood. Now she
really had no reason to stay in New York. After all, she had learned that Garbo
was also leaving the country in July, sailing to Sweden with George Schlee.
Luckily, she was still receiving her monthly alimony from her ex-husband,
so she could afford to travel. In her last poem to Garbo she may have fan-
tasized, "You and me. There is no other way. You belong to me." Now, fifteen years after she had begun her intense obsession, she must have known
on some level that Garbo would never really belong to her. She continued
to delude herself on this futile voyage, however, yearning for an icon who
seemed to have as many personal problems as herself.

~10~

"Looking over My Shoulder for Something Else"

Soon after she arrived in Paris, Mercedes traveled to Cannes, where she stayed for two weeks with her old friend Isabel Pell. After experiencing the war-torn devastation in London and Paris, Mercedes welcomed with relief the calm of the Mediterranean. One evening, she met Claire, the Marquise de Forbin, and was "struck by her extreme fragility."[1] After a moonlit dinner, they walked onto the terrace to take in the sea, which was "shimmering like quicksilver." Mercedes was excited by "the delicate modeling of her brow, the exquisite chiseling of her nose." She learned that Claire had been born in Avignon but raised in Morocco. She had been active in the resistance movement and had even received a citation by the Strategic Services Unit of the United States Forces in the European Theatre. Mercedes was captivated and soon began yet another affair.

During the months she was courting Claire, Mercedes received three messages from Garbo, who had not communicated in several years. The first was a rather oddly worded birthday note. Garbo wished Mercedes a happy birthday but made it clear that she was not yet prepared to call on her or anyone else. In the second, Garbo apologized for not having telephoned Mercedes before she left the United States for Sweden but quickly noted that her decision to leave was a sudden one. She hoped to see Mercedes in the near future. They were together sometime in 1946, since the third letter refers to their meeting. It must not have been a pleasant reunion, for

Garbo penned in her message almost verbatim her famous "I vant to be alone." Garbo pleaded with Mercedes not to bother her. She was simply not up to it.[2]

Certainly a further stress for Mercedes was Garbo's being courted not only by George Schlee but also by Cecil Beaton. Cecil was immediately smitten when he met Garbo at a party hosted by the editor of *Vogue* in the spring of 1946. He sent her dozens of love letters, invited her to visit him in England, and even proposed marriage. When she visited him at his hotel room in early November 1947, he recorded in his diary that they "were suddenly together in unexplained, unexpected and inevitable intimacy.... I had to throw my mind back to the times ... when in my wildest dreams I had invented the scenes that were now taking place."[3]

One day they discussed Mercedes. Garbo complained, "She's done me such harm, such mischief, has gossiped so and been so vulgar. She's always trying to scheme and find out things and you can't shut her up." When Cecil told Garbo that Mercedes had asked him point blank whether he was having an affair with her, Garbo snapped, "That's just like her. It's so vulgar."[4]

Claire joined Mercedes back in New York for the Christmas holidays of 1947, arriving Christmas Eve, the night of a great blizzard. Although the city was buried in snow, they attended a holiday party and then walked to see the spectacular Christmas tree at Radio City.

Through Cecil's intercession, Christmas morning found Mercedes, Cecil, and Garbo dining together. Although Mercedes was nervous about hosting the breakfast, she was optimistic, since she had not received any communication from Garbo for the entire year. There is no record of Claire's being present. Cecil has described the unique meal: "Mercedes, unable to hide her anxiety, was extremely preoccupied with the thought of having to prepare a meal. Greta, sensing the climate, at once took control and entertained us all with a most amusing and adroit performance."[5] She sang a medley of Salvation hymns and then proceeded to tie a towel around her waist and cooked ham and eggs for them all. Cecil noticed, "Greta has a paralyzing effect on her best friend, who becomes tactless and silly in the presence of her high priestess."[6]

Claire's absence from the breakfast hardly meant that Mercedes had ended their relationship. A few days later, she and Claire attended a screening of *A Duel in the Sun,* starring Lillian Gish. Soon after, Claire returned to Paris and Mercedes followed.

Shortly before she joined Claire, Mercedes arranged to have dinner alone with Cecil. According to the account in his diary, Cecil was apprehensive about the reasons for the dinner and had planned to be vague and evasive if Mercedes asked about Garbo. He was astonished that she "never once asked me any questions or seemed to be curious or indiscreet in fact to show herself as anything but the most wonderful & loyal friend of 20 years devotion—in the face of many setbacks & raw deals—for Greta is really unkind to her & gives her terrible mental beatings."[7] Mercedes expressed sincere concern for Garbo, that her life and career were at a crossroads. If she did not soon reconcile herself to making films, she insisted, Garbo would be finished in Hollywood. Mercedes thought that both Stokowski and Schlee exploited her. After the dinner, Cecil concluded that Mercedes "had no personal axe to grind, nothing to offer in fact except the great desire to help Greta all she can—& Greta has few people who can help her."[8]

Back in France, Mercedes resumed her romance with Claire. In early autumn, they traveled together to Avignon, going by way of Nîmes and Arles. A highlight of the trip was seeing the church where Claire had been christened and married.

Not long after Mercedes returned to Paris, she was invited to accompany Princess Dilkusha de Rohan to a dinner hosted by Maria Annunziata Sartori, better known as Poppy Kirk.[9] The daughter of the United States vice consul in Livorno, Italy, Poppy had been raised in France and England. Her first marriage at an early age ended in divorce after the birth of her son, Victor, in 1923. She had worked as a model for several years as well as for Schiaparelli, the Ballets Russes, and the well-known couturier Molyneux. In 1935 she had married Geoffrey Kirk, who worked for the British Foreign Office.

Mercedes was enchanted by Poppy's cooking, her intellect, and particularly her interest in Oriental philosophy. As the dinner guests began to depart, Mercedes learned that Poppy was leaving with her husband within a week for Washington, D.C., New York, and then on to Mexico City, where her husband was taking on a new government post. They made plans to rendezvous in New York in late December.

Their month together was a whirlwind of adventure—going to the theater, dining out, sightseeing, taking long strolls along Fifth Avenue, and meeting many of Mercedes's old friends, especially Natacha Rambova. By the time Poppy finally left to join her husband in Mexico, Mercedes had once again committed herself to another woman. As Poppy disclosed a few weeks later, "Since those few moments on the sofa when I held you in my arms—ever still—my thoughts, my whole reason for living has been you."[10] In another letter, she remembered their first night together. "I don't think I had moved from your arms all night. I did wake up several times, but only to move nearer to you."[11] Mercedes agreed to sublet her New York apartment to Carol Channing and move to Paris. Poppy agreed that she would go to Mexico and tell her husband that she was leaving him.[12]

What followed was a torrent of letters that Poppy mailed to Mercedes in Paris between the first of February 1949 and when they were finally united in early April. In her first letter she writes, "If you had told me a year ago in London when I promised Geoffrey that I would come here for a little to try and start our live [sic] again—that it would be in a hot smart night club in Mexico that I would ask him to release me of that promise—I would not have believed you. But I am free—how long now it will take me to cure the bitterness I cannot tell—Geoffrey treats me with icy politeness."[13]

In her next letter, however, Poppy indicates a problem brewing. "You had covered me so closely—with such very soft wings—that I was not prepared for this. But don't worry. I hold my head very high with great pride for you, and am very calm—so there can be nothing you can reproach me with—I kiss the tips of your ten fingers."[14] The problem stemmed from Princess Dilkusha. Even though she and Poppy had ended their relationship years earlier and had remained friends, the Princess had invited Mercedes to Poppy's for dinner because she wanted to initiate an affair with Mercedes. Apparently, the jealous Princess was showing Mercedes the love letters that Poppy had written to her. Poppy was so disturbed that between February 15 and 20 she sent several cables to Mercedes, trying to reassure her about her undying love.

At one point, Poppy described an awkward moment she had experienced with her husband. In an earlier letter, she had assured Mercedes that all of her mail went directly to a woman at the Embassy by the name of Fiona, who did not open letters and sealed all cables before sending them directly to Poppy. This particular day, however, Geoffrey opened one of the cables from Mercedes and confronted Poppy over dinner. Did she want to marry the person who sent the cable? "It was very sweetly asked," Poppy explained, "and I answered vaguely and the subject was dropped."[15]

By early March, Mercedes had been back in Paris for more than a month and, with Claire's assistance, had rented a small flat at 5 Quai Voltaire. There was only a bedroom, living room, and kitchen, but she installed a modern toilet in the hallway and a tub in the kitchen. In anticipation of Poppy's arrival, she had redecorated it and purchased some antique furniture. When she expressed doubt about their future together and her jealousy, Poppy responded, "[I]f I have spoiled your love for me I am sorry. . . . [I]f my love— you feel that we must start out life together by eliminating doubts and shadows, then I think you must have the courage not to go through with our plans—and leave our few weeks of infinite happiness unspoiled. . . . I beg of you, please don't let me come to Paris and find you love me less or in a different way."[16] Apparently the trip to Paris was fruitful. Two weeks later, they were together.

For several months, Mercedes experienced for the first time the joys of actually living with a woman she loved. Because of Poppy's skillful cooking, they entertained often. Dinners would have a color scheme. If the floral centerpiece was pink, the soup was pink—borscht or tomato. They might have radishes, shrimp with rice, and strawberries for dessert. Poppy could plan yellow, green, or purple dinners. Summer days they often strolled along the Seine, visited the flower markets, and basked in the sun. They enjoyed concerts and dining out. By early autumn, with their finances running low, Poppy decided to accept a job with fashion designer Schiaparelli.

Though it was a necessary decision, it was a challenge to their relationship. "I was suddenly left alone all day," Mercedes complained. "I had been most of my life alone, but these few months with Poppy had spoiled me. . . . I became very nervous and I hated being left alone in the flat."[17] She developed severe headaches and a recurrence of her deep depressions.

But her mood soon changed. Quite unexpectedly, she received a letter from Garbo who was vacationing in Italy with George Schlee. She promised to telephone the minute she arrived in Paris.[18] She arrived in early September. During their days together, and when Poppy was working, Mercedes and Garbo took long walks in the Bois and the Tuileries Gardens. At one point, Mercedes even orchestrated a dinner for the three of them. Unfortunately, the evening did not progress as Mercedes had hoped. Several years later, her friend Ram Gopal mentioned the story she had told him of how Poppy and "Greta fought at your flat."[19] Because of her heavy workload leading up to the Christmas holidays, Poppy began putting in many long days at the Schiaparelli shop, leaving Mercedes alone more than ever. Soon after Christmas, Mercedes hurried back to New York to attend the funeral of her old friend Eleanora von Mendelssohn, who had committed suicide by leaping from a window. Eleanora had been instrumental in introducing Mercedes to Salka Viertel and Garbo. Mercedes had often visited her in Salzburg. And now, another suicide, following that of her father and brother. She confided it had "a terrible effect on me."[20]

In the next three months, while Mercedes remained in New York, Poppy mailed her almost two dozen letters that describe their deteriorating relationship as well as Mercedes's uneven temperament. Poppy admitted that although she hated to see Mercedes leave, "This separation may be good. You needed it."[21] Two days later, she clarified herself, "Please don't think I shall ever try and hold you my darling. I must get used to your flights and wait for you to come back. But don't do it too often." She confessed that she hated "to turn around in my bed . . . and not see my lovely one near me. . . . I need you my boy. Never forget it day or night. . . . Your girl needs you and loves you with all her heart." She admitted that when she received Mercedes's letters she would lock herself in the bathroom where she could read them undisturbed.[22]

By early February, Poppy had come to a clearer understanding of Mercedes's needs. "Your only love will be for people who are dependent on you, and who you will love and really devote yourself with happiness to those who will take everything from you and though you can love me, I will never I think make you happy." She ended the letter with this poignant observation: "However closely I hold you in my arms, you will be looking over my shoulder for something else."[23] Mercedes's response cannot be found. However, she must have mentioned that she and Garbo were again seeing each other, for Poppy replied, "I am so glad you are happy and have Greta so close to you again." And then she made herself painfully clear:

> Your incredibly selfish decisions about our life and love—must keep in a place of their own so that it does not create in me either an immediate desire to break with you or to make me bitter and unhappy. So I will not ask your advice on any decisions I may take and of course not expect you [to] share in what I will decide. You in return will do exactly as you wish. I cannot say to you it is to me my ideal of what I hoped our love would be, but between your soul in New York, and my work in Paris and New York, we may find a meeting place sometimes.[24]

In another letter a few weeks later, Poppy repeated her feelings. "Some decisions concerning my life will have now to be taken without you. I warned you about that. You have nothing to reproach me about. You have created the separation . . . in return I have taken my freedom. This you will have to respect."[25]

But Mercedes did not seem to understand. Why could she not have both Poppy and Garbo as lovers at the same time? Poppy tried to explain, "Have you ever thought if our situations were changed—reversed—suppose you were working and I suddenly told you I was leaving two or three times a year—to stay with Geoffrey—to go to my house in London—because of many trivial reasons—I wonder how you would feel about it."[26]

The very weeks that Mercedes was corresponding with Poppy about their future together, Mercedes was receiving encouraging mail from Garbo, who was in California with George Schlee. Garbo asked Mercedes what she was

planning to do about her depressions. Speaking from her own personal experience, she understood the difficulty Mercedes might have of getting well
when she was feeling vulnerable and without a focus. Undoubtedly, Garbo's
concern must have pleased Mercedes, but what probably pleased her more
was being asked to help her find an apartment in New York.[27] As Poppy had
insisted, Mercedes needed people to be dependent on her. By mid-May Mercedes had decided to return to Paris in October. Even though her relationship with Poppy had no future, it was still better than nothing. Maybe she
could somehow make it work. After Mercedes left New York, Garbo wrote
her one of her warmest, most intimate messages. She implored Mercedes
to take care of herself, acknowledging that life is full of challenges and
troubles. She hoped Mercedes's difficulties would all work out for the best.[28]

Back in Paris, Mercedes tried to revive her relationship with Poppy, as
they were now living together in a small flat on the Quai Saint Michel. In
December, their excursion to London proved to be ill fated. Mercedes's
decision to spend a few nights with her friend Ram Gopal infuriated Poppy.
When Mercedes returned to their room at the Hotel Savoy, Poppy grabbed
her, banged her head against the wall, threw her to the floor, and tried lock-
ing her up.[29]

It was around this time that Poppy began renting a farmhouse in Normandy, in the tiny village of Aincourt. The place had a pastoral setting of
fields and cattle. Still trying to build a life together, the two of them escaped
there almost every weekend and sometimes, especially in the summer, they
would drive down in the evening and return to Paris in the morning. An
addition to the household was La Linda, a small Siamese kitten named after Mercedes's grandmother. When in Paris, they resumed their dinner parties. One was with Eva Le Gallienne and her lover Margaret Webster. "The
evening passed pleasantly," Mercedes wrote, "and we laughed about the old
days of *Jehanne d'Arc.*"

Occasionally, Mercedes received letters from Garbo, requesting to see her.
Although Garbo knew Poppy did not want her around, she still hoped
Mercedes could serve as her escort while she was in Paris. A year later, Garbo
wrote again that she realized Poppy would be depressed to learn of her plan
to visit Paris. However, Garbo felt that she would not interfere with Mercedes's schedule overly much, since her good friend George Schlee would
be accompanying her.[30] At one point, Garbo even indicated that she and Mercedes might live together.[31] As the letters from Garbo became more intimate
and personal, the relationship between Mercedes and Poppy grew cooler.

By March 1953 Poppy was living again with her husband. On August 3,
1953, Poppy wrote to Mercedes in New York, "You are mistaken in my

affection for you. It is a deep and lasting one. You will not find me lacking in friendship—and my tender understanding. Just things have taken their proper place—we should and could always have been good friends—had you been generous in your affection for me."[32] Then Poppy began to refuse Mercedes's telephone calls. "The time has come," wrote Poppy, "when I must have time to myself."[33]

Poppy had tolerated all she could of Mercedes's obsession with and devotion to Garbo. Mercedes's close friends were rather expecting to see the breakup. When Hope Williams learned of it, she wrote to Mercedes, "I am not really very surprised to hear about Poppy. She spoke rather independently in Paris about the future. . . . Probably it is for the best but that doesn't make it less hard to take."[34]

Poppy was certainly not blameless for their breakup. Ram Gopal found her a "bitchy, small person. Her whole attitude was one of egotism. She always tried to make Mercedes jealous and constantly reminded her that she had a husband she could return to." Ram felt so unwelcome around her that one time he screamed at her, "You mean fuck nothing to me! You are a fucking bitch!" Mercedes would often complain to him that "she felt her life was being squeezed to death by Poppy." She and Poppy never stopped fighting. Ram advised Mercedes, "Don't for god's sake give up Garbo for this whorish Poppy Kirk."[35]

At almost the same time as the letter from Poppy, Mercedes had yet another falling out with Garbo. In mid-July, the night before Garbo was sailing for Europe, she accused Mercedes of furnishing Cecil Beaton with some details that he used in his 1937 *Scrapbook*. Mercedes informed Cecil three months later, "We got into a row and I told her one or two truths. She was angry and left without calling me the next morning or saying good-bye. . . . It is really so idiotic and unnatural that after years of friendship, one has to still go on handling her with absurd 'kid gloves,' or else suffer a falling out of some kind. Naturally I miss her and not seeing her makes me unhappy. Life is rushing by so quickly it is a pity to miss any moments with people one loves!"[36] Cecil replied within a week. "I don't know why she should turn against either of us. . . . I trust she will have got in touch with you, as I'm sure she needs you—& I've always thought that the two of you would end your days together."[37] For more than a year, the only communication Mercedes had with Garbo was a New Year's card.

Through most of 1954, Mercedes sent both Garbo and Poppy letters of despair. How ironic that she had wanted to retain the love of both and yet had now lost them both at about the same time. In July, Poppy mentioned that she had received two depressing letters from Mercedes. "I am sorry you are letting yourself go like this—as you have so much both in yourself and to give to others—and depression doesn't help."[38] Garbo's response to her depression was less sympathetic. In a particularly cantankerous mood, Garbo demanded that Mercedes stop assaulting her with letters, especially when she was facing personal problems herself. She did not want to talk to Mercedes about her personal life, and she refused any future meeting until she was more prepared to deal with Mercedes.[39]

One of her friends was more supportive. Mercedes had met Alice B. Toklas several years earlier and on at least one occasion had visited her in Paris with Cecil and Garbo. Beginning in April 1953, they began a steady correspondence, sharing, among other things, their favorite vegetarian recipes. Needing again to be needed, Mercedes sent her flowers, a purse, and newspaper clippings. She also shipped her a copy of Alfred Kinsey's 1948 *Sexual Behavior in the Human Male,* which was a survey of sexual behavior in men and popularly known as "The Kinsey Report." Alice responded, "The Kinsey reports are so hopelessly dull. . . . As you say so rightly American sex is the most banal point from which to study our compatriots. . . . Sex is perhaps like culture—a luxury that only becomes an art after generations of leisurely acquaintance."[40] Sensing that Mercedes was quite depressed and searching for some focus in her life, Alice encouraged her to concentrate on her writing and suggested she write a biography of Igor Stravinsky or an autobiography of her own life. "The temptation to be able to read it [her autobiography] is the excuse for pursuing you," she wrote. "You will understand the eagerness."[41]

Mercedes actually had never given up on her writing. In 1949, when she was in Paris waiting for Poppy to join her, she had worked on a play about Duse. Whether it was that script or another one, Mercedes wrote to Poppy about her attempts in trying to get a production mounted in London. In 1955, it looked as if she had persuaded Lillian Gish to star in a New York production of *The Mother of Christ.*[42] When Ram Gopal heard of the possibilities, he was overjoyed and urged Mercedes to bring it to London where he was living. "Why not over here, there is in a way more mature producers to GET that sort of thing GOING here. . . . I hope to GOD you get your play done, YOU like I, NEED it, for our inner self confidences and for the feeling of knowing that someone WANTS what we GIVE in spirit thru the drama of the Theatre, be it an Indian temple platform, or a New York stage."[43]

Once again, a production never materialized. At some point, Mercedes must have adopted Igor Stravinsky's earlier idea to have the role of the Virgin Mary suggested by a bright light instead of by an actress. By 1963, when she approached Flora Robson about starring in a production, the play had been retitled *The Infinite Light*. Robson turned down the project, however, saying it is "a moving and beautiful play, but I fear it is not for the commercial theatre."[44]

There is no evidence that Mercedes received any correspondence from Poppy or Alice in either 1955 or 1956 nor anything more than two Easter cards from Garbo. Unfortunately, it was a period when she needed emotional support as never before. Not only had her thirty-year attempt to stage *The Mother of Christ* collapsed yet another time, but also one of her former lovers, Ona Munson, had committed suicide. Shortly after Ona had married Eugene Berman in 1949, the couple had moved to Paris, renting a flat just a few doors from Mercedes and Poppy. Ona hated Paris and always seemed unhappy. Whenever Mercedes visited her, she always left feeling worse herself. After she returned to Los Angeles, Ona wrote to Mercedes, "I have not changed in my feelings toward you but my life has changed and I do not have the vitality or strength to extend it further."[45] On February 11, 1955, she was found dead from an overdose of sleeping pills. On a table near the bed where she died was a suicide note that was published in her *New York Times* obituary: "This is the only way I know to be free again. Please don't follow me."[46]

Mercedes does not mention this suicide in her autobiography, but she was devastated. Her father, her brother, her good friend Eleanora von Mendelssohn, and now her former lover—four suicides. Too many for any one person to bear. So many outrageous thoughts and questions overwhelmed her. As before, she felt rage at having been deserted and abandoned by persons she loved. Why should she have to suffer so many tragic deaths? Was God punishing her for some reason? She found herself reaching back in time to those blissful days when she and Ona had slept in each other's arms, but questions kept plaguing her. "Why did this happen?" "Why did Ona feel that ending her life was her only answer?" Mercedes kept reliving the weeks before Ona's death, wondering whether she could have prevented it. Were there signs she should have recognized? Had she done anything to precipitate the suicide? Her first reactions of shock, disbelief, and numbness quickly wore off, and were replaced by intense pain, as if someone had ripped open her chest and torn out her heart. Mercedes became obsessed with "what ifs" and "if onlys." If only she had known, if only she had been in New York at the time, if only she had been more attentive. What if, if only. What sadness, what guilt she was feeling. There was no one close to understand her loss or the nightmare she was living. A nervous breakdown followed, as she fell into a severe state of depression and contemplated suicide herself.

✑ 11 ✑

"Just Damned Bewildered"

As soon as he heard of Mercedes's collapse, Cecil immediately wrote:

'm sorry not to have heard more cheerful news from you. Why did Ona Munson kill herself? Was her life a failure? The marriage no go? Did she use drug—drink? I'm also terribly sad about Greta not seeing you—I'm afraid she has very little gratitude in her disposition—takes everything as her due—& gives mighty little to others. I'm afraid nothing will alter her, it's no good scolding—the only thing is to protect oneself against useless suffering. Life must go on, & there is much to interest & stimulate one each day. One cannot regret, too much, the past. I'm afraid Greta isn't going to have a happy old age—but then who is? It's difficult. I quite agree that unless one does kindnesses to others that one becomes paid out for one's selfishness.[1]

And just a month later, he repeated his frustration with Garbo. "It is monstrous of her [Greta] not to see you—I fear she takes friendship for granted. I suppose having such a success wherever she goes makes her feel that it is her due to have people do her bidding. I trust it may always be her lot to find people who are willing to do what she wants without anything from her in return."[2]

Making Mercedes feel even more threatened was the recurrence of an old eye infection. Back in the late 1940s, before she had met Poppy, Mercedes

161

had accidentally poured cleaning fluid into her right eye instead of eye wash. She continued to have so many infections that she was forced at times to wear an eye patch. Added to her already eccentric costumes, it gave her the look of a pirate. For some reason, the infection now returned and caused considerable discomfort. Alice B. Toklas agonized over her suffering, writing, "It is ghastly that your beautiful, your uniquely beautiful eyes, should have played you so wicked a trick."[3] With no income except for her alimony and with mounting medical bills, she was forced to move into a much smaller apartment at 315 E. Sixty-eighth Street.

Her old friend Tamara Karsavina was so worried about Mercedes's well-being she advised, "What you need is someone who might help you to pull through, to some objective." She invited Mercedes to visit her in London: "With your fear of being alone it might help you to have someone to talk to."[4]

Another old friend who tried to pull her through was Ram Gopal. Adjoining the lounge of his apartment overlooking London's Hyde Park was "a magnificent room of warm Himalayan blue, bright but soothing.... This room will be Mercedes's room, your room my darling." He begged her to join him. "We will pray together, meditate, and I can massage your spine, play you music, or just sit quietly, and no noise or person will disturb you."[5] A few weeks later, he repeated his invitation. "Yes Alba you will stay with me, and when you come I'll have the room filled with flowers, and incense and prayers BEFORE you come so that you may enter in peace.... Sometimes when you feel like it I will attempt to cure you with my dance therapy—movements of Yoga and rhythm down in the studio, but Come darling, don't stay there, New York for you is not good for too long; only in small doses." He indicated his plans to travel to India to the Hill of Arunachala and invited her to accompany him. He stressed his gratitude for their intimate relationship.

> Yes there is a lot about you in my blood darling. you've been such an ever present ghost—flitting just a little beyond my physical vision, but ever present and Living in my inner vision of Truth, Beauty and elegance.... How much richer my life has been in KNOWING and LOVING (spiritually) you, and what a love I've learnt, by comparison and not rudely either, the others AFTER you of both sexes that I've known (not all) but most, seem as empty as tin cans on a rubbish heap, valueless Cyphers, giving, doing, learning and being just NOTHING.

In closing, he acknowledged, "You've certainly put a lot of YOUR power and self into GRETA, who certainly absorbed YOU.... all my purest thoughts and pale pink, violet, and rose gardens full of LOVE. Yours darling, Ram."[6] Even her ex-husband, Abram Poole, was concerned for her health and wrote, asking why he never heard from her.[7]

Mercedes, who was now in her early sixties, was simply not able to accept assistance. Her possessive, controlling behavior coupled with her yearning for Garbo had wreaked havoc on so many of her past relationships—with Dietrich, Munson, Claire, and Poppy. And now, even though she was at the end of her resources, she could not acquiesce to Ram's offer. He offered love, a beautiful room overlooking Hyde Park that he would fill with flowers and incense, a peaceful environment, and total security. She could even have returned to India with him. What a perfect solution from a sincere friend, but she turned her back, only to persist with her fantasy for a reunion with Garbo.

Ram Gopal understood Mercedes's attraction to Garbo. "She had a magnetic personality," he said, "and she and Mercedes possessed the same aura. Once Mercedes met Garbo, all she did was dream of Garbo." But Garbo was afraid of having her life exposed. "Be careful. Don't let people know about us," she would say to Mercedes. "Garbo needed to dominate. When she felt someone else dominating, she'd pull back. Poor Mercedes," Ram sighed. "She had to love. Loving was like breathing. She gave all of herself in a relationship and wanted back all that she gave."[8]

Her excessive preoccupation with Garbo certainly approached clinical obsession. According to the American Psychiatric Association, an obsessive disorder diagnosis calls for "recurrent and persistent ideas, thoughts, impulses, or images that are experienced, at least initially, as intrusive." A person suffering from this illness "recognizes that the obsessions are the product of his or her own mind, not imposed from without." Such obsessions "cause marked distress, are time-consuming . . . or significantly interfere with the person's normal routine, occupational functioning, or usual social activities or relationships with others." The only diagnostic criteria that Mercedes did not seem to exhibit was that the obsessive person "attempts to ignore or suppress such thoughts or impulses or to neutralize them."[9] Mercedes's condition, therefore, would probably have fit the description that psychiatrist Judith L. Rapoport designated as "on the boundaries" of obsessive behavior.[10]

Indeed, contemporary analysts may have diagnosed Mercedes's suffering as the delusional disorder of "erotomania." "The central theme of an erotic delusion is that one is loved by another. The delusion usually concerns idealized romantic love and spiritual union rather than sexual attraction. The person about whom this conviction is held is usually of higher

status, such as a famous person or superior at work. Efforts to contact the
object of delusion, through telephone calls, letters, gifts . . . are common.
The prevalence of erotic delusions is such as to be a significant source of
harassment to public figures."[11] The average age of onset of this disorder
has been found to be between 40 and 55. Mercedes was 39 when she met
Garbo. The main impairment it causes is in "social and marital functioning."[12] In the case of Mercedes, it definitely impaired her relationships with
other women.

Whether or not she suffered from these specific diseases, Mercedes could
not forsake the woman she adored. Garbo, who certainly had relationship
issues of her own, did not help with her occasional appearances. Around
1958, Mercedes again had reasons for joy—a totally unexpected visit from
Garbo! According to Cecil, Garbo telephoned first and then went to Mercedes's apartment, where she burst "into floods of tears."[13] "I have no one
to look after me." "You don't *want* anyone to look after you," Mercedes
responded. Garbo replied, "I'm frightened. I'm so *lost!*" Cecil then recorded
in his diary, "Mercedes is her very best friend & for 30 years has stood by
her, willing to devote her life to her. Once again she rallied. She prevailed
upon a little Italian doctor to break his rule of not having private clients to
come to New York from Rochester each day to look after Greta. . . . In spite
of everything Mercedes continues to do all she can for Greta."[14] Mercedes
wrote enthusiastically to Ram Gopal about this turn of events with Garbo.
He was thrilled.

> Even though you are far away, I feel your sufferings, anguishes and
> disturbed states in an alarmingly life-like manner. . . . There is only
> one place for you and for me to go from the dark depths of the bot-
> toms to which our past karmas have perhaps cast us—and the place
> to go is right up to the top in the light, love and realization of the
> golden fire of God, success and all good things. You should try very
> hard, as I try very hard, not to look back at my shadow as I walk
> towards the sun, but rather with chin up to walk forward and thought-
> constructively into a determined and absolute realization of the
> bounty, wealth, love, beauty and plentifulness that is ours by right from
> God. . . . Much love, darling. . . . The sword of your spirit has been
> cast into hellish fires, but, darling, you have triumphed, and now you
> have, I believe, arisen in God's realization triumphant, strong, calm and
> prepared for the finality of the years ahead to create, serve and realize
> in the arts. . . . Much, much love—and a kiss from my spirit to yours
> my beautiful, sweet Alba.[15]

Knowing that Garbo was going to be in Monte Carlo, Mercedes decided that she, too, would go to Europe. From June through October of 1957, she stayed part of the time with Poppy in Paris and part of the time with Ram in London. During those months, she received at least two letters from Garbo. Inquiring about her eyes, Garbo sympathized with Mercedes's suffering. She hoped a miracle would appear that would relieve her pain. About five weeks later, Garbo repeated her concern and indicated that if nothing unexpected happened she would see Mercedes soon in Paris.[16] There is no evidence that this meeting ever took place.

Mercedes's optimism did not last long. Back in New York and taking cortisone and suffering from depression, she planned her suicide, telling her friend Wilder Luke Burnap that she had a gun just for that purpose. She yearned to spend time alone with Garbo, but it never happened. For the first part of 1958, Mercedes was in New York, but Garbo was in California. During the summer, Mercedes was back in Europe, but Garbo was in New York or Monte Carlo. In the autumn, Mercedes returned to New York, but Garbo was in Paris. The letters Mercedes received from Garbo during these long months were not comforting. Garbo discussed her boredom and her diet. She thanked Mercedes for sending her slippers that she had ordered, and she asked Mercedes to arrange for a woman to clean her apartment prior to her return to New York. In one letter, Garbo complained about Mercedes's incessant snooping and prying into her life and demanded that Mercedes stop at once. She reminded Mercedes that she had little regard for people who intruded in her private life. She might feel closer to Mercedes if she would only stop probing.[17]

Sadly, no sign of affection, no genuine concern. And at a time when Mercedes desperately needed something more from Garbo. Ram Gopal was frightened by her mood. He warned, "you've simply got to pull yourself out of the RUT of ILL health and nerves, and the disastrous effects of that ghastly killer drug you took."[18]

To pull herself "out of the rut," she took his advice and returned to writing her autobiography. Thirty years earlier, Bessie Marbury had encouraged her to keep a notebook or diary so that one day she would have some of the necessary details to write her life story. At the time, this might have sounded pretentious. But with a wealth of adventure, ecstasy, and pain behind her, this now seemed like the perfect solution. In the early 1950s she had begun the composition, but now she worked on it with zeal. Mercedes had not taken Bessie's advice at the time, so now she had to work from memory and her accumulation of correspondence and memorabilia. By June 1958 she had secured a publisher.[19]

As she worked on her book, she sent drafts to former lover Marlene Dietrich to examine. She suggested that Mercedes expand the section about Broadway producer Augustin Daly entering her life when she was four. It is "interesting because theatre plays big part in your story. Theatre people are unusual people. . . . Granted they hold fascination for everybody, but you became acustomed [sic] to be drawn into the inner circle. Leave it as a maybe but touch on it. It silences any suspicion of 'celebrity hunting' later on."

Also, Dietrich thought Mercedes should make much more of her relationship with her sister Rita. "This is too interesting a woman not to mention her relationship with you," she stressed. "If there was none that is important too. But keep the red thread from Daly to Rita. Delight—Beauty—Magical people inhabited your world. You became used to beauty from the day you were grown up enough to recognize it."

She also gave advice about how Mercedes should discuss her relationship with Garbo. "Talk about her dominant or willfull [sic] side or child like taking refuge in shunning reality and her attitude of make-believe to overcome disappointment. Don't say what you felt other than you felt you were the cause of some disappointment."[20] It's quite possible that Garbo got wind of how she was discussed in the book prior to its publication. She had always warned people not to write about her, and only a few years earlier had been angry that Mercedes had supplied information about her for Cecil's book. Now she was enraged that Mercedes was producing a book herself. Even worse, Mercedes included topless photos of Garbo that she had taken during their trip to Silver Lake in 1931. The very last message Mercedes ever received from Garbo stated very bluntly Garbo's demand that Mercedes should not dismiss other people's needs. Her selfish actions, wrote Garbo, were thoughtless and were driving Garbo crazy.[21]

When her autobiography, *Here Lies the Heart,* finally appeared in 1960, reaction was certainly positive. Her close friends praised the book. Cecil Beaton wrote her that "there is so much good stuff in it & I have enjoyed it a lot."[22] Alice B. Toklas was another fan: "Your book has left me breathless—excited and very happy. No matter how much I expected, you have exceeded that by atomic distance. . . . I curtsey before your tremendous accomplishment."[23] Asked to write a promotional pitch for the book, Alice pointed out, "To those of us who have lived in the world Miss de Acosta revives it for us. For those who have only looked at it, she makes it come alive. It is a fascinating book of rare beauty."[24]

All signs pointed to a major success. On May 18, 1960, Mercedes was interviewed about her book by ABC-TV. In August, BBC-TV taped an interview as well. Jan Mostowski, in charge of window displays at the prestigious Brentano's bookstore on Forty-seventh Street and Fifth Avenue, recalls a luncheon with Mercedes. A mutual friend, author Alexander Janta, set up the meeting to discuss promotional possibilities. Back in 1938 when Janta was Ram Gopal's lover, Mercedes had stayed at his country estate in Poland. Mostowski remembers that he was so charmed by this dark, intriguing woman that he returned to the store and set up a major display in the Fifth Avenue windows.[25]

Reviews of the book were extremely enthusiastic. Arthur Todd of the *New York Times* called it "a fascinatingly readable memoir of a quite extraordinary personality.... On a deeper level, it presents a penetrating view of a rare and individual human being."[26] A critic for *Dance* magazine declared that the book was "in the realm of great literature."[27] And Richard McLaughlin of the *New Leader* proclaimed that

> the reader almost immediately understands that he is in the presence of a forceful, sensitive woman.... It is one thing to know a great many celebrities by their first names, but it quite rare to find someone with the empathy with which Miss de Acosta has been endowed. This to me is but one of the extraordinary facets of her many-faceted and unique autobiography.... I think her book's significance as a historical document, as an authentic social history, cannot be stressed enough.[28]

The review that undoubtedly would have alarmed Garbo, however, appeared in the *Miami Herald*. Betsy Buffington's headline read "Greta Garbo's Pal Has Much to Tell." "Mercedes knew everybody," she concluded. "She doesn't tell all by any means—but what she does tell is right fine reading.... Whatever else it may be, her book definitely isn't boring."[29]

One afternoon after the book appeared, Garbo was shopping in a health food store in New York City. She suddenly recognized on the floor in front of her a long-toed, silver-buckled shoe a woman was wearing, looked up, and then noticed the black cape. "Aren't we on speaking terms today?" asked Mercedes. Without saying a word, Garbo quickly turned and walked out the door. Even though Mercedes had very little money those days, she still managed to send Garbo a small blue spruce tree at Christmas and a basket full of toys, mistletoe, and vodka. Garbo kept the tree and vodka, returning everything else without even a brief note of thanks. When Mercedes telephoned Garbo to wish her a happy new year, Garbo slammed the phone down, shouting that she did not want to talk to Mercedes.[30]

Other people mentioned in the book were equally angry. Eva Le Gallienne, for instance, told friends that the book should have been called "Here the Heart Lies and Lies and Lies."[31] She became so enraged that if someone mentioned Mercedes's name, she would storm from the room in disgust. She and Mercedes had worshiped Duse. They had met Duse together and later had stood vigil with their arms linked at her coffin. Yet in 1966 when Le Gallienne wrote her memories of Duse in *The Mystic in the Theatre,* she did not give Mercedes even a footnote reference. Even though Mercedes's finished book discusses all of her female friends with no direct reference to their sexual orientation, many readers were outraged by the various implications. In 1960 the subject of lesbianism was still awkward at best.

Although Mercedes was encouraged by the initial publication and publicity, royalties were slim. Even excellent reviews do not guarantee sales. In fact, one historian claims she did not earn a penny.[32] Besides the snubbing and rejection from old friends, the book's financial failure threw her into a deeper depression. By now, she was living a threadbare existence. She had been receiving her monthly alimony from Abram Poole since their divorce in 1935, but when he died in 1961 her allowance was frozen.[33] Years earlier, she had pleaded for more money from Abram, but he had refused. She had even helped arrange for an exhibit of his paintings at the Century Club in December 1958, hoping that would convince him. He would not budge. With no income, no savings, no prospects for employment, she was forced to sell her treasured family Spanish diamond bracelets to the highest bidder in order to pay for serious brain surgery and a painful operation on one of her legs.

Still another plan came to mind. Ingrid Bergman had starred in a film about Joan of Arc in 1948, and Jean Seberg had starred in Otto Preminger's version in 1957. Maybe now was finally the right time for a Broadway production of her thirty-five-year-old script. Even before her autobiography appeared, Mercedes sent a copy of it along with her play to actress Eva Bartok. A Hungarian-born film actress, she had starred in numerous films in the 1950s, including *The Crimson Pirate* (1952) with Burt Lancaster. Bartok was grateful for the offer.

> Thank you so much for your book & the play. . . . I do think that the play is wonderful & I realize that one mustn't give it to just anyone to read because, as you say, the 'idea' is free. . . . I had been most moved by it, & of course as a film it could be also magnificent. I am deeply grateful for your faith in me as to my ability to play the part, but I wonder if we can find someone who will share your belief. It should be a great and beautiful task, I wonder myself—could I do it?[34]

Within a few weeks, the actress had piqued the interest of producer John Martin and sent him the script. She told Mercedes, "I feel that if you have enough faith to offer it to me & we find someone who'd have faith to back it—I'd risk my going 'to the stake of the mess & be buried' for it, either on stage or film."[35] Again, once again, nothing ever materialized. It was the last time Mercedes sought a production for one of her plays.

She was in desperate need of money and was now faced with the somber possibility of having to apply for welfare and move into even smaller living quarters. It was during this bleak period that Mercedes contacted William H. McCarthy, curator of Philadelphia's Rosenbach Museum and Library, to see whether they might be interested in purchasing her papers. She couldn't have made a better choice. Not only was McCarthy a gay man and therefore sympathetic with Mercedes's plight, but also the Rosenbach was fast becoming one of the premiere museums of literary masterpieces in the country. The Rosenbach brothers had achieved international fame in the early 1900s as dealers in rare books and manuscripts, having purchased priceless works by Geoffrey Chaucer, Charles Dickens, and James Joyce. In 1954 they had founded a museum and library, housed in their former home on Delancey Place, adjacent to the fashionable Rittenhouse Square. What a coup if she could have her papers placed alongside such international giants.

In the summer of 1959, she vowed she would not sell her Garbo papers separately and pleaded with McCarthy to purchase her entire collection. "I need this money quite desperately so I would appreciate your getting me all you can. And please do not think me grabbing in asking you this. These are my only chance for making a little money as I now have nothing further to sell and as I hate so selling them at all and would rather, by far, give them—I might just as well be taken for a goose as a gander—or as a knave rather than a thief—or how does the saying go?"[36] By June 1960, they had come to an agreement. Mercedes sold to the museum for an undisclosed sum all of her Garbo materials, her books, manuscripts, photographs, collection of correspondence, and other memorabilia. The museum promised that "the gift is to be kept absolutely private and the whole collection is to be sealed and put in our vault, clearly identified and marked that it is not to be opened until ten years after the deaths of Miss Garbo and yourself, whichever shall be later. The Foundation accepts this agreement as a trust. It is clearly understood that this material is not to be seen or handled by anyone but Mr. McCarthy." The bulk of the letters of Marlene Dietrich, Eva Le Gallienne, Poppy Kirk, and Claire, the Marquise de Forbin, were to be sealed and not opened until after Mercedes's death and the death of each of the writers respectively.[37] Reluctantly, she was forced to also sell her love letters. "I would not have had the heart or courage to have burned these letters. I mean, of course, Eva, Greta's and Marlene's who were lovers. So it seemed a God-sent moment when you took them. I only hope, as the years go on, and you are no longer there that they will be respected and protected from the eyes of vulgar people."[38]

The sale, she hoped, would end her financial difficulties. Regretfully, it did not. "Never in all my life have I been so broke," she wrote. "I have not even money for bus fare."[39] Fortunately, old lovers and friends—Hope Williams, Marlene Dietrich, Poppy Kirk, Malvina Hoffman—sent her money to cover some of her bills. As Malvina said, "I hope you will accept this small check just as a little friendly souvenir of my affection. . . . It would please me if you would use the check for a few taxis when you get stronger. It's nice to feel you can blow yourself to a few rides. Be a good girl & balance your check book month by month then you will feel relieved."[40] When Mercedes yearned to see the Broadway hit *Camelot* in January 1961, she begged for a free ticket from Janet Gaynor, wife of the designer.[41] To repay Mercedes who had helped her find a publisher for her autobiography, Tamara Karsavina sent her money and hosted her at her home in London for the month of August.[42]

In mid-October 1961 she wrote to McCarthy at the Rosenbach Museum, "I am embarrassed to ask you to help me out but I am actually without any money at all. I have never been in such sad straits. . . . It seems idiotic to believe that yesterday and today I had exactly .40 in my purse and in consequence walked everywhere not even daring the luxury of a bus!"[43] By December she was feeling particularly morose, confiding in Cecil Beaton, "I see so many people round me ageing and so many people ill. It makes me feel it would be wise to die at the age of 45 and I wish I had. Only Anita Loos still seems spry and Gloria Swanson—they seem to be the eternal young ones!!"[44]

She panicked when she learned that Garbo might be moving permanently to Sweden. This news "gave me a *terrific* heart stab because I cannot imagine New York without her. . . . It is strange how lonely I feel now that I know she is not in New York. Even though I do not see her there was always the possibility of running into her, of hearing some news of her or even of her calling up. . . . *Do let me know if you have news of her plans.*"[45]

One loyal friend was Malvina Hoffman, whom she had lived with briefly in 1960. Mercedes was very appreciative, writing to William McCarthy, "Certainly as we grow older life becomes increasingly sad and difficult. I never so much realized this when I was young. But now I do. . . . Friends, either by death or otherwise, have gone out of ones life. This is why I cherish so much your friendship and Malvina's too, who has gone through so many years with me."[46] McCarthy committed suicide in 1965, and Malvina died the following year.

She was so gratified that Alice B. Toklas continued to correspond from Paris. In letters that were usually signed "devotedly," "fondest love," or "my love to you," Alice always reassured Mercedes of her devotion. In one, she wrote, "You are unique, generous, in the way you love. God's blessing is upon you for it shines through you." When Alice learned in 1963 that Mercedes was ill, though she herself was eighty-six years old at the time, she invited Mercedes to live with her for a while in Paris.[47] Unfortunately, Mercedes's health and lack of money prevented her from making the journey.

Even though in failing health and financial misery, Mercedes had managed to develop a few new friendships. In September 1961 she had initiated an affair with a tubercular young British actress who was a waitress at a New York coffee shop. She shared Thanksgiving dinners with Andy Warhol and his friends. Certainly one of her favorites was author Kieran Tunney, who had written a biography of Tallulah Bankhead. They went for long walks, and they talked on the telephone two or three times daily. He remembers that the first time he went to her apartment she apologized, "Horrid little flat—I'll never get used to it." An enormous black cat leapt into her arms. "My darling Linda," she said to her cat, "what would I do without you in this lousy dump. My angel, my pet, my gorgeous one, the only remaining light left in my life!"[48]

Soon after he had met Mercedes, Tunney attended a dinner party that included Garbo and when he mentioned Mercedes's name, Garbo sighed, "We've drifted apart.... My fault, I suppose. I must always be free. To come and go as I choose. And despite Mercedes' wonderful courage and strength . . . she is hopelessly feminine. Needs to possess and envelop one—with marriage or the equivalent."[49] Tunney soon found out himself how demanding Mercedes could be.

> If sleep failed her, she thought nothing of calling one at two or three in the morning to discuss the meaning of existence, sleeping and waking, or a tract on a Far Eastern religion that she believed could change all our lives. And if one was invited to Southampton or Bridgehampton for a weekend Mercedes expected one to arrange that she too was included even if the host had never met or heard of her; and if and when one succeeded in such an awkward task, it was quite on the cards she might sulk for the entire weekend if the household couldn't or wouldn't cope with whatever diet she was on at that particular time![50]

He finally was forced to limit their meetings.

He concluded that Mercedes "though a delight in all sorts of ways—intelligent, interested in every aspect of the arts, generous to a fault . . . and possessing great bravery and courage—she was destructive to those she loved if they valued the faintest hint of privacy, balance or order in their lives."[51]

Two other occasional visitors were Wilder Luke Burnap and Abram Poole Jr., son of her ex-husband and his second wife. Both men claim that as they would leave Mercedes's apartment after tea, they would often see Garbo standing across the street. It appeared as if she was waiting so that she could go up to see Mercedes. They never waited to see if she did.[52]

Most of her visitors at the very end were "Les Girls," young women hoping they would be introduced to Garbo. Although she had been labeled a social butterfly and tagged "the dyke at the top of the stairs," Mercedes whispered to one of the few friends who still visited her, "I'm sitting here all alone."[53] She pointed to the autographed photographs in her room signed "To Dearest Mercedes," "To the One and Only Mercedes," and others, and admitted that she had been forgotten by all the famous personalities in her past now that she was penniless. "I don't think it's made me bitter—just damned bewildered. And I'm not ashamed to say I'm lonely."[54]

When Cecil telephoned Mercedes in April 1966, she told him she was "dying by slow degrees." "Just out of cantankerousness" she was fighting to live.[55] When he asked if he could come to see her, she replied, "It would give you too much of a shock. You see the pain has been so great behind the eye that it has entirely turned my hair white."[56]

He pleaded with Garbo to send her a note or flowers. But she still harbored resentment and anger. "Why must you bring up such a subject?" she charged. "I've got enough to cope with. I'm in trouble enough. I can't tell you what it is. But it's enough! I don't want any more troubles."[57] Kieran Tunney, however, remembers a moment when Garbo was more compassionate. When he learned that Mercedes was ailing, he hurried to her apartment with some flowers. As he stepped from the elevator, he saw "a slender figure which had been bending over a plant on the ground outside Mercedes' door, straightened up with a muffled gasp. It was Garbo. Putting a finger to her lips, she pointed to the gift and whispered: 'I read the poor dear is suffering. This plant I know will appeal to her. but please don't say I've left it.'"[58] How truly sad that the woman she worshiped for nearly forty years could not bring herself to acknowledge her feelings, even at the end of Mercedes's life.

At the age of seventy-five, Mercedes died of "natural causes" in her apartment at 2:15 AM on May 9, 1968. Even though her doctor, Luis A. Amill, had attended her the night before and had concluded that death was imminent, the only person at her bedside at the end was her sister Maria Chandler.[59] Her body was cremated the next day, and her ashes were buried at Trinity Cemetery alongside the vault containing the bodies of her mother and sister Rita. The small stone that marks the site of her ashes overlooks the Astor mausoleum and is on a hillside surrounded by towering maple trees.

The nine years between 1919 and 1928 had been extremely productive for Mercedes: three books of poetry, two novels, and four produced plays—two Off-Broadway, another in Paris, and a fourth both on Broadway and in London. However, with the exception of her 1960 autobiography, her last forty years were devoid of any literary accomplishment. The early promise she had shown as a poet, novelist, and playwright never truly materialized. In the pantheon of theater history, she is now practically unknown, except perhaps as a starstruck social butterfly and confidante of the superstars of her day.

In recent years, playwrights have attempted to portray her life on stage. In London, Christie Ryan, using *Here Lies the Heart* as her primary reference, wrote both a play and a screenplay that she titled "Mercedes." Although they have been critiqued extensively by notables such as actress–director Estelle Parsons, literary agent Lindsay Granger, and film writer–producer Lee Thuna, they remain unproduced except for a private reading at the Pleasance Theatre in 2000. More successful was the play *Garbo's Cuban Lover*, written by Odalys Nanin and performed in Studio City, California, in the fall of 2001 by Macha Theatre. With a cast of characters including not only Mercedes and Garbo but also Dietrich, Irving Thalberg, Salka Viertel, Poppy Kirk, and Isadora Duncan, the drama was described by a critic for the *Los Angeles Times* as "an intriguing, well-performed portrait of romantic obsession and the attraction of opposites."[60] It was selected by the *Advocate* magazine as one of the ten best plays of 2001.

Although Mercedes's literary work has been forgotten, her story provides an important study on how a writer's same-sex desire can mold a career. Her love for other women and her struggle for acceptance were certainly sources of her originality and fueled her writing. But her need to find her dream woman, along with the cloying emotionalism with which she suffocated her lovers, turned to fanaticism, clouding her vision, taste, and artistic decisions. She was blinded by sexual passion. When he learned of her death, Cecil Beaton wrote an epitaph in his diary: "I cannot be sorry at her death. I am only sorry that she should have been so unfulfilled as a character. In her youth she showed zest and originality. She was one of the most rebellious & brazen of Lesbians. . . . I am relieved that her long drawn out unhappiness has at last come to an end."[61] Thirty-three years after her death, Ram Gopal sat alone in his private room at the Norbury Hall residential home, surrounded by memories—photographs of his parents, his family home in India, Jesus Christ, Ramana Maharshi, Nijinsky, Anna Pavlova, his meeting with the Dalai Lama. Prominently displayed was a large photograph of Mercedes, which she presented to him in 1959. The inscription read, "For Ram, Whose True Self will always shine. Alba." He remembered how she always wanted to be a man. If he were able to speak to her, he would have said, "I hope you've come to some peace with yourself."[62]

It is almost ironic that just one year after her death, on June 28, 1969, riots erupted outside a gay bar in Greenwich Village as city police raided the popular Stonewall Inn. Prior to this time, organizations such as the Mattachine Society had advocated that homosexuals needed to assimilate and to remain invisible. But within weeks of the riots, the new Gay Liberation Front, chanting "out of the closets and into the streets," marked the undisputed birth of the contemporary lesbian and gay rights movement. Unfortunately, Mercedes, a rebellious and brazen lesbian who was a forerunner of the movement, was never able to enjoy the benefits.

At her bedside when she died was her Bible. The front page reveals six snapshots of Garbo, and on the facing page is a quotation from the book of Matthew written in Mercedes's handwriting and dated 1922. It reads, "He that findeth his life shall lose it: and he that loseth his life shall find it. . . . Come unto me, all ye that labour and are heavy laden, and I will give you rest. . . . Take my yoke upon you, and learn of me; for I am meek and lowly in heart: and ye shall find rest unto your souls. . . . For my yoke is easy, and my burden light."

Mercedes died with so many unfulfilled dreams. She had ceaselessly battled and labored to reach them—fame as a successful novelist and poet, a career as a playwright and screenwriter, acceptance as an independent woman, financial security, approval of her desire for other women, gratitude and devotion from her lovers, love and acceptance from Garbo. What tragedy—she achieved none of them.

At the top of the page in the Bible where Mercedes had written the passage from Matthew, there is another image of Garbo. It appears to be from a scene in *Camille* in which she kisses her costar, Robert Taylor, though his face has been carefully cut out. Turning the page exposes still more photos of Garbo. On the page opposite are photos of other women she loved—Eva Le Gallienne, Eleonora Duse, Isadora Duncan, her sister Rita, and her mother.[63] Although several of these women had preceded her in death and two of them—Garbo and Le Gallienne—refused to see Mercedes at the end of her life, they all remained close to her heart.

In the final pages of her autobiography, Mercedes writes,

Today, I realize that my view of life is very different from what it was when I was young, or what it was a few years ago, or even only yesterday. Life is nothing but a continual process of change. Thanks to my many mistakes along the way, I have learned some lessons. . . . Many people I have written about in this book are now dead. Death—that supreme sculptor—has chiselled much of my heart away with the dying of each one. And yet the core of my heart remains. It remains to battle, to struggle, and ever to seek peace. Perhaps just this lesson I in the end must learn: that struggle itself is the peace of life, and that real peace—that envied peace—belongs to another shore. Another shore so close that it is within ourselves. But we must become mariners to reach it. . . . Some things are never to be more than dreamed.[64]

Notes
Index

Notes

Preface

1. Eva Le Gallienne, *At 33* (New York: Longmans, Green, 1939), 161.

2. Anne Kaufman Schneider, interview by author, New York City, May 18, 1989; Diana McLellan, *The Girls: Sappho Goes to Hollywood* (New York: St. Martin's Press, 2000), 16.

3. Robert A. Schanke, *Shattered Applause: The Lives of Eva Le Gallienne* (Carbondale: Southern Illinois University Press, 1992), 278.

4. Kim Marra and Robert A. Schanke, eds., *Staging Desire: Queer Readings of American Theater History* (Ann Arbor: University of Michigan Press, 2002), 4.

5. Edward Burns, ed., *Staying On Alone—The Letters of Alice B. Toklas* (New York: Random House, 1974), 319.

6. S. Smith, *A Poetics of Woman's Autobiography* (Bloomington: Indiana University Press, 1987), 46.

7. Morton Hunt, *The Universe Within* (New York: Simon and Schuster, 1982), 90.

8. McLellan, *The Girls,* 361.

9. Mercedes de Acosta, *Here Lies the Heart* (New York: William Morrow, 1960), 357.

10. Garbo to Mercedes, paraphrase of a letter, September 19, 1935, Rosenbach Museum.

11. John F. Kihlstrom and Nancy Kantor, "Mental Representation of the Self," in *Advances in Experimental Social Psychology,* vol. 17, ed. Leonard Berkowitz (New York: Academic Press, 1984), 13.

12. Cecil Beaton, unpublished diary entry, February 3, 1930.

13. Mercedes de Acosta, *Here Lies the Heart* (North Stratford, NH: Ayer Company Publishers, 1998).

14. Katz to the author, e-mail, October 8, 2001.

15. Georges Gusdorf, "Conditions and Limits of Autobiography," in *Autobiography: Essays Theoretical and Critical,* ed. James Olney (Princeton, NJ: Princeton University Press, 1980), 35.

1. "Mother Complex"

1. Cecil Beaton, unpublished diary entry, February 3, 1930.

2. The last two quotations are from the dust jacket of Diana McLellan's book *The*

Girls: Sappho Goes to Hollywood (New York: St. Martin's Press, 2000) and from an interview of Gavin Lambert by Ron Hogan found at <www.beatrice.com/interviews/lambert/index.html>, respectively.

3. Hugo Vickers, *Loving Garbo: The Story of Greta Garbo, Cecil Beaton, and Mercedes de Acosta* (New York: Random House, 1994), 12.

4. Ibid.

5. Quoted in Steven Bach, *Marlene Dietrich: Life and Legend* (New York: William Morrow, 1992), 172.

6. Lillian Faderman, *Odd Girls and Twilight Lovers: A History of Lesbian Life in Twentieth-Century America* (New York: Columbia University Press, 1991), 64, 67.

7. David Van Leer, *The Queening of America* (New York: Routledge, 1995), 19. See also Laurence Senelick, *Gender in Performance* (Hanover, NH: University Press of New England, 1992), xi, 39.

8. Ram Gopal, interview by author, Norbury Hall, Norbury, England, November 4, 2001.

9. See Felicia Londré, "Money Without Glory: Turn-of-the-Century America's Women Playwrights," in *The American Stage,* ed. Ron Engle and Tice L. Miller (New York: Cambridge University Press, 1993), 131.

10. See J. K. Curry, "Rachel Crothers: An Exceptional Woman in a Man's World," in *Staging Desire: Queer Readings of American Theater History,* ed. Kim Marra and Robert A. Schanke (Ann Arbor: University of Michigan Press, 2002), 55–80.

11. Gopal, interview, November 4, 2001.

12. *Cleveland Plain Dealer,* July 23, 1911.

13. Quoted in George Chauncey, *Gay New York: Gender, Urban Culture, and the Making of the Gay Male World* (New York: BasicBooks, 1994), 352.

14. Faderman, *Odd Girls,* 119.

15. Abram Poole Jr., telephone conversation with author, August 14, 2001. This information was corroborated during an interview with Ram Gopal on November 14, 2001.

16. Quoted in Faderman, *Odd Girls,* 131.

17. Ibid., 145.

18. Family genealogy, Rosenbach Museum, Philadelphia. Each page is edged in gold and is handwritten in Spanish.

19. Louis A. Pérez, *Cuba: Between Reform and Revolution* (New York: Oxford University Press, 1988), 100.

20. Basil Rauch, *American Interest in Cuba: 1848–1855* (New York: Columbia University Press, 1948), 42.

21. Mercedes de Acosta, "Here Lies the Heart," typescript with corrections, folder 03:01, 22, Rosenbach Museum.

22. Mercedes de Acosta, *Here Lies the Heart* (New York: William Morrow, 1960), 12.

23. Philip S. Foner, *A History of Cuba and Its Relations with the United States,* vol. 1, *1492–1845* (New York: International Publishers, 1962), 125.

24. Ibid., 10.

25. On April 18–22, 2001, I visited Morro Castle and, with the assistance of an interpreter, Dr. George Ann Huck, talked with several guides.

26. Nephew of Mercedes, telephone interview by author, August 6, 2001.

27. The exact birth date of Mercedes's mother and the date of her marriage to

Mercedes's father are unclear. As far as I can determine, the dates are as follows: Mercedes's father was born in 1837 and fled to the United States in 1852. Mercedes's mother was born in 1853 and arrived in New York in 1868. They married in 1870, when he was thirty-three years old and she was seventeen.

28. *Here Lies the Heart,* 16.

29. 1870 *New York Census Index,* vol. 1 (Bountiful, UT: Precision Indexing, 1997). Ricardo de Acosta was listed as an importer of Sigars [*sic*].

30. This calculation was provided by Dr. Richard Glendening, professor of economics, Central College, Pella, IA.

31. *Here Lies the Heart,* 19.

32. Jerry E. Patterson, *The Vanderbilts* (New York: Harry N. Abrams, 1989), 126–31.

33. This calculation was provided by Glendening.

34. Her exact birth year is unclear. Her death certificate lists 1892; her application for a social security account number lists 1900; her *New York Times* obituary lists 1893; her passports list 1900.

35. *Here Lies the Heart,* 26–27.

36. In a telephone interview I conducted with Patricia Andre on September 1, 2000, she stated that her grandmother, Bridget Burns Eagan, who had been born in Ireland on November 28, 1856, migrated to America and was wet nurse for the de Acostas, possibly from 1888 to 1899. It is unclear whether Bridget Eagan and Bridget Sweeney are the same woman.

37. *Here Lies the Heart,* 28–29.

38. Ibid., 23.

39. Ibid., 29.

40. Ibid.

41. *New York Times,* May 23, 1897.

42. *Here Lies the Heart,* 11, 24.

43. Ibid., 11.

44. Mercedes de Acosta, book of poems, folder 04:11, Rosenbach Museum.

45. *Here Lies the Heart,* 24.

46. Typescript with corrections, folder 03:01, 11, Rosenbach Museum.

47. Brooks Atkinson, *Broadway* (New York: Macmillan, 1970), 17.

48. *Here Lies the Heart,* 43.

49. *New York Times,* November 7, 1905.

50. *Here Lies the Heart,* 17.

51. Stacy Wolf, "Mary Martin: Washin' That Man Right Outta Her Hair," in *Passing Performances: Queer Readings of Leading Players in American Theater History,* ed. Robert A. Schanke and Kim Marra (Ann Arbor: University of Michigan Press, 1998), 295.

2. "I Will Be Lonely All My Life"

1. Frank Crowninshield, "An Elegante of Another Era," in *Appreciations of Rita de Acosta Lydig with Notes on an Exhibition Held at the Museum of Costume Art* (New York: N.p., March 12, 1940), n.p.

2. The exact year is impossible to determine. When she married in 1895, the press variously reported that she was fifteen, sixteen, eighteen, or twenty. Most sources set her birth date in 1880. However, a copy of her marriage certificate, found in her divorce decree from William E. D. Stokes, lists her as being twenty years old when they

married in 1895. The decree is registered with the Supreme Court, New York County, and is on file at the County Clerk's office, New York City.

3. Mercedes de Acosta, "Here Lies the Heart," typescript with corrections, folder 03:01, 43, Rosenbach Museum.

4. *New York Times,* November 18, 1894.

5. *New York Times,* January 4, 1895.

6. *New York Times,* January 6, 1895; Mercedes de Acosta, *Here Lies the Heart* (New York: William Morrow, 1960), 5.

7. M.K.L., "Profiles: Lady of an Antique World," *New Yorker,* November 19, 1927, 28.

8. Typescript with corrections, folder 02:01, 37, Rosenbach Museum.

9. *New York Times,* April 22 and May 15, 1895.

10. *New York Times,* April 4, 1895, and October 9, 1896.

11. *New York Times,* October 16 and November 15, 1896, and January 7, 1897.

12. *New York Times,* October 3, 1897.

13. Mrs. Philip Lydig, *Tragic Mansions* (New York: Boni and Liveright, 1927), 144–45.

14. *New York Times,* November 18, 1894.

15. *Here Lies the Heart,* 22.

16. *New York Times,* August 19, 1899.

17. A complete transcript of the court testimony and the divorce decree is on file at the County Clerk's office, New York City.

18. *New York Times,* May 3 and May 8, 1900; divorce decree registered with the Supreme Court, New York County; Annette Tapert and Diana Edkins, *The Power of Style: The Women Who Defined the Art of Living Well* (New York: Crown Publishers, 1994), 17.

19. *New York Times,* April 20, 1927; Tapert and Edkins, 17.

20. *Here Lies the Heart,* 22.

21. Tapert and Edkins, 17.

22. *Here Lies the Heart,* 23.

23. Typescript with corrections, folder 02:01, 38, Rosenbach Museum. On page 95 of Helen Sheehy's *Eva Le Gallienne: A Biography* (New York: Alfred A. Knopf, 1996), the author supplies a parenthetical criticism of Mercedes's memory: "Never mind that photographs of Mercedes with her brothers and sisters show her in long curls and ruffled dresses." The accusation seems odd, since there is only one extant photograph of Mercedes as a young girl. Indeed, that photograph, which is included in Mercedes's autobiography, shows her with long curls and a ruffled dress. However, she is clearly older than seven years, the age when Mercedes claims she discovered she was not a boy. But the important point here is not whether she dressed as a boy or even believed she was a boy. Rather, it is more important that Mercedes wanted her readers to believe this account of her childhood, whether or not it was true.

24. Mercedes de Acosta, "First Writing," typed manuscript of her autobiography, folder 01:05, 30–32, Rosenbach Museum. In both Hugo Vickers's *Loving Garbo: The Story of Greta Garbo, Cecil Beaton, and Mercedes de Acosta* (New York: Random House, 1994) and Karen Swenson's *Greta Garbo: A Life Apart* (New York: Scribner, 1997), the authors cite as sources the "First Draft" and the "Second Draft" of *Here Lies the Heart.* The librarian at the Rosenbach Museum, Elizabeth Fuller, has confirmed that those citations are not accurate. The museum has no manuscripts labeled "First Draft" or "Second Draft." The citations I provide here are the correct ones.

25. Quoted in Lillian Faderman, ed., *Chloe Plus Olivia: An Anthology of Lesbian Literature from the Seventeenth Century to the Present* (New York: Penguin, 1994), 164–76.

26. Typescript with corrections, folder 03:01, 66, Rosenbach Museum.

27. William Lee Howard, "Effeminate Men and Masculine Women," *New York Medical Journal* 77 (May 5, 1900): 686–87.

28. *New York Times,* January 26 and 29, 1892.

29. *Here Lies the Heart,* 36.

30. "First Writing," 30–32.

31. Ibid., 33–34.

32. Typescript with corrections, folder 02:04, 338.

33. *Here Lies the Heart,* 41.

34. M.K.L., "Profiles," 28–29.

35. *The Rita Lydig Collection of Notable Art* (New York: American Art Association, 1913), ix–x.

36. Crowninshield, "An Elegante of Another Era," n.p.

37. William Harlan Hale, *The World of Rodin: 1840–1917* (New York: Time-Life Books, 1969), 10.

38. Isadora Duncan, *My Life* (Boni and Liveright, 1927), 285.

39. *Here Lies the Heart,* 48. Unfortunately, the bust of Rita Lydig by Rodin cannot be located.

40. There is no evidence that Mercedes's father ever visited Cuba after he emigrated to the United States. Even though he was in New York when the Cuban revolutionary Josef Marti visited the city, there is no record of their meeting or of her father's response to the revolution.

41. Alfred Allen Lewis, *Ladies and Not-So-Gentle Women* (New York: Viking, 2000), 160.

42. *New York Times,* August 28, 1907.

43. *Here Lies the Heart,* 54.

44. Typescript with corrections, folder 02:01, 95, Rosenbach Museum.

45. Mercedes Hernandez de Acosta prayer book from 1908, Rosenbach Museum.

46. Mercedes de Acosta, book of poems, folder 04:11, Rosenbach Museum.

47. Typescript with corrections, folder 03:02, 205–7, Rosenbach Museum.

48. Ibid.

49. Quoted in Louis A. Pérez, *Cuba: Between Reform and Revolution* (New York: Oxford University Press, 1988), 166.

50. Quoted in Geoff Simons, *Cuba: From Conquistador to Castro* (New York: St. Martin's Press, 1996), 221.

51. Mercedes de Acosta, book of poems, folder 04:11, Rosenbach Museum.

52. *Here Lies the Heart,* 65.

53. Typescript with corrections, folder 03:02, 140, Rosenbach Museum.

54. *Here Lies the Heart,* 61–62.

55. *New York Times,* October 19, 1911.

3. "Beauty She Achieved"

1. Paris telephone numbers and addresses for Natalie Barney and Alice B. Toklas are written in Rita's address book, box 2, folder 4, Special Collections, Georgetown University Library, Washington, DC.

2. Elisabeth Marbury, *My Crystal Ball* (New York: Boni and Liveright, 1923), 261.

3. *New York Times,* April 1, 1913.

4. The Costume Institute of the Metropolitan Museum of Art and the Museum of the City of New York own a considerable amount of her costume collection.

5. Annette Tapert and Diana Edkins, *The Power of Style: The Women Who Defined the Art of Living Well* (New York: Crown Publishers, 1994), 23.

6. Mercedes de Acosta, *Here Lies the Heart* (New York: William Morrow, 1960), 46.

7. Tapert and Edkins, 22–23.

8. "Rita de Acosta Lydig (1880–1929)," a tribute written by the Costume Institute of the Metropolitan Museum of Art, June 23, 2000, <http://www.costumeinstitute.org/ritade.htm>.

9. Arnold Genthe, *As I Remember* (New York: Reynal and Hitchcock, 1936), 221–22.

10. Alfred Allen Lewis, *Ladies and Not-So-Gentle Women* (New York: Viking, 2000), 229.

11. *New York Times,* June 6, 1922.

12. Lue Allen, review of *Ladies and Not-So-Gentle Women,* by Alfred Allen Lewis, <http://www.thedailypage.com/features/books/archive>.

13. Quoted in Lewis, 55.

14. On page 209 of *Ladies and Not-So-Gentle Women,* Lewis cites Marbury's *My Crystal Ball* when he claims that Bessie came up with the club's coat of arms, "a beaver, signifying activity, and a crown, suggesting that in democratic America each woman was a queen." Given the symbolic connotations of the beaver, such a choice would have been ironic, indeed. However, my examination of Marbury's book did not uncover this fact. Since I have not discovered such a reference in any other source, I question its validity.

15. *New York Times,* December 16, 1909.

16. Quoted in Robert A. Schanke, "Mary Shaw: A Fighting Champion," in *Women in American Theatre,* ed. Helen Krich Chinoy and Linda Walsh Jenkins (New York: Theatre Communications Group, 1987), 103.

17. Mrs. Philip Lydig, *Tragic Mansions* (New York: Boni and Liveright, 1927), 15, 46–47, 66–67, 72.

18. Ibid., 143–44.

19. *Here Lies the Heart,* 22.

20. Mercedes de Acosta, "First Writing," typed manuscript of her autobiography, folder 01:05, 196–97, Rosenbach Museum.

21. *New York Times,* April 5, 1913.

22. *New York Times,* March 23, 1913. When I contacted the Mayo Clinic to determine the exact nature of her illness, I learned that Minnesota state law prohibits disclosing any patient information, except to relatives, even though there are no living relatives and Rita died in 1929.

23. *New York Times,* April 2, 1913.

24. *New York Times,* August 8, 1914.

25. Axel Madsen, *The Sewing Circle: Hollywood's Greatest Secret, Female Stars Who Loved Other Women* (New York: Birch Lane Press, 1995), 41.

26. See Robert A. Schanke, *Shattered Applause: The Lives of Eva Le Gallienne* (Carbondale: Southern Illinois University Press, 1992), as well as his essay on Nazimova in

Passing Performances: Queer Readings of Leading Players in American Theater History, ed. Robert A. Schanke and Kim Marra (Ann Arbor: University of Michigan Press, 1998).

27. For more information about the Orlenev-Nazimova tour, see Laurence Senelick, "The American Tour of Orlenev and Nazimova, 1905–1906" in *Wandering Stars: Russian Emigré Theatre, 1905–1940,* ed. Laurence Senelick (Iowa City: University of Iowa Press, 1992), 1–15. Emma Goldman describes her work for Orlenev and Nazimova in her autobiography, *Living My Life: Emma Goldman,* vol. 1 (New York: Dover Publications, 1970), 373–79. Her experience served as the cornerstone for her book *The Social Significance of the Modern Drama.*

28. Louis Untermeyer's "Nazimova as Hedda Gabler" appears in Ada Patterson's "An Interview with a Multiple Woman," *Theatre Magazine* 7 (August 1907): 219; Sigismond de Ivanowski's portraits of her as Nora and Hedda appeared in Owen Johnson's essay, "Mme. Alla Nazimova," *Century Magazine* 74 (June 1907): 221, 223–26.

29. Madsen, *The Sewing Circle,* 117, 146.

30. Canby to Lee Shubert, December 29, 1908, Shubert Archive, New York City.

31. Ibid.

32. *New York Evening Star,* n.d., Shubert Archive.

33. "Nazimova in *War Brides,*" *Theatre Magazine* 22 (March 1915): 116.

34. Mercedes de Acosta, "Here Lies the Heart," typescript with corrections, folder 02:02, 121–22, Rosenbach Museum.

35. Quoted in Gavin Lambert, *Nazimova: A Biography* (New York: Alfred A. Knopf, 1997), 173.

36. Ibid., 178.

37. For a discussion of their meeting, see *Here Lies the Heart,* 72–75.

38. Typescript with corrections, folder 02:02, 121, Rosenbach Museum.

39. Ann Daly, *Done into Dance: Isadora Duncan in America* (Bloomington: Indiana University Press, 1995), 185.

40. Ibid., 187.

41. "First Writing," 64.

42. Ibid., 75.

43. Ram Gopal, interview by author, Norbury, England, November 14, 2001.

4. "Strange Turmoil"

1. Mrs. Philip Lydig, *Tragic Mansions* (New York: Boni and Liveright, 1927), 143–44.

2. Joseph Wood Krutch, *The American Drama Since 1918: An Informal History,* rev. ed. (New York: G. Braziller, 1957), 7–8.

3. Since it is impossible to know when she actually completed writing her plays, I have provided the dates when they were copyrighted or published. The Library of Congress copyright registration number for *Loneliness* is 44123; © copyright June 10, 1916. Unless otherwise noted, all direct quotations are from the actual scripts. All copyrights of Mercedes's plays, published and unpublished, have expired.

4. Library of Congress copyright registration number, 45349; © copyright November 4, 1916.

5. Paul Kennedy to Mercedes, November 20, 1919, folder 09:14, Rosenbach Museum, quotes a letter Kennedy had received from Williams. Kennedy's letter is on letterhead of the Foreign Press Service.

6. *Somewhere in France: A Play in 1 Act* © copyright June 15, 1916; registration number, 44149.

7. Mercedes de Acosta and Stuart Benson, *"For France,"* Outlook, July 25, 1917, 483. In January 1921, Stuart Benson married Mary "Mimsey" Duggett, an actress who had been the emotional center of Eva Le Gallienne's life for three years. A few months earlier, Mercedes had initiated her own relationship with Le Gallienne.

8. Mercedes de Acosta, *Here Lies the Heart* (New York: William Morrow, 1960), 76.

9. Ibid., 85.

10. Mercedes de Acosta, *Moods* (New York: Moffat, Yard, 1919), 45.

11. *Vogue,* March 15, 1920, n.p.

12. Ibid., 2.

13. *What Next!* © copyright February 3, 1920; Library of Congress registration number, 53757.

14. *Here Lies the Heart,* 95.

15. Richard Kislan, *The Musical* (New York: Applause Books, 1995), 117–19.

16. Mercedes de Acosta, "Here Lies the Heart," typescript with corrections, folder 02:02, 173, Rosenbach Museum. In the typescript of the play, this song is in act 3.

17. *New York Herald,* January 27, 1920; *New York American,* January 27, 1920. It seems odd that there are no extant photos of the production, nor is the production ever mentioned in any discussions of the Princess musicals.

18. *Here Lies the Heart,* 108.

19. Ibid.

20. *Here Lies the Heart,* 109.

21. Elisabeth Marbury, *My Crystal Ball* (New York: Boni and Liveright, 1923), 36.

22. *New York Times,* May 12, 1920.

23. *New York Sun,* February 27, 1922.

24. Hugo Vickers, *Loving Garbo: The Story of Greta Garbo, Cecil Beaton, and Mercedes de Acosta* (New York: Random House, 1994), 12.

25. *New York Times,* August 15, 1919.

26. *Here Lies the Heart,* 124.

27. See J. K. Curry, "Rachel Crothers: An Exceptional Woman in a Man's World," in *Passing Performances: Queer Readings of Leading Players in American Theater History,* ed. Robert A. Schanke and Kim Marra (Ann Arbor: University of Michigan Press, 1998).

28. Mercedes de Acosta, *Wind Chaff* (New York: Moffat, Yard, 1920), 11–12, 188–89, 225, 232.

29. "Many Women of Society Win Fame in the World of Literature and Art," *New York Herald,* n.d. Unmarked clipping in file 06:04, de Acosta Collection, Rosenbach Museum.

30. Typescript with corrections, folder 02:03, 216, Rosenbach Museum.

31. *The Moon Flower,* © copyright September 24, 1920; Library of Congress registration number, 55585.

5. "Love Goes On"

1. See Robert A. Schanke, *Shattered Applause: The Lives of Eva Le Gallienne* (Carbondale: Southern Illinois University Press, 1992). In my discussion of the relationship between Mercedes and Le Gallienne, there are discrepancies between what I have written in this book and what I wrote in *Shattered Applause.* When I was writing

the earlier biography, Le Gallienne was still alive and the letters that she wrote to Mercedes were sealed at the Rosenbach Museum. Those letters, which were made available to readers after she died in 1991, provide more accurate information than was earlier available.

2. *New York Times,* May 4, 1920.

3. In my biography of Le Gallienne, *Shattered Applause,* 53–54, and in Helen Sheehy's biography *Eva Le Gallienne: A Biography* (New York: Alfred A. Knopf, 1996), 95, we both state that Mercedes met Le Gallienne in 1921 when she was starring in *Liliom.* But if they met a few days prior to Mercedes's wedding, as Mercedes claims, the year had to be 1920 and not 1921.

4. Mercedes de Acosta, "Here Lies the Heart," typescript with corrections, folder 02:02, 200, Rosenbach Museum.

5. Mercedes de Acosta, *Archways of Life* (New York: Moffat, Yard, 1921), 13.

6. *New York Times,* May 1, 1921; *Cleveland Plain Dealer,* October 17, 1922.

7. *Austin Statesman,* November 17, 1924.

8. Typescript with corrections, folder 02:03, 221, Rosenbach Museum.

9. In *Here Lies the Heart* (New York: William Morrow, 1960), Mercedes lists the date of death as December 21. However, her mother's obituary appeared in the *New York Times* on December 6, 1921, and records her death as having occurred on December 5.

10. *Here Lies the Heart,* 134–35.

11. Mercedes de Acosta, *Sandro Botticelli* (New York: Moffat, Yard, 1923).

12. *Here Lies the Heart,* 136.

13. Ibid., 103.

14. Typescript with corrections, folder 02:02, 180, Rosenbach Museum.

15. Ibid.

16. Michael Strange to Mercedes, poem, Christmas 1921, folder 11:09, Rosenbach Museum.

17. Le Gallienne to Mercedes, paraphrase of a poem, January 12, 1922, Rosenbach Museum.

18. All letters from Le Gallienne to Mercedes paraphrased in this chapter are at the Rosenbach Museum.

19. Le Gallienne to Mercedes, paraphrase of a poem written in 1922, Rosenbach Museum.

20. Le Gallienne to Mercedes, paraphrase of letters, May 2, 13, 22, and 23, 1922, Rosenbach Museum.

21. *Here Lies the Heart,* 122; Le Gallienne to Mercedes, paraphrase of a letter, May 18, 1922, Rosenbach Museum.

22. Le Gallienne to Mercedes, paraphrase of a poem written in 1922, Rosenbach Museum.

23. Le Gallienne to Mercedes, paraphrase of a letter, June 13, 1922.

24. Ibid., June 12, 1922.

25. *Archways of Life,* 14.

26. Ibid., 33.

27. Ibid., 13, 14, 33, 24.

28. Mercedes de Acosta, *Streets and Shadows* (New York: Moffat, Yard, 1922), 33.

29. *Archways of Life,* 18.

30. Marjorie Allen Seiffert, "A Warm-Hearted Book," *Poetry: A Magazine of Verse,* January 1924, 222–23.

31. Le Gallienne to Mercedes, paraphrase of a letter, September 19, 1922.

32. Ibid., July 24, 1922.

33. *Archways of Life,* 34.

34. Le Gallienne to Mercedes, paraphrase of letters, August 2 and 22, 1922.

35. Ibid., August 24, 1922.

36. Ibid., September 29 and October 4, 1922.

37. Ibid., October 11, 1922.

38. Ibid., October 18, 1922.

39. Ibid., November 10, 1922.

40. Ibid., March 4, 1923.

41. *Jehanne d'Arc* © copyright March 3, 1922; Library of Congress registration number, 60141.

42. Le Gallienne to Mercedes, paraphrase of a letter, May 13, 1922.

43. Le Gallienne to Mercedes, paraphrase of letters, March 1 and 8, 1923.

44. *Sandro Botticelli* © copyright February 20, 1923; Library of Congress registration number, 63688; published by Moffat, Yard, and Company in 1923.

45. Hope Williams to Mercedes, card, folder 11:19, de Acosta Collection, Rosenbach Museum; Jesse Lynch Williams to Mercedes, telegram, March 26, 1923, de Acosta Collection, Rosenbach Museum.

46. Percy Hammond, "The Theaters," *New York Tribune,* March 27, 1923; Heywood Broun, *Democrat Chronicle,* April 1, 1923; Gordon Whyte, *Billboard,* April 7, 1923.

47. Typescript with corrections, folder 02:02, 101, Rosenbach Museum.

48. Ibid., folder 02:03, 247, Rosenbach Museum.

49. *Jacob Slovak* © copyright February 20, 1923; Library of Congress registration number, 63687.

50. *Here Lies the Heart,* 148.

51. Ibid., 149.

52. Le Gallienne to Mercedes, paraphrase of a letter, June 23, 1924.

53. *Streets and Shadows,* 26, 36.

54. Le Gallienne to Mercedes, paraphrase of a letter, April 14, 1923.

55. *Here Lies the Heart,* 149.

56. Typescript with corrections, folder 03:04, 338–39, Rosenbach Museum.

57. *Mother of Christ* © copyright April 5, 1924; Library of Congress registration number, 67345.

58. Typescript with corrections, folder 03:04, 323–24, Rosenbach Museum. A copy of the Italian translation intended for Duse is in the de Acosta Collection of the Rosenbach Museum with the title *La Luce Infinita* (The Infinite Light) and dated 1924, folder 04:01.

59. Mercedes's ticket to the solemn requiem mass, as well as the palm leaf, is in the Rosenbach Museum.

60. de Wolfe to Mercedes, 1923, Rosenbach Museum.

61. Le Gallienne to Mercedes, paraphrase of a letter, September 26, 1924.

62. Ibid., February 6, 1922.

63. Ibid., April 6, 1922.

64. Typed manuscript of *Jehanne d'Arc,* Rosenbach Museum.

65. Le Gallienne to Mercedes, paraphrase of a letter, November 16, 1924.

66. Ibid., February 18, 1925.

67. Correspondence from Mercedes to Speiser, as well as from O'Neill to Speiser, is in the Speiser Collection, University of Pennsylvania Rare Book and Manuscript Library, Philadelphia.

68. Mercedes de Acosta, "First Writing," typed manuscript of her autobiography, folder 01:05, 175–76, Rosenbach Museum.

69. *Theatre Magazine,* May 1925.

70. *Chicago Tribune* (Paris edition), June 11, 1925.

71. Norman Bel Geddes, *Miracle in the Evening: An Autobiography,* ed. William Kelley (Garden City, NY: Doubleday, 1960), 329–30.

72. Quoted in Sheehy, *Eva Le Gallienne,* 99.

73. *L'Action Française* (Paris), June 18, 1925.

74. *New York Review,* July 11, 1925.

75. Flanner to Mercedes, poem, n.d., folder 08:14, Rosenbach Museum.

76. Noel Coward, *Present Indicative* (New York: Doubleday, 1937), 216.

77. Karsavina to Mercedes, July 23, 1926, folder 09:12, Rosenbach Museum.

78. Le Gallienne to her mother, July 27, 1925, and June 24, 1928; and quoted in Sheehy, *Eva Le Gallienne,* 127–28.

79. *Here Lies the Heart,* 166.

80. "First Writing," 181. Le Gallienne founded the Civic Repertory Theatre in New York City in October 1926.

81. Le Gallienne to Mercedes, paraphrase of a letter, March 1, 1926, Rosenbach Museum.

82. *Streets and Shadows,* 26.

6. "Bound to Blunder"

1. Mercedes de Acosta, *Here Lies the Heart* (New York: William Morrow, 1960), 170.

2. Duncan to Mercedes, poem, 1927, folder 08:07, Rosenbach Museum.

3. Duncan to Mercedes, n.d., Rosenbach Museum.

4. Isadora Duncan, *My Life* (New York: Boni and Liveright, 1927), 285.

5. *New York Times,* September 21 and 22 and October 30, 1926.

6. *They That Walk Enchained* © copyright November 4, 1916; Library of Congress registration number, 45349.

7. *The Better Life* © copyright January 12, 1925; Library of Congress registration number, 70040.

8. *Illusion* © copyright March 14, 1928; Library of Congress registration number, 83146.

9. *The Dark Light* © copyright February 6, 1926; Library of Congress registration number, 74466. A copy of this script can be found in the Georgetown University Library, Washington, DC.

10. "The Arrow of Longing," typescript, Rosenbach Museum.

11. Mercedes de Acosta, "Here Lies the Heart," typescript with corrections, folder 02:04, 316, Rosenbach Museum.

12. Bel Geddes to Le Gallienne, November 26, 1924, folder 08:18, Rosenbach Museum.

13. In Philip Hoare, *Noel Coward* (University of Chicago Press, 1998), 151, the

author refers to Bickerton as the "sometime lover of Mercedes de Acosta." This relationship is highly unlikely. Mercedes was a committed lesbian who never had her name linked with any man except her husband, Abram Poole. Abram's son by a second marriage maintains that the marriage between his father and Mercedes was never consummated.

14. *New York Times,* October 6, 1927; *New York World,* October 6, 1927; *Billboard,* n.d.

15. The stage manager's working copy of *Jacob Slovak* is in the Rosenbach Museum, folder 04:02. It is almost identical to the typescript for *Prejudice,* folder 04:10, which was used for the subsequent London production.

16. *Here Lies the Heart,* 173.

17. The correspondence between Mercedes and Edward Gordon Craig can be found in the Billy Rose Theatre Collection, New York Public Library. The letters are not dated. On several of Mercedes's letters to him, Craig has scribbled caustic remarks in the margins.

18. Perhaps Craig did not care for the way Duncan described him so vividly. At one point, she writes, "In him I had met the flesh of my flesh, the blood of my blood. . . . I always see him . . . when his white, lithe, gleaming body emerged from the chrysalis of clothes and shone upon my dazzled eyes in all his splendour." See Duncan, *My Life,* 182–83.

19. There is a copy of *The Mother of Christ* in the Max Reinhardt Archives and Library in the Special Collections at the State University of New York in Binghamton. In German, it is called *Die Mutter Gottes.* The curator of the Archives, Herbert Poetzl, has noted that it was probably sent to the Reinhardt theater organization and that Reinhardt himself rarely read these submissions. There is no further evidence that Reinhardt was considering a production.

20. These last two quotations are printed on the front and back covers of the paperback edition published by Liveright Publishing Corporation in 1995.

21. In Ronald Hayman's *John Gielgud* (New York: Random House, 1971), there is no mention of the production in the text, although it is listed in the chronological list of productions at the end of the book. Soon after the production, he was invited to join the Old Vic, where he starred as Romeo.

22. *Daily Sketch,* June 18, 1928; *Evening Standard,* June 18, 1928; *Morning Post,* June 18, 1928; *Western Morning News and Mercury* (Plymouth), June 19, 1928.

23. *Outlook,* June 23, 1928; *Times* (London), June 18, 1928.

24. John Gielgud to the author, August 7, 1995.

25. *Here Lies the Heart,* 119, 138.

26. Karsavina to Mercedes, telegram, folder 09:13; Karsavina to Mercedes, telegram, July 13, 1928, folder 09:12, Rosenbach Museum.

27. Diana McLellan, *The Girls: Sappho Goes to Hollywood* (New York: St. Martin's Press, 2000), 93.

28. Le Gallienne to her mother, May 9 and June 24, 1928, and quoted in Helen Sheehy, *Eva Le Gallienne: A Biography* (New York: Alfred A. Knopf, 1996), 176.

29. All the essays are at the Rosenbach Museum.

30. Mercedes de Acosta, *Until the Day Break* (New York: Longmans, Green, 1928).

31. This message by Elisabeth Marbury seems to have been intended as a promotional quotation for Mercedes's new book and is in the de Acosta Collection, Rosenbach Museum.

32. "Latest Works of Fiction," *New York Times,* April 29, 1928; Anne Kulique Kramer, "Mercedes de Acosta: Poet and Dramatist," *American Hebrew,* May 4, 1928, 982; "With

Silent Friends," *Tatler,* May 30, 1928, 398; Neil Lyons, "Footprints," *Bookman,* July 1928, n.p.

33. Vern L. Bullough, *Homosexuality: A History* (New York: New American Library, 1979), 124–25.

34. *New York Times,* September 30, 1926; *New York Morning Telegraph,* October 10, 1926; Arthur Hornblow, "Mr. Hornblow Goes to the Play," *Theatre Magazine* 44 (December 1926): 16; George Jean Nathan, "The Theatre," *American Mercury* 12 (March 1927): 373.

35. McLellan, *The Girls,* 85.

36. Cecil Beaton, unpublished diary, December 13, 1928, and quoted in Hugo Vickers, *Loving Garbo: The Story of Greta Garbo, Cecil Beaton, and Mercedes de Acosta* (New York: Random House, 1994), 39.

37. Beaton, unpublished diary, December 15, 1928.

38. Ibid., December 16, 1928.

39. The Library of Congress registration number for *Himself* is 5669. It was copyrighted on May 16, 1930.

40. *New York Times,* October 3, 1921.

41. *New York Times,* September 2, 1922.

42. *New York Times,* September 24, 1922.

43. *New York Times,* May 26, 1924.

44. *New York Times,* September 10, 1926. This statement was later used in her book *Tragic Mansions.*

45. *New York Times,* March 18 and April 7, 1927.

46. *New York Times,* April 20, 1927.

47. *New York Times,* May 8 and 11, July 13, and August 25, 1927.

48. *New York Times,* May 3, June 3 and 22, and October 18, 1927.

49. *New York Times,* March 26, August 11, and December 7, 1925.

50. *New York Times,* October 7, 1927; June 21, 1928; October 20, 1929; Standard Certificate of Death, Bureau of Records, Department of Health of the City of New York.

51. Typescript with corrections, folder 03:02, 110, Rosenbach Museum.

52. *Here Lies the Heart,* 205.

53. Craig to Mercedes, January 23, 1928, Rosenbach Museum.

7. "My Beloved"

1. Marbury to Mercedes, May 6, 1929, Rosenbach Museum.

2. Mercedes de Acosta, *Here Lies the Heart* (New York: William Morrow, 1960), 206.

3. *East River,* film script, Rosenbach Museum.

4. Poole to Mercedes, card, n.d., folder 10:26, 242, Rosenbach Museum.

5. *Here Lies the Heart,* 209.

6. Mercedes de Acosta, "First Writing," typed manuscript of her autobiography, folder 01:05, n.p., Rosenbach Museum.

7. Mercedes de Acosta, "Here Lies the Heart," typescript with corrections, folder 03:05, 452–53, Rosenbach Museum.

8. Leila J. Rupp, "'Imagine My Surprise': Women's Relationships in Mid-Twentieth-Century America," in *Hidden from History: Reclaiming the Gay and Lesbian Past,* ed. Martin Bauml Duberman, Martha Vicinus, and George Chauncey Jr. (New York: Penguin, 1989), 399–404.

9. *Here Lies the Heart,* 214.

10. Typescript with corrections, folder 02:04, 345.

11. *Here Lies the Heart,* 215–18.

12. Antoni Gronowicz, *Garbo: Her Story* (New York: Simon and Schuster, 1990), 311–17.

13. Ibid.

14. Ibid., 224, 226.

15. "*Susan Lenox* Sent Back for Retakes," *Hollywood Reporter,* August 11, 1931, n.p.; "It's Funny About My Face," *American Magazine,* June 1934.

16. Mercedes de Acosta, "In New Mexico," *Poetry: A Magazine of Verse* 38 (June 1931): 143.

17. Mercedes de Acosta, "Poems to Greta Garbo," folder 23:113, Rosenbach Museum. On page 127 of Diana McLellan's *The Girls: Sappho Goes to Hollywood* (New York: St. Martin's Press, 2000), the author suggests that Mercedes "presented Greta with a book of her poems, lovingly inscribed" with this particular poem. Since this scrapbook of poems is handwritten, was not completed until 1944, and is in the Mercedes de Acosta Collection at the Rosenbach Museum, it is doubtful that Mercedes ever presented it to Garbo.

18. Karen Swenson, *Greta Garbo: A Life Apart* (New York: Scribner, 1997), 260.

19. The source for this information is found in Swenson, *Greta Garbo,* 259–60.

20. Garbo to Mercedes, card, folder 23:01, Rosenbach Museum.

21. *Desperate,* film script, Rosenbach Museum.

22. *Here Lies the Heart,* 233.

23. *Hollywood Citizen-News,* June 6, 1932.

24. Mercedes to President Hoover, telegram, June 16, 1932, National Archives.

25. Gronowicz, *Garbo: Her Story,* 317–21.

26. Ibid.

27. Comic strip, folder 23:02, Rosenbach Museum.

28. Loos to Beaton, September 29, 1932, and quoted in Hugo Vickers, *Loving Garbo: The Story of Greta Garbo, Cecil Beaton, and Mercedes de Acosta* (New York: Random House, 1994), 3.

29. McLellan, *The Girls,* 196.

30. "Poems to Greta Garbo," folder 23:113, Rosenbach Museum.

31. *Here Lies the Heart,* 240.

8. "State of Slavery"

1. Dietrich to her husband, quoted in Maria Riva, *Marlene Dietrich* (New York: Alfred A. Knopf, 1992), 154. In *Here Lies the Heart* (New York: William Morrow, 1960), 241, Mercedes writes that she met Dietrich when she accompanied Cecil Beaton to a dance concert. Dietrich's letter to her husband, however, says they met at a party.

2. Quoted in Riva, *Marlene Dietrich,* 154.

3. Kenneth Tynan, *The Sound of Two Hands Clapping* (New York: Holt, Rinehart, Winston, 1975), 84.

4. Dietrich to Mercedes, telegram, September 19, 1932, and cited in Hugo Vickers, *Loving Garbo: The Story of Greta Garbo, Cecil Beaton, and Mercedes de Acosta* (New York: Random House, 1994), 60.

5. Dietrich to Mercedes, September 15, 1932, folder 08:24, Rosenbach Museum.

6. Ibid., September 29, 1932.

7. Ibid., November 6, 1932.

8. Ibid., n.d.

9. Mercedes de Acosta, "Here Lies the Heart," typescript with corrections, folder 02:04, 391, Rosenbach Museum.

10. Quoted in Vickers, *Loving Garbo,* 60.

11. Maddy Vegtel, "Blonde Venus and Swedish Sphinx," *Vanity Fair,* June 1934.

12. Quoted in Riva, *Marlene Dietrich,* 154.

13. Mercedes de Acosta, note in her address book, Georgetown University Library, Washington, DC.

14. Mercedes to Dietrich, ca. 1932, quoted in Riva, *Marlene Dietrich,* 168.

15. Quoted in Alfred Allen Lewis, *Ladies and Not-So-Gentle Women* (New York: Viking, 2000), 429.

16. Quoted in Riva, *Marlene Dietrich,* 157.

17. Ibid., 168–69.

18. Garbo to Mercedes, paraphrase of notes and telegrams, folders 23:03–23:08, Rosenbach Museum.

19. Mercedes de Acosta, "Poems to Greta Garbo," folder 23:113, Rosenbach Museum.

20. *Here Lies the Heart,* 250–51. In the de Acosta Collection at the Rosenbach Museum are dozens of letters and telegrams, even pieces of cardboard, with Garbo's handwriting. It would seem as if Mercedes treasured everything she ever received from Garbo. Yet there is nothing that indicates any kind of communication from Garbo between March 2, 1933, and September 19, 1935. In the March 2 telegram Garbo sent from Stockholm, all she writes is that she will be returning soon.

21. Garbo to Viertel, April 17, 1933; quoted in Karen Swenson, *Greta Garbo: A Life Apart* (New York: Scribner, 1997), 294.

22. The letters between Salka and her husband are quoted in Salka Viertel, *The Kindness of Strangers* (New York: Holt, Rinehart, Winston, 1969), 187, 193.

23. *Here Lies the Heart,* 251.

24. Swenson, *Greta Garbo,* 301.

25. Viertel, *The Kindness of Strangers,* 152.

26. Ibid., 173–74. According to the MGM script files, the first draft of the script was dated June 10, 1932.

27. Quoted in Swenson, *Greta Garbo,* 287.

28. Mercedes to Dietrich, quoted in Diana McLellan, *The Girls: Sappho Goes to Hollywood* (New York: St. Martin's Press, 2000), 190.

29. Swenson, *Greta Garbo,* 317–18.

30. *Here Lies the Heart,* 253.

31. Ibid.

32. Ibid., 258.

33. Ibid.

34. Typescript with corrections, folder 02:05, 415, Rosenbach Museum.

35. Le Gallienne to her mother, March 7, 1934, and quoted in Helen Sheehy, *Eva Le Gallienne: A Biography* (New York: Alfred A. Knopf, 1996), 231.

36. "Rambling Reporter," *Hollywood Reporter,* June 12, 1934.

37. "Historic Facts on the Life of Jehanne d'Arc," comp. Mercedes de Acosta, submitted to Irving Thalberg on August 4, 1934, folder 04:06, 23, Rosenbach Museum.

38. *Here Lies the Heart,* 259.

39. Ibid., 259–60.

40. Typescript with corrections, folder 02:04, 390, Rosenbach Museum.

41. In a telephone conversation with Abram Poole Jr. on August 14, 2001, he mentioned that his mother, Janice Fair, had modeled for one of the statues in St. Patrick's Cathedral.

42. *Here Lies the Heart,* 261.

43. Typescript with corrections, folder 02:05, 419–21, Rosenbach Museum.

44. *Here Lies the Heart,* 191.

45. In a telephone conversation with Mercedes's nephew, Nathaniel Weyl, on August 6, 2001, he suggested that family members always wondered whether the other woman was Greta Garbo. He indicated, however, that he believed that Garbo "would have had more sense."

46. File no. 50, 567, September 19, 1935, Second Judicial District Court of the State of Nevada in the County of Washoe.

47. This calculation was provided by Dr. Richard Glendening, professor of economics, Central College, Pella, IA.

48. "Abram Poole Divorced," *New York Times,* September 24, 1935.

49. M. S. Irani to Mercedes, folder 10:10, December 31, 1934, Rosenbach Museum. Since the folder that included this letter by M. S. Irani contained only letters written by Meher Baba, M. S. Irani is probably another name he used.

50. "Rambling Reporter," *Hollywood Reporter,* July 31, 1935.

51. The information about her visit to this monastery is found in an essay she wrote called "Study in Sainthood," *Tomorrow* 1 (May 1942): 37–40.

52. Meher Baba to Mercedes, folder 10:10, January 16, 1935, Rosenbach Museum.

53. Ibid., June 6, 1935.

54. Ibid., July 10, 1935.

55. Ibid.

56. Ibid., September 12 and October 11, 1935.

57. Garbo to Mercedes, paraphrase of a letter, September 19, 1935, folder 23:09, Rosenbach Museum.

58. Meher Baba to Mercedes, cable, October 19, 1935.

59. *Here Lies the Heart,* 272.

60. Meher Baba to Mercedes, November 7, 1935.

61. *Here Lies the Heart,* 271.

62. "Poems to Greta Garbo."

63. In 1939 Marie Doro set this poem to music with the title "Dedication." It was published as sheet music by G. Schirmer, Inc., New York.

64. Garbo to Salka Viertel, November 22, 1935, and quoted in Swenson, *Greta Garbo,* 344.

65. "Poems to Greta Garbo."

66. Sheilah Graham, "Everything's Fixed at Studio to Welcome Mysterious Guest," *Los Angeles Times,* April 27, 1936.

67. Sorella Maria to Mercedes, February 6, 1936, folder 10:08, Rosenbach Museum.

68. Garbo to Count Wachtmeister, December 1936, and quoted in Sven Broman, *Greta Garbo berätter* (Stockholm: Wahlstrom and Widstrand, 1990), 182.

69. In letters from Garbo to Mercedes written in March or April of 1938, she thanks

Mercedes for sending shoes, asks her to take sample fabric to a seamstress, and refers to a house that Mercedes has suggested she rent. Folder 23:11–14, Rosenbach Museum.

70. Sorella Maria to Mercedes, January 11, 1937, Rosenbach Museum.

71. Ibid., March 18, 1937.

72. Another difficulty was the settling of a lawsuit. She had been fined and sued for thirty thousand dollars for the wrongful death of a woman she had hit with her car on November 26, 1934. Mercedes finally settled out of court for $2,150 in June 1937. See *New York Daily News,* June 9, 1937.

73. "Divorce Rumor Links Garbo and Stokowski," *New York Post,* October 20, 1937.

74. Quoted in the *New York Post,* August 11, 1954.

75. Meher Baba to Mercedes, folder 10:10, October 2, 1937, Rosenbach Museum.

76. Typescript with corrections, folder 03:06, 591, Rosenbach Museum.

77. Her passport, which is at the Rosenbach Museum, is stamped October 20, 1937.

78. "Poems to Greta Garbo."

9. "There Is No Other Way"

1. Paul Brunton, *A Search in Secret India* (London: Rider, 1934).

2. For a more complete discussion of his teachings, see Sri Ramana Maharshi, *Truth Revealed* (Tiruvannamalai, India: Sri Ramanasramam, 1935).

3. T. M. P. Mahadevan, "Bhagavan Ramana," <www.realization.org>, reprinted from T. M. P. Mahadevan, *Ramana Maharshi and His Philosophy of Existence* (Tiruvannamalai, India: Sri Ramanasramam, 1989).

4. Thomas Berry, *Religions of India: Hinduism, Yoga, Buddhism* (New York: Bruce Publishing, 1971), 76–80.

5. Ibid., 82.

6. Maharshi, *Truth Revealed,* i, 20, 21–22. Mercedes's copy of this book is in box 4, folder 5, of the Georgetown University Library, Washington, DC. Other items of hers that deal with yoga and were donated to the library in 1986 include Sri Deva Ram Sukul, *Pilgrimage Lessons* (New York: Yoga Institute of America, n.d.); *Talks with Sri Ramana Maharshi,* vols. 1–3 (Tiruvannamalai, India, 1955); a small pamphlet entitled *Self Inquiry: Being Original Instructions of Bhagavan Sri Ramana Maharshi* (1952); and Bhagavan Sri Ramana Maharshi, *Who Am I* (rev. ed., 1939). Mercedes inscribed her name, along with the words *India 1938,* on the front cover of this last item.

7. Susheela Misra, *Some Dancers of India* (New Delhi: Harman Publishing, 1992), 63.

8. Ram Gopal, interview by author, Norbury, England, November 14, 2001.

9. Ibid.

10. Mercedes de Acosta, *Here Lies the Heart* (New York: William Morrow, 1960), 119.

11. For more discussion on Orientalism, see Emily Apter, "Acting Out Orientalism: Sapphic Theatricality in Turn-of-the-Century Paris" in *Performance and Cultural Politics,* ed. Elin Diamond (New York: Routledge, 1996), 15–34.

12. Gopal, interview by author, Norbury, England, November 4, 2001.

13. Meher Baba to Mercedes, folder 10:10, n.d., Rosenbach Museum.

14. Garbo to Mercedes, paraphrase of a letter, no clear date but probably September 13, 1938, folder 23:15, Rosenbach Museum.

15. Quoted in Ram Gopal, *Rhythm in the Heavens* (London: N.p., 1957), 77.

16. Gopal to Mercedes, October 12, 1939, folder 11:01, Rosenbach Museum.

17. Ibid., January 30, 1940.

18. Gopal, interview, November 14, 2001.

19. *Here Lies the Heart,* 290.

20. Ibid., 292–94.

21. Ibid., frontispiece.

22. "Elsa Maxwell's Party Line," *New York Post,* April 20, 1943.

23. Gopal, interview, November 4, 2001.

24. Several years later, Hauser published his *Gayelord Hauser's Treasury of Secrets* (New York: Farrar, Strauss, 1963). On page 336, he describes his first meeting with Garbo, to whom he served wild rice burgers, a salad of fresh vegetables, and broiled honeyed grapefruit. He does not mention that Mercedes was present. In fact, he claims that Garbo telephoned him for an appointment at the suggestion of Stoki. He includes the recipe for "Potatoes A la Garbo."

25. Garbo to Hauser, ca. 1940, quoted in Karen Swenson, *Greta Garbo: A Life Apart* (New York: Scribner, 1997), 399.

26. Hauser to Mercedes, November 9, 1939, Rosenbach Museum.

27. Hauser, *Treasury of Secrets,* 336.

28. *Los Angeles Times,* January 15, 1941.

29. Mercedes de Acosta, "Here Lies the Heart," typescript with corrections, folder 02:05, 487, Rosenbach Museum.

30. Mercedes had kept all of Rita's clothes but eventually donated them to various museums.

31. Frank Crowninshield, "The Fabulous Mrs. Lydig," *Vanity Fair,* April 1940, 61–63, 106, 108.

32. Munson to Mercedes, February 20, 1940, Rosenbach Museum.

33. Ibid., February 26, March 11, and March 20, 1940.

34. Ibid., March 6, 1940.

35. Quoted in Hugo Vickers, *Loving Garbo: The Story of Greta Garbo, Cecil Beaton, and Mercedes de Acosta* (New York: Random House, 1994), 76.

36. Munson to Mercedes, March 1, 1940, Rosenbach Museum.

37. Ibid., March 6, 1940.

38. Ibid., January 5, 1942.

39. Although the inclination would be to identify "Dorothy A." as film director Dorothy Arzner, there is no evidence for that claim.

40. Munson to Mercedes, November 10, 1941, Rosenbach Museum.

41. Gopal, interview, November 14, 2001.

42. Typescript with corrections, folder 03:07, 614, Rosenbach Museum.

43. Larry Ceplair and Steven Englund, *The Inquisition in Hollywood: Politics in the Film Community, 1930–1960* (Berkeley: University of California Press, 1983), 4.

44. Ibid., 8.

45. *Here Lies the Heart,* 323.

46. Ceplair and Englund, *The Inquisition in Hollywood,* 156.

47. *Variety,* July 28, 1941.

48. Ibid., 139.

49. Leo C. Rosten, *Hollywood: The Movie Colony, The Movie Makers* (New York: Harcourt, Brace, 1941), 160–61.

50. Nazimova to Mercedes, Easter Monday, 1942, folder 10:18, Rosenbach Museum.

51. Typescript with corrections, folder 02:06, 517–18, Rosenbach Museum.

52. "Robinson Jeffers," *Victory*, n.d., Rosenbach Museum.

53. "Hall of Man Shows Peoples of the World," *Victory*, n.d., 44, 46–47, 73; folder 09:07, de Acosta Collection, Rosenbach Museum.

54. The archives of the Parapsychology Foundation that sponsored *Tomorrow* magazine indicate that Mercedes's first publication for them was her July 1942 essay "Study in Sainthood," which described her meeting with Sister Sorella Maria in Italy. Her name was on the masthead as an associate editor March through June 1943. During her tenure with *Tomorrow*, she also wrote several book reviews, as well as an essay in the May 1943 issue entitled "Holy India," in which she discusses her 1938 visit with Sri Ramana Maharshi and several other spiritual leaders.

55. *Here Lies the Heart*, 324.

56. Eileen J. Garrett, "Editorial," *Tomorrow* 2 (March 1943): 3.

57. Pablo Neruda, "Seventh of November," *Tomorrow* 2 (March 1943): 31, 33.

58. In 1953, Salka Viertel's application for a passport was not approved because she was alleged to be a Communist. Only after she went to Washington, DC, and appeared before the State Department's Passport Division was she granted a temporary, four-month passport. See Salka Viertel, *The Kindness of Strangers* (New York: Holt, Rinehart, Winston, 1969), 325–34.

59. Mercedes de Acosta, "The Challenge of a Changing World," Rosenbach Museum.

60. Contract for *The Leader*, folder 11:02, April 24, 1944, Rosenbach Museum.

61. Mercedes to Igor Stravinsky, January 16, 1944, folder 11:10, Rosenbach Museum.

62. Stravinsky to Mercedes, folder 11:10, February 22, 1944, Rosenbach Museum. Translation is mine.

63. Swenson, *Greta Garbo*, 421.

64. Typescript with corrections, folder 04:303, Rosenbach Museum. One source, Diana McLellan, *The Girls: Sappho Goes to Hollywood* (New York: St. Martin's Press), 300, suggests Valentina "was an old amour" of Mercedes.

65. Quoted in Vickers, *Loving Garbo*, 80.

66. *Here Lies the Heart*, 325.

67. Ibid., 326.

68. In *Here Lies the Heart*, 326, Mercedes writes that she "got a job to go to Europe and write articles for a syndicated newspaper." I have found no evidence supporting that claim.

10. "Looking over My Shoulder for Something Else"

1. The account of their first meeting is recorded in Mercedes de Acosta, *Here Lies the Heart* (New York: William Morrow, 1960), 331–32. The letters from Claire to Mercedes are sealed in a vault at the Rosenbach Museum. They may not be read until the museum can confirm the death of the writer. As of this writing, the museum has been unsuccessful.

2. Garbo to Mercedes, paraphrases of letters and telegrams, March 1, September 24, and n.d., 1946, folders 23:19–23:21, Rosenbach Museum.

3. Cecil Beaton, unpublished diary, November 3, 1947, and quoted in Hugo Vickers, *Loving Garbo: The Story of Greta Garbo, Cecil Beaton, and Mercedes de Acosta* (New York: Random House, 1994), 110.

4. Beaton, unpublished diary, December 11, 1947, and quoted in Vickers, *Loving Garbo*, 114.

5. Cecil Beaton, *Memoirs of the 40's* (New York: McGraw-Hill, 1972), 222–23.

6. Ibid., 245.

7. Beaton, unpublished diary, February 6, 1948, and quoted in Vickers, *Loving Garbo,* 119–22.

8. Ibid.

9. Dilkusha de Rohan, the daughter of a British Army officer stationed in India, married French Prince Carlos de Rohan in 1922. For a short time, the Princess and Poppy lived together.

10. Poppy to Mercedes, April 2, 1949, folder 13:01, Rosenbach Museum.

11. Ibid., March 24, 1949.

12. Mercedes indicates in *Here Lies the Heart,* 343, that after she had returned to Paris she "suddenly had a letter from Poppy saying she wanted to return to Paris and suggesting we share a flat together." Their correspondence, however, suggests they had made the decision prior to Poppy's going to Mexico.

13. Poppy to Mercedes, n.d., folder 13:01, Rosenbach Museum.

14. Ibid., February 1949.

15. Ibid., February 22, 1949.

16. Ibid., April 2, 1949.

17. *Here Lies the Heart,* 346.

18. Garbo to Mercedes, paraphrase of a letter, August 15, 1949, folder 23:28, Rosenbach Museum.

19. Gopal to Mercedes, May 16, 1955, folder 11:01, Rosenbach Museum.

20. *Here Lies the Heart,* 347.

21. Poppy Kirk to Mercedes, January 19, 1950, folder 13:01, Rosenbach Museum.

22. Ibid., January 25, 1950.

23. Ibid., February 4, 1950.

24. Ibid., February 15, 1950.

25. Ibid., April 18, 1950.

26. Ibid., February 23, 1950.

27. Garbo to Mercedes, paraphrase of a letter, May 12, 1950, folder 23:31, Rosenbach Museum.

28. Ibid., May 18 (?), 1950, folder 23:32, Rosenbach Museum.

29. Gopal to Mercedes, May 16, 1955, folder 11:01, Rosenbach Museum.

30. Garbo to Mercedes, paraphrase of letters, July 29, 1951, and April 2, 1952, folders 23:38 and 23:42, Rosenbach Museum.

31. Ibid., June 7, 1952.

32. Kirk to Mercedes, August 3, 1953, folder 13:01, Rosenbach Museum.

33. Ibid., August 23, 1954.

34. Hope Williams to Mercedes, September 1, 1953, folder 11:19, Rosenbach Museum.

35. Ram Gopal, interview by author, Norbury, England, November 14, 2001.

36. Mercedes to Beaton, October 5, 1953, and quoted in Vickers, *Loving Garbo,* 209–10.

37. Beaton to Mercedes, October 11, 1953, folder 07:06, Rosenbach Museum.

38. Kirk to Mercedes, July 17, 1954, folder 13:01, Rosenbach Museum.

39. Garbo to Mercedes, paraphrase of a letter, December 22, 1954, folder 23:59, Rosenbach Museum.

40. Toklas to Mercedes, September 26, 1953, folder 11:13, Rosenbach Museum.
41. Ibid.
42. Rambova to Mercedes, October 9, 1955, folder 11:02, Rosenbach Museum.
43. Gopal to Mercedes, folder 11:01, August 11, 1955, Rosenbach Museum.
44. Robson to Mercedes, folder 11:05, October 5, 1963, Rosenbach Museum.
45. Munson to Mercedes, July 24, 1954, Rosenbach Museum.
46. *New York Times,* February 12, 1955.

11. "Just Damned Bewildered"

1. Beaton to Mercedes, March 23, 1955, folder 07:06, Rosenbach Museum.
2. Ibid., May 1, 1955.
3. Toklas to Mercedes, March 12, 1957, folder 11:13, Rosenbach Museum.
4. Karsavina to Mercedes, August 12, 1956, folder 09:12, Rosenbach Museum.
5. Gopal to Mercedes, June 3, 1955, folder 11:01, Rosenbach Museum.
6. Ibid., August 11, 1955.
7. Poole to Mercedes, January 3, 1956, folder 10:26, Rosenbach Museum.
8. Ram Gopal, interview by author, Norbury, England, November 14, 2001.
9. *Diagnostic and Statistical Manual of Mental Disorders,* 3rd ed., rev. (Washington, DC: American Psychiatric Association, 1987), 247.
10. Judith L. Rapoport, *The Boy Who Couldn't Stop Washing* (New York: New American Library, 1989), 176.
11. *Diagnostic and Statistical Manual,* 199.
12. Ibid., 200–201.
13. The account of this reunion is found in Cecil Beaton, unpublished diary, winter 1958, and quoted in Hugo Vickers, *Loving Garbo: The Story of Greta Garbo, Cecil Beaton, and Mercedes de Acosta* (New York: Random House, 1994), 243.
14. Ibid.
15. Gopal to Mercedes, May 16, 1957, folder 11:01, Rosenbach Museum.
16. Garbo to Mercedes, paraphrase of letters, August 7 and September 14, 1957, folders 23:67 and 23:68, Rosenbach Museum.
17. Ibid., February 25, 1958, folder 23:73.
18. Gopal to Mercedes, December 23, 1957, folder 11:01, Rosenbach Museum.
19. Toklas to Mercedes, June 30, 1958, folder 11:13, Rosenbach Museum.
20. Dietrich to Mercedes, notes about Mercedes's autobiography, n.d., folder 08;04, Rosenbach Museum.
21. Garbo to Mercedes, paraphrase of a letter, n.d., folder 23:88, Rosenbach Museum.
22. Beaton to Mercedes, March 26, 1960, Rosenbach Museum.
23. Toklas to Mercedes, April 17, 1960, folder 11:13, Rosenbach Museum.
24. Ibid., August 19, 1960.
25. Jan Mostowski, telephone interview by author, September 25, 2001.
26. Arthur Todd, "The Place Cards Read Like an All Star Cast at a Benefit," *New York Times Book Review,* May 29, 1960, 6.
27. "The Book Shelf," *Dance,* May 1960, n.p.
28. Richard McLaughlin, "Adventures of an Esthete," *New Leader,* June 13, 1960, 29.
29. *Miami Herald,* n.d.
30. Beaton, unpublished diary, winter 1961, and quoted in Vickers, *Loving Garbo,* 256.

31. When I asked Gopal why people say her book is full of lies, he replied, "It's jealousy. They will say the same thing about your book." Interview, November 14, 2001.

32. Vickers, *Loving Garbo,* 254.

33. After their divorce in 1935, Poole won the Altman prize for figure painting in displays of the National Academy of Design—in 1938 for his *Spanish Sisters* and in 1940 for *Young Dancer.* He is one of the portrait artists featured in John Head, "Framing Society," *Social Register Observer,* winter 2001, 88–93.

34. Bartok to Mercedes, February 28, 1960, folder 07:05, Rosenbach Museum.

35. Ibid., May 2, 1960.

36. Mercedes to McCarthy, June 29, 1959, folder 07:01, Rosenbach Museum.

37. These agreements were made in two separate letters, both written by McCarthy to Mercedes on June 1, 1960, and approved by her on June 5, 1960.

38. Mercedes to McCarthy, October 31, 1964, folder 07:01, Rosenbach Museum. I can certainly confirm that the museum kept their promise. When I tried to see the letters of Claire, the Marquise de Forbin, in June 2001, they were still sealed in the vault because nobody could confirm that she had died. Even though I received letters from two of her relatives confirming her death, these letters were not considered official documents. The museum staff could not tell me the size of this collection of letters nor whether they were written in English or in French. No one had looked at them since they had been deposited in 1960.

39. Mercedes to McCarthy, December 14, 1960, folder 07:01, Rosenbach Museum.

40. Hoffman to Mercedes, May 18, 1961, folder 09:07, Rosenbach Museum. Evidence of the gift from Hope Williams is found in a letter to Mercedes, July 21, 1962, folder 11:19, Rosenbach Museum.

41. Gaynor to Mercedes, January 12, 1961, Rosenbach Museum.

42. Karsavina to Mercedes, November 27, 1961, Rosenbach Museum.

43. Mercedes to McCarthy, October 17, 1961, folder 07:01, Rosenbach Museum.

44. Mercedes to Beaton, December 11, 1961, and quoted in Vickers, *Loving Garbo,* 278.

45. Ibid.

46. Mercedes to McCarthy, October 31, 1964, folder 07:01, Rosenbach Museum.

47. Toklas to Mercedes, September 9, 1959, and April 21, 1963, folder 11:13, Rosenbach Museum.

48. Kieran Tunney, *Interrupted Autobiography and Aurora* (London: Quartet Books, 1989), 35.

49. Ibid., 33.

50. Ibid., 42.

51. Ibid.

52. Burnap's observation is mentioned in Vickers, *Loving Garbo,* 244. Poole's observation was through a telephone interview by the author on August 14, 2001.

53. Tunney, *Interrupted Autobiography and Aurora,* 37; Burnap to Vickers, September 30, 1992, quoted in Vickers, *Loving Garbo,* 280.

54. Quoted in Tunney, 37.

55. Beaton, unpublished diary, April 1966, and quoted in Vickers, *Loving Garbo,* 280.

56. Beaton, unpublished diary, May 1968, and quoted in Vickers, *Loving Garbo,* 281–82.

57. Beaton, unpublished diary, April 1966.

58. Tunney, 43.

59. Certificate of death no. 156-68-110185, filed May 9, 1968, at 8:47 P.M., Department of Health, City of New York.

60. Philip Brandes, "Theater Beat: 'Garbo' Probes Real Lives with Sensitivity," *Los Angeles Times,* October 5, 2001. As this book was being completed, Odalys Nanin was planning to revive the play at the Ford Amphitheatre in October 2003 and was writing a screenplay adaptation.

61. Beaton, unpublished diary, May 1968, quoted in Vickers, *Loving Garbo,* 281–82.

62. Gopal, interview, November 14, 2001. Ram Gopal died on October 12, 2003, just a few months after the hardback edition of this volume was published.

63. Bible, Rosenbach Museum.

64. Mercedes de Acosta, *Here Lies the Heart* (New York: William Morrow, 1960), 357–58.

Index

A Professor Emeritus of Theater at Central College in Pella, Iowa, ROBERT A. SCHANKE is the editor of the international journal *Theatre History Studies* and the Southern Illinois University Press series Theater in the Americas. His previous books include *Women in Turmoil: Six Plays by Mercedes de Acosta* and *Shattered Applause: The Lives of Eva Le Gallienne,* a finalist for both the Lambda Literary Award and the Barnard Hewitt Award for theater research.

THEATER IN THE AMERICAS

The goal of the series is to publish a wide range of scholarship on theater and performance, defining theater in its broadest terms and including subjects that encompass all of the Americas.

The series focuses on the performance and production of theater and theater artists and practitioners but welcomes studies of dramatic literature as well. Meant to be inclusive, the series invites studies of traditional, experimental, and ethnic forms of theater; celebrations, festivals, and rituals that perform culture; and acts of civil disobedience that are performative in nature. We publish studies of theater and performance activities of all cultural groups within the Americas, including biographies of individuals, histories of theater companies, studies of cultural traditions, and collections of plays.